The Wisdom of
Thomas Starr King

The Wisdom of Thomas Starr King

Thomas Starr King's
Substance and Show

Edited and introduced by
Paul Rich

WESTPHALIA PRESS
An imprint of Policy Studies Organization

The Wisdom of Thomas Starr King:
Thomas Starr King's
Substance and Show

Westphalia Press
An imprint of Policy Studies Organization
dgutierrezs@ipsonet.org

For information:
Westphalia Press
1527 New Hampshire Ave., N.W.
Washington, D.C. 20036

ISBN-13: 978-0944285909
ISBN-10: 0944285902

Updated material and comments on this edition can be
found at the Policy Studies Organization website:
http://www.ipsonet.org/

**This edition is dedicated to Arthur Shurcliff,
remembering mountain days**

Also from Westphalia Press

westphaliapress.org

*The Idea of the
Digital University*

*Masonic Tombstones and
Masonic Secrets*

Treasures of London

The History of Photography

L'Enfant and the Freemasons

Baronial Bedrooms

Making Trouble for Muslims

*Material History and
Ritual Objects*

Paddle Your Own Canoe

*Opportunity and
Horatio Alger*

*Careers in the Face of
Challenge*

Bookplates of the Kings

*Collecting American
Presidential Autographs*

Freemasonry in Old Buffalo

*Original Cables from the
Pearl Harbor Attack*

*Social Satire and the
Modern Novel*

The Essence of Harvard

The Genius of Freemasonry

*A Definitive Commentary
on Bookplates*

*James Martineau and
Rebuilding Theology*

No Bird Lacks Feathers

*Earthworms, Horses, and
Living Things*

*The Man Who Killed
President Garfield*

*Anti-Masonry and the Murder
of Morgan*

Understanding Art

Homeopathy

Ancient Masonic Mysteries

Collecting Old Books

*Masonic Secret Signs and
Passwords*

*The Thomas Starr
King Dispute*

Earl Warren's Masonic Lodge

Lariats and Lassos

Mr. Garfield of Ohio

The French Foreign Legion

War in Syria

*Naturism Comes to the United
States*

*New Sources on Women and
Freemasonry*

*Designing, Adapting,
Strategizing in Online
Education*

Policy Diagnosis

*Meeting Minutes of Naval
Lodge No. 4 F.A.A.M.*

THE WISDOM OF THOMAS STARR KING'S
SUBSTANCE AND SHOW
PREFACE TO THIS EDITION

A S mentioned in several Westphalia new editions related to Thomas Starr King, a feature of the Capitol in Washington is the collection of statues representing each state. Normally a state may have two of its worthies on display, and in case of California for many years the couple had been Junipero Serra and Thomas Starr King. The theological balance achieved by having a Roman Catholic and a Unitarian as the state's representatives seemed apt.

Starr King achieved that distinction because he spent himself in stumping California to keep the state on the Union side during the Civil War. An estimated forty percent of the population were Southerners and whether California would leave the Union was a real issue.

As we note in other Starr King reprints, in 2006, the California Legislature decided to

E

remove the statue of Thomas Starr King and replace it with a statue of Ronald Reagan. Of course Ronald Reagan is not unnoticed in Washington, and represented by a statue at the airport named after him, by several paintings in the Congressional offices, and by the giving of his name to a massive Federal office and conference complex.

In removing Starr King, one reason offered was that he was not born in California. Ronald Reagan was born in Illinois and Father Serra was born in Majorca, so that seemed a spurious excuse. About the affair, the *Los Angeles Times* (May 29, 2009), commented:

"It's never pleasant watching politicians try to manipulate history. Whether it's an ex-president blocking release of incriminating White House tapes, the Russian government closing a KGB archive to foreign researchers or Japanese officials forcing a school textbook author to excise references to World War II-era atrocities, the public's ability to learn the truth about historic events is hobbled.

The imminent removal from the U.S. Capitol of a statue of Thomas Starr King, a charismatic San Francisco minister and orator credited with

F

helping keep California in the Union during the run-up to the Civil War, hardly qualifies as a major crime against history. Yet the successful effort by California Republicans to replace him in the National Statuary Hall Collection with a larger-than-life sculpture of Ronald Reagan is troubling nonetheless."

Included in this volume is the Starr King lecture on Socrates. He liked to tell how two miners saw a poster advertising his coming lecture on "Socrates and his Age". One asked the other, "Bill, who was this fellow Socrates and who the hell cares about his age?"

It remains troubling but probably inevitable that history can become a political football. When the statue was dedicated, its placement was done with great honor and dignity. A new edition of some of his writings may give pause about the furtive way it was removed.

Paul Rich

G

SUBSTANCE AND SHOW,

AND OTHER LECTURES.

BY

THOMAS STARR KING.

EDITED, WITH AN INTRODUCTION,

By EDWIN P. WHIPPLE.

BOSTON:
JAMES R. OSGOOD AND COMPANY
LATE TICKNOR & FIELDS, AND FIELDS, OSGOOD, & CO.
1877.

CONTENTS.

———◆———

		PAGE
INTRODUCTION		vii
I.	SUBSTANCE AND SHOW; OR, FACTS AND FORCES	1
II.	THE LAWS OF DISORDER	34
III.	SOCRATES	78
IV.	SIGHT AND INSIGHT	148
V.	HILDEBRAND	190
VI.	MUSIC	231
VII.	EXISTENCE AND LIFE	254
VIII.	THE EARTH AND THE MECHANIC ARTS .	275
IX.	DANIEL WEBSTER	299
X.	BOOKS AND READING	354
XI.	THE PRIVILEGE AND DUTIES OF PATRIOTISM	389
XII.	INTELLECTUAL DUTIES OF STUDENTS IN THEIR ACADEMIC YEARS	413

INTRODUCTION.

THOSE who have read the biographical preface to Mr. King's sermons, published about a month ago under the general title of " Christianity and Humanity," do not need to be informed that his influence extended far beyond his parish and his denomination, and included that vast multitude of listeners who are more or less magnetically affected by the lyceum lecturer. Indeed, he was one of the foremost speakers who followed in the train of Ralph Waldo Emerson in erecting the lecture platform into a kind of free pulpit, from which the advanced ideas of spiritual thinkers, philanthropists, and reformers were diffused through the community. It is needless to speak of Emerson's supremacy in this line of thought and endeavor, for it is now universally acknowledged. By carefully avoiding all controversy with the good and learned men who were both shocked by his radicalism and charmed by his genius and character, he made his simple affirmations felt as forces wherever his voice was heard in our multitudinous lyceums. In the course of a few years he did much to emancipate the popular mind from its ingrained theological and politi-

cal prejudices, and he did this without severely
wounding or insulting the feelings and opinions
of the champions of the established order. In
spite of his occasional indulgence in certain
caprices and audacities of his individuality, he
commonly confined himself to the glad work of
shedding _light_ on the questions he treated ; and
the main object of his teaching was directed to
disentangling the imperative ideas of truth and
goodness, of beauty and justice, from the partial
views of all forcible individualities, including his
own. He aimed to purify his intellect and moral
sentiment from all personal bias, and to make his
reason and conscience worthy to receive and announce the inspirations of impersonal truth and
morality. His constitution of mind and character instinctively led him to avoid controversy as
something which would inevitably enfeeble his
faculty of spiritual insight, and give him a cheap
victory over opponents at the immense expense
of interrupting his work of patient self-discipline
as a seer. Then his friend, Theodore Parker, was
always at hand to concentrate on himself every
element of pugnacious opposition to the new ideas
with a pugnacity that no controversies could appease, and who was incapable of feeling any persecution so keenly as the persecution of silence,
especially when it came from the Unitarian brethren whom he criticised. Both of these men labored, each after his particular fashion, to make the
lecture-room a place where both independence of

opinion and peculiarity of character could be freely expressed ; and a third, Wendell Phillips, needed nothing but his incomparable power of eloquence, which was at once seductive and smiting, to recommend himself to any audience which he consented to address, whether he spoke on "The Lost Arts," or on subjects connected with the reform movements of the time.

Mr. King became a force in the lecture-room, as he became a force in the pulpit, by the happy union in his nature of brilliancy of talent with beneficence of character. Few persons will stand the test of that pitiless analysis which austerely probes down through intellect and conscience to the roots of individual disposition, regardless of all the "grafts" which culture or "grace" have added to the original stock ; but those who knew King intimately must admit that, in penetrating to the heart of his being, they found nothing there which contradicted the first impression that he was sound to the core, — that he was instinctively sympathetic, unselfish, and humane. This essential goodness made him loved and respected even by those who most violently disagreed with him in opinion ; for there was nothing of the sullen and arrogant self-sufficiency of the dogmatist and egotist in his most confident, masculine, and joyous utterance of his own perceptions of truth. Only such persons as were under the slavery of fear, envy, and malignity could suspect that his intellect ever became the organ of such ignoble passions.

As a result of this original felicity of nature, his eloquence was as persuasive as it was inspiring and instructive. It had that subtle element of influence which can only come from a humane disposition, underlying thought and style, and vitalizing both. What King said was excellent; but the spirit in which he said it was felt by persons of all grades of culture as a precious something which abolished all distinctions of social " clanship," and, for the time, bound them together in the kinship of a common humanity. In short, his eloquence had that nameless charm which made it universally *attractive.* It will be observed, by the reader of the present volume, that this personal attractiveness was accompanied by knowledge, thought, wit, humor, fancy, and imagination ; that every faculty of the lecturer's mind and every feeling of his heart was engaged in the task of fastening the attention of his hearers to the subject he discussed ; but still, even in the reading, we feel that the great beauty of the performance streaming through all the minor beauties of detail, is the beautiful character of Starr King unconsciously impressed upon it.

There are many lecturers still living who will remember the effect of the lecture on " Substance and Show " by their experience in following King the week after its delivery. As soon as they arrived, the Lecture Committee inevitably began to talk about King's " Substance and Show " ; as soon as each had concluded his particular address,

the Lecture Committee, after the briefest of all
polite pauses, recurred to the more pleasing topic
of King and his "Substance and Show." The
popularity of this admirable lecture was one of
the finest of all tributes ever paid to the average
taste and intelligence of the lecture audiences of
the country. In a letter to a friend, in December
1851, King says : " My lecture has become a fact
and a show ; whether it is a substance and a force
is questionable. . . . . You do not, I think, take
the antithesis I make, or exactly appreciate the
drift of the plan. The aim of it is wholly practical, — to break down, in the popular mind, the
inveterate association of strength and permanence
with the visible side of the world and things we
can 'sense.' The illustrations from science are
taken to buttress faith in the invisible and intangible as being the causal and productive agencies.
Substance is that which stands under, supports,
moulds, etc. ; and the whole visible universe really
leans upon secret impalpable energies, to which it
owes shape, color, and its myriad varieties. I make
no antithesis between material and immaterial
forces, but show how all the glories and differences
in nature are due to the secret working of electric,
actinic, magnetic powers, and that the whole order
and science of nature is in the last analysis the
expression of Divine ideas. With this aid from
nature, I go into the historic world and moral life,
to show that ideas, sentiments, moral truth, are
the most vigorous, despotic, unwasting substances,

since nations lean on them; and character, the great reality and most efficient force we know, is the organization of these. It is a Lyceum Sermon." As to his figurative style, he tells his correspondent that rhetoric, considered "as jewelry and *rouge*, is sufficiently contemptible," but that it is legitimate when it is the expression of what is in itself beautiful. "You are not," he adds, "charitable enough to rhetoric. Equations, plus and minus, algebraic signs and diagrams, are not the ideals of the perfection of speech. God is a glorious rhetorician. How he hides his mathematics and bald geometry! Does n't he ornament all the truth he states to us through nature, and when he teaches a chemical and vegetable science in the oak, the elm, and the palm, does n't he perorate in their bossy, waving canopy of leaves?"

In the lectures on "The Laws of Disorder," "Sight and Insight," and "Existence and Life," the same general tendency is observable which lends so much attractiveness to "Substance and Show." In reading them we are constantly witnessing the transformation of physical into spiritual laws, or, as Emerson would say, "the metamorphosis of natural into spiritual facts." The fertility of the writer's mind in illustrations, analogies, and images compels the reader to follow the course of the thinking with a pleased and ever-expectant attention to the end. These lectures, as originally delivered before lyceums, met the

wants of all the classes huddled together in a
lecture audience.   The general strain was so high
and noble that everybody who listened felt uplifted and ennobled.   It was not merely, in the
case of King's discourse, that

> " Rustic life and poverty
> Grew beautiful beneath his touch,"

but that wealth and poverty were alike made to
admit the superiority of mental and moral " good"
over mere worldly " goods."   The expressions of
satisfaction varied with the grammatical rather
than the human peculiarities of the persons who
were addressed.   "What a grand, inspiring, and
instructive lecture ! " was the verdict of those clad
in silk and broadcloth, after the speaker had concluded.   " *Them* 's idees," was the judgment of one
hard-headed, horny-handed workman in home-
spun, as he came out of the hall by the side of
King.

The lecture on " Socrates " attained a popularity
nearly as great as that on " Substance and Show."
This was the more remarkable because the subject might be supposed foreign to the sympathies
of those who made up the bulk of the audience
of a village or town lyceum.   But King, though
necessarily not a profound Greek scholar, was
passionately attracted to Plato at an early age,
and had so absorbed Cousin's French translation
of that great master in p ilosophy that he ventured, when he had hardly attained legal manhood, to contribute a critical exposition of Plato's

doctrine of immortality to the " Universalist Review," and in the course of it to question the accuracy and the insight of so accomplished a scholar as Professor Andrews Norton. The figure of Socrates, in the Platonic dialogues, had been impressed so vividly on his imagination, that Socrates at last became to him as actual a personage as any acquaintance he daily passed in the streets of Charlestown or Boston. He thought he could contrive to transfer to other minds the image of this heathen saint and sage as it existed, warm, glowing, and lifelike, in his own. His success was complete. Indeed, the lecture is a masterpiece of its kind. Scholarship can doubtless paint a finer portrait of Socrates ; but to naturalize him, morally and intellectually, so as to make him a sort of fellow-citizen of the honest inhabitants of ordinary American towns and villages, is a task which mere scholarship is incompetent to perform ; yet King succeeded in doing this difficult work. In English literature the most admirable exposition of the life, character, and method of Socrates is doubtless to be found in Grote's " History of Greece" ; but no Cape Cod fisherman or Western pioneer could have been induced to read Grote, whereas both heard King with delight. In the records of our American lyceums there is probably no other instance of such a subject being made universally popular by the attractive genius of the speaker.

The lecture on " Hildebrand " was written for a

special occasion, and its interest was not tested
by being repeated before miscellaneous audiences. It is a favorable specimen of King's
power of dealing with the great crises and characters of ecclesiastical history. The editor had
intended to include in this volume a still more
elaborate lecture on "Constantine and his Times";
but the publication of that, as well as of two addresses on the "Life and Writings of St. Paul,"
is reluctantly postponed for the present. Indeed,
an editor who thoroughly explores the mass of
manuscripts which Mr. King left behind him, for
the purpose of selecting a few for publication,
finds his task all the more difficult on account
of the very richness of the materials. He knows
what he would like to print, but his literary conscience is troubled by the thought of those which
he is compelled to omit.

Mr. King was intensely sensitive to the influences of music, though he had no technical knowledge of it as a science, and could not
read its language. One of the most eloquent
discourses in his volume of sermons is that on
"The Organ and its Symbolism"; and readers
of the present volume cannot fail to be impressed
by the address on "Music," recording, as it does,
the ideas and emotions awakened in the writer by
listening to the works of the great composers.
It was a privilege to sit near him when a work of
Handel, Mozart, or Beethoven was performed;
for the ecstasy which thrilled his own frame

became infectious, and one enjoyed the double delight of hearing the music and of participating in the rapture of a companion whose soul was in most delicious accord with it.

Five of the lectures in the present volume were written and delivered in California. That on "Books and Reading" speaks for itself as one of the best of all addresses ever delivered on a topic which has seemingly been worn threadbare by the efforts equally of genius and mediocrity, but which, in King's hands, comes out fresh and new, as though he were the first man who had ever discoursed about it. As far as advice on such a subject is ever an aid to intellectual education, it may be said that King succeeded in his aim ; for the lecture had not only a surprising popularity, but numbers of his hearers really adopted his plan of reading, and doubtless found it to be of much practical value. The other four lectures refer more or less to the Rebellion. King, while he was in California, could no more keep Jefferson Davis and the secessionists out of his sermons and addresses, than Dickens's Mr. Dick could keep Charles the First out of his "Memorial." The lecture on "Daniel Webster" was one of three which he delivered to immense audiences in California before the war broke out. It is now printed, not for its literary merit, but because it contains many felicitous touches of characterization, unfolds and forecasts the principles on which the impending struggle must be conducted, and was a cause of much irritation to those "conservatives" who could not openly oppose the doctrines of such an apostle of conservatism as Webster, but who were still doubtful whether, in the event of a war, they should cast their fortunes with the free or the slave States. The lecture was written in headlong haste, and some of the paragraphs are evidently mere notes of what the lecturer afterwards expanded in the delivery; but it did its appointed work more effectually than if it had been a perfect specimen of rhetoric; for it brought into the discussion the authoritative name of Webster, as the one statesman of the country who had not only crushed and trampled under foot all the sophisms of the most redoubtable logicians of disunion and of liberticide, but had made the preservation of the Union the one practical object and supreme ideal of American statesmanship. King's "Webster" was not only denouncedby politicians in newspapers, but gently rebuked by priests in the pulpit. As to the latter, they professed to have no objection to the eulogy of any prominent statesman of the past, but they thought it indecorous to apply Webster's principles in a satirical and offensive way to the problems of the present. When the war actually burst out, King plainly told his parishioners that his religion was identical with his patriotism; and he referred, in a strain of bitter-sweet eloquence, to the theological rancor which had ostracized him as a dis-

turber of the public peace, because he had foreseen and stated those perversions of constitutional
law which alone endangered it.

Up to the time of Mr. King's death it was generally believed that he, more than any other man,
had prevented California and the whole Pacific
coast from falling into the gulf of disunion.   It is
certain that Abraham Lincoln held this opinion ;
and it was an opinion which the President shared
with thousands of prominent men in all sections
of the country, including those California sympa-
thizers with the South who were most vexed by
King's opposition to their schemes.   The usual
answer to this general impression of the effect
of his work comes, of course, from patriots who
maintain that California was sound for the Union
from the first ; that King merely felt the pulse of
the people, and gave eloquent expression to the
general sentiment of the State.   But in fact he did
not merely feel the people's pulse ; he gave incessantly an *im*-pulse to the vague Union feeling, and
directed it to a definite object.   Doubtless a large
majority of the population were Unionists.   Had it
been otherwise, it would not have been necessary
for some of the most unscrupulous politicians of
the State to conceal their treasonable designs under patriotic professions of loyalty.   Then there
was a large body of honest men who insisted that
the war should be conducted on principles which
would insure the defeat of the Union armies.
Miracles are now banished from authentic secular

history ; but still there is something almost miraculous in the triumph of the national cause against
the wrong-headiness of those well-meaning patriots
who contended that the war should be prosecuted
on the constitutional principles which Jefferson
Davis and Alexander Stephens laid down for the
edification and guidance of Federal statesmen and
generals. The leading opponents of the Constitution, armed to overturn both *it* and the government founded *on* it, still managed to steal some
time from their conferences with foreign powers,
and their direction of military operations, to instruct the loyal people as to the proper limitations
of their power in putting down the most formida-
ble of all rebellions ; and there is something comical in the thought that these admonitions not to
violate the provisions of the Constitution were
keenly felt, not merely by secret traitors in the
loyal States, but by a large body of Unionists who
were eager and ready to sacrifice life and property
to sustain the Union and the Constitution.

> " Pleased to the last they cropped the flowery food,
> And licked the hands just raised to shed their blood."

When therefore we say that King kept California
strong for the Union, we do not mean that he simply was the eloquent voice through which the general Union sentiment found expression, but that
he guided Union opinion ; that he both anticipated
and defended the measures which eventually made
the cause of the Union successful. He became a
power in California, because he had the sagacity

to detect, and the intrepidity to denounce, the
treason that skulked under loyal phrases and
catchwords; and his influence was measured,
not by his bursts of declamatory eloquence on
the blessings of union, but by the skill with which
he took the people, as it were, out of the hands
of disloyal politicians, and induced them to give
their vigorous support to the administration of the
national government.

It has not been the intention of the editor of
this volume to publish any lecture which specially
represents King's deadly animosity to the enemies
of the country; indeed, it has now become
fashionable to speak of treason as an amiable
weakness of generous and susceptible natures;
but the reader will note that this animosity
bursts forth here and there in the noble lecture
on "The Earth and the Mechanic Arts," and
even affords the occasion for a sublime image
of "the earthquake wave," in the college address on "The Intellectual Duties of Students."
The grand spirit which animates the oration on
"The Privilege and Duties of Patriotism" will
be felt, appreciated, and acknowledged by hundreds who may be irked by the relentless assault
made in it on the old aristocracy of Southern
slaveholders. But King, during the whole period
of his life in California, was so penetrated,
through and through, with the sentiment of patriotism, that his hostility to the enemies of the
Union and the Federal government broke out,

not merely in such addresses as this to Union soldiers, but in every form in which his moral and intellectual activity found expression.

Throughout the lectures in the present volume the reader can hardly fail to be impressed by King's broad humanity. He had a horror of all social arrangements which tended to confirm sterile and stunted natures in the self-satisfaction they derived from contemplating their own little-ness of soul. He ranked men and women, not according to their social position, but according to their place in the ascending scale of intellect and virtue. " Think," he says, in speaking of the future life, — " think of the poor exclusives from this sphere carrying their petty measures, which limit their sympathies on earth, into the world of substance, setting up their little coteries to cut Gabriel if he did not belong to their set, or ex-clude some spirit whose brow is freighted with truth, if he was not born quite high enough to suit their fancy ! " The one unmistakable mark of vulgarity was, in his view, narrowness of mind and insensibility of heart, — the stupid prejudice which rails at ideas, and the inhuman selfishness which scoffs at philanthropy.

In his lectures, as in his sermons, the largeness, liberality, and humanity of his disposition found their natural expression in genial breadth of thought and beneficence of feeling. Everything small and mean was as abhorrent to his soul as was everything base and cruel. His heart and brain agreed in instinctively rejecting whatever had a tendency to degrade humanity, and in instinctively admitting whatever was calculated to purify, enrich, elevate, and invigorate it. Throughout the present volume, on whatever subject he exercises his bright and joyous faculties, it will ever be found that he is a teacher of manliness as well as of godliness. " Circumstances," he says, " may determine how much show a man shall make. To be famous, depends on some fortuities ; to be a president, depends on the acute smellers of a few politicians and a mysterious set of wires ; to be rich, depends upon birth or luck ; to be intellectually eminent, may depend on the appointment of Providence ; but to be a man, in the sense of substance, depends solely on one's own noble ambition and determination to live in contact with God's open atmosphere of truth and right, from which all true manliness is inspired and fed."

And again he says, in reference to the three methods of observing the material universe which are so prominent in all his lectures : " Out of three roots grows the great tree of nature,—truth, beauty, good. The man of science follows up its mighty stem, measures it, and sees its branches in the silver-leaved boughs of the firmament. The poet delights in the symmetry of its strength, the grace of its arches, the flush of its fruit. Only to the man with finer eye than both is the secret of its glory unveiled ; for his vision discerns how it is fed and in what air it thrives. To him it is only an expansion of the burning bush on Horeb, seen by the solemn prophet, glowing continually with the presence of Infinite Law and Love, yet remaining forever unconsumed."

I.

SUBSTANCE AND SHOW; OR, FACTS AND FORCES.

I PROPOSE to speak on the difference between *substance* and *show*, or the distinction
we should make between the facts of the world
and life, and the causal forces which lie behind
and beneath them. No mind which comprehends
the issues involved in the distinction will fail to see
that the topic is vitally practical; for scepticism,
or mistaken conceptions of the truth upon this
point, must degrade our whole theory of life,
demoralize our reverence, and make the region
with which our faith should be in constant contact
thin, dreamy, and spectral.

Most persons, doubtless, if you place before
them a paving-stone and a slip of paper with some
writing on it, would not hesitate to say that there
is as much more substance in the rock than in
the paper as there is heaviness. Yet they might
make a great mistake. Suppose that the slip of
paper contains the sentence, " God is love " ; or,
" Thou shalt love thy neighbor as thyself " ; or,
" All men have moral rights by reason of heavenly parentage," then the paper represents more

I   A

force and substance than the stone. Heaven and earth may pass away, but such words can never die out or become less real.

The word "substance" means that which stands under and supports anything else. Whatever then creates, upholds, classifies anything which our senses behold, though we cannot handle, see, taste, or smell it, is more substantial than the object itself. In this way the soul, which vivifies, moves, and supports the body, is a more potent substance than the hard bones and heavy flesh which it vitalizes. A ten-pound weight falling on your head affects you unpleasantly as substance, much more so than a leaf of the New Testament, if dropped in the same direction ; but there is a way in which a page of the New Testament may fall upon a nation and split it, or infuse itself into its bulk and give it strength and permanence. We should be careful, therefore, what test we adopt in order to decide the relative stability of things.

There is a very general tendency to deny that ideal forces have any practical power. But there have been several thinkers whose scepticism has an opposite direction. "We cannot," they say, "attribute external reality to the sensations we feel." We need not wonder that this theory has failed to convince the unmetaphysical common-sense of people that a stone post is merely a stubborn thought, and that the bite of a dog is nothing but an acquaintance with a pugnacious, four-footed conception. When a man falls down stairs it is not easy to convince him that his thought simply tumbles along an inclined series of perceptions and comes to a conclusion that breaks his head ; least of all, can you induce a man to believe that the scolding of his wife is nothing but the buzzing of his own waspish thoughts, and her use of his purse only the loss of some golden fancies from his memory. We are all safe against such idealism as Bishop Berkeley reasoned out so logically. Byron's refutation of it is neat and witty : —

> " When Bishop Berkeley says there is no matter,
> It is no matter what Bishop Berkeley says."

And yet, by more satisfactory evidence than that which the idealists propose, we are warned against confounding the conception of substance with matter, and confining it to things we can see and grasp. Science steps in and shows us that the physical system of things leans on spirit. We talk of the world of matter, but there is no such world. Everything about us is a mixture or marriage of matter and spirit. A world of matter simply would be a huge heap of sandy atoms or an infinite continent of stagnant vapor. There would be no motion, no force, no form, no order, no beauty, in the universe as it now is ; organization meets us at every step and wherever we look ; organization implies spirit, — something that rules, disposes, penetrates, and vivifies matter.

See what a sermon Astronomy preaches as to

the substantial power of invisible things. If the
visible universe is so stupendous, what shall we
think of the unseen force and vitality in whose
arms all its splendors rest? It is no gigantic Atlas,
as the Greeks fancied, that upholds the celestial
sphere ; all the constellations are kept from falling by an impalpable energy that uses no muscles
and no masonry. The ancient mathematician,
Archimedes, once said, "Give me a foot of ground
outside the globe to stand upon, and I will make
a lever that will lift the world." The invisible
lever of gravitation, however, without any fulcrum
or purchase, does lift the globe, and make it waltz
too, with its blond lunar partner, twelve hundred
miles a minute to the music of the sun, — ay,
and heaves sun and systems and milky-way in
majestic cotillons on its ethereal floor.

You grasp an iron ball, and call it hard ; it is
not the iron that is hard, but cohesive force that
packs the particles of metal into intense socia-
bility. Let the force abate, and the same metal
becomes like mush ; let it disappear, and the ball
is a heap of powder which your breath scatters in
the air. If the cohesive energy in nature should
get tired and unclench its grasp of matter, our
earth — to use an expressive New-England phrase
— would instantly become " a great slump " ; so
that what we tread on is not material substance,
but matter braced up by a spiritual substance, for
which it serves as the form and show.

All the peculiarities of rock and glass, diamond,

ice, and crystal are due to the working of unseen military forces that employ themselves under ground, — in caverns, beneath rivers, in mountain crypts, and through the coldest nights, drilling companies of atoms into crystalline battalions and squares, and every caprice of a fantastic order.

When we turn to the vegetable kingdom, is not the revelation still more wonderful? The forms which we see grow out of substances and are supported by forces which we do not see. The stuff out of which all vegetable appearances are made is reducible to oxygen, hydrogen, carbon, and nitrogen. How does it happen that this common stock is worked up in such different ways? Why is a lily woven out of it in one place and a dahlia in another, a grape-vine here, and a honeysuckle there, — the orange in Italy, the palm in Egypt, the olive in Greece, and the pine in Maine? Simply because a subtile force of a peculiar kind is at work wherever any vegetable structure adorns the ground, and takes to itself its favorite robe. We have outgrown the charming fancy of the Greeks that every tree has its Dryad that lives in it, animates it, and dies when the tree withers. But we ought, for the truth's sake, to believe that a life-spirit inhabits every flower and shrub, and protects it against the prowling forces of destruction. Look at a full-sized oak, the rooted Leviathan of the fields. Judging by your senses and by the scales, you would say that the substance of the noble tree was its bulk of bark and bough and

branch and leaves and sap, the cords of woody
and moist matter that compose it and make it
heavy. But really its substance is that which
makes it an oak, that which weaves its bark and
glues it to the stem, and wraps its rings of fresh
wood around the trunk every year, and pushes
out its boughs and clothes its twigs with digestive
leaves and sucks up nutriment from the soil continually, and makes the roots clench the ground
with their fibrous fingers as a purchase against the
storm wind, and at last holds aloft its tons of matter
against the constant tug and wrath of gravitation,
and swings its Briarean arms in triumph over the
globe and in defiance of the gale. Were it not for
this energetic essence that crouches in the acorn
and stretches its limbs every year, there would be
no oak ; the matter that clothes it would enjoy its
stupid slumber ; and when the forest monarch
stands up in his sinewy lordliest pride, let the
pervading life power, and its vassal forces that
weigh nothing at all, be annihilated, and the whole
structure would wither in a second to inorganic
dust. So every gigantic fact in nature is the index
and vesture of a gigantic force. Everything which
we call organization that spots the landscape of
nature is a revelation of secret force that has
been wedded to matter, and if the spiritual powers
that have thus domesticated themselves around
us should be cancelled, the whole planet would
be a huge desert of Sahara, — a black sand-ball
without a shrub, a grass-blade, or a moss.

As we rise in the scale of forces towards greater subtility the forces become more important and efficient. Water is more intimately concerned with life than rock, air higher in the rank of service than water, electric and magnetic agencies more powerful than air, and light, the most delicate, is the supreme magician of all. Just think how much expenditure of mechanical strength. is necessary to water a city in the hot summer months. What pumping and tugging and wearisome trudging of horses with the great sprinklers over the tedious pavement! But see with what beautiful and noiseless force nature waters the cities! The sun looks steadily on the ocean, and its beams lift lakes of water into the air, tossing it up thousands of feet with their delicate fingers, and carefully picking every grain of salt from it before they let it go. No granite reservoirs are needed to hold in the Cochituates and Crotons of the atmosphere, but the soft outlines of the clouds hem in the vast weight of the upper tides that are to cool the globe, and the winds harness themselves as steeds to these silken caldrons and hurry them along through space, while they disburse their rivers of moisture from their great height so lightly that seldom a violet is crushed by the rudeness with which the stream descends.

Our conceptions of strength and endurance are so associated with visible implements and mechanical arrangements that it is hard to divorce them, and yet the stream of electric fire that splits an ash is not a ponderable thing, and the way in which the loadstone reaches the ten-pound weight and makes it jump is not perceptible. You would think the man had pretty good molars that should gnaw a spike like a stick of candy, but a bottle of innocent-looking hydrogen gas will chew up a piece of bar-iron as though it were some favorite Cavendish ; and Mr. Faraday, the great chemist, claims to have demonstrated that each drop of water is the sheath of electric force sufficient to charge eight hundred thousand Leyden jars. In spite of Maine liquor laws, therefore, the most temperate man is a pretty hard drinker, for he is compelled to slake his thirst with a condensed thunder-storm. The difference in power between a woman's scolding and a woman's tears is explained now. Chemistry has put it into formulas. When a lady scolds a man has to face only a few puffs of articulate carbonic acid, but her weeping is liquid lightning.

The prominent lesson of science to men, therefore, is faith in the intangible and invisible. Shall we talk of matter as the great reality of the world, the prominent substance? It is nothing but the battle-ground of terrific forces. Every particle of matter, the chemists tell us, is strained up to its last degree of endurance. The glistening bead of dew from which the daisy gently nurses its strength, and which a sunbeam may dissipate, is the globular compromise of antagonistic powers that would shake this building in their unchained rage. And so every atom of matter is the slave of imperious masters that never let it alone. It is nursed and caressed, next bandied about, and soon cuffed and kicked by its invisible overseers. Poor atoms! no abolition societies will ever free them from their bondage, no colonization movement waft them to any physical Liberia. For every particle of matter is bound by eternal fealty to some spiritual lords, to be pinched by one and squeezed by another and torn asunder by a third; now to be painted by this and now blistered by that; now tormented with heat and soon chilled with cold; hurried from the Arctic Circle to sweat at the Equator, and then sent on an errand to the Southern Pole; forced through transmigrations of fish, fowl, and flesh; and, if in some corner of creation the poor thing finds leisure to die, searched out and whipped to life again and kept in its constant round.

Thus the stuff that we weigh, handle, and tread upon is only the show of invisible substances, the facts over which subtle and mighty forces rule.

Next, let us look at ideas as substantial things. If the true definition of substance is causal and sustaining force, then ideas take the first rank as substances, for the whole universe was thought into order and beauty. The word was, "Let there be light, and there was light." Nature is the language and imagery of Divine ideas. A Persian poet said : "The world is a bud from the bower of his beauty; the sun is a spark from the light of his wisdom; the sky is a bubble on the

1 *

sea of his power." A row of types, as arranged
by a compositor, not only present to the eye certain shapes, colors, and other sensible qualities,
but also intimate to the mind some thought that
once arose in a human intellect, and which they
have been selected to represent to others. So all
the objects of nature constitute a hieroglyphic
alphabet, which states great truths and sentiments that dwell in the Infinite intellect ; with
this difference, that the objects of nature are created and upheld by the idea or sentiment which
possesses them. They would fall away and dissolve if the eternal truth they represent should
vanish, just as the body would crumble if the soul
should leave it. Not a planet that wheels its circle
around its controlling flame, not a sun that pours its
blaze upon the black ether, not one of all the con-
stellated chandeliers that burn in the dome of
heaven, not a firmament that spots the robe of
space with a fringe of light, but is a visible
statement of a conception, wish, or purpose in
the mind of God, from which it was born, and to
which alone it owes its continuance and form.
Jonathan Edwards imagined that the Almighty
creates and upholds the universe, as a reflection
on a mirror is caused and sustained by the person
or object that stands before it. The rays fall
from the object upon the mirror every moment,
and the reflection would cease as soon as the
object should remove ; so, he conceived, the universe is the continuous image of the Creator's

constant thought, and would change instantly if the expression of his purpose varied, and would fade from space if his ideas should be dismissed. The mind cannot entertain a more sublime thought than this, and we learn from it that the man who does not delight in the beauty of the universe, and does not receive into his soul some impressions of the meaning of nature, has no contact with the world of Divine Substance, but lives in a vast baby-house of Show.

Let us see, next, how applicable the principle we are considering is to the world of man and history. All the shows of social life are manifestations of a secret and impalpable substance. Every house, workshop, church, school-room, athenæum, theatre, is the representative of an opinion. What the eye sees of them is built of bricks, iron, wood, and mortar by carpenters, smiths, and masons ; but the seed from which they grew and the forces by which they are upheld are ideas, affections, conceptions of utility, sentiments of worship. Strike these out of a people's mind and heart, and its homes, temples, colleges, and art-rooms fall away, like the trunk of the oak when its life-power is smitten, and only the bald, sandy surface of savage life remains.

What a difference it would make in the physical and moral landscape of a new country, whether a race of Saxons or of Turks were dropped upon it ! In the latter case the timber and stone are slowly conjured into the form of mosques and minarets,

Sultan's palaces and harems, and the various features of a lazy Moslem civilization; while the coming of the Saxon genius bids the forests prepare to be hewn for homes and factories, humble shrines of learning, and thickly strewn domes for Sabbath praise and prayer. The iron can no longer sleep in its hiding-places; the coal — the only black slave whose labor the white man may rightfully impress — must bring its hot temperament to human service; the streams are compelled to pour their strength upon muscular and busy wheels, that weave fabrics of comfort and luxury; valleys are exalted, and mountains bend their necks; steam hurries with monstrous burdens; magnetism shoots thoughts along its slender veins; mighty piles that stand for justice, law, and equal government overlook a thousand cities; and the white wings of commerce, vying in number and in speed with the pinions of the sea-birds, flap in every breeze that stirs the polar, the moderate, or the tropic waves. There may be as many men, as much bodily strength, among the Turks as with the Saxons; but there is not the spirit, there are not the ideas, to make the fingers so cunning and the muscles so strong. It is the hidden spiritual substance in the Saxon frames that makes their bones and blood its purchase and pulleys, to lift up the myriad structures that bear witness to Saxon civilization. All that we see in England and America, so different from what Calcutta and Canton exhibit to the eye, is the clothing and show of different ideas, principles, and sentiments that pervade our vigorous blood.

Thus, each nation of the globe is a huge battery of spiritual forces to which each individual contributes something. The oneness of the nation is the unity of the galvanic current that is generated from the many layers of metal and acid. And the question of the superior power of one nation over another is not at all to be decided by the relative numbers of population and armies, nor by the forts, guns, and magazines, but rather by the relative mental and moral energies of the lands. France, for instance, is a magnificent incarnation of a certain temperament, and the generations that rise up in her borders continually supply the same mental and social forces, thus giving her one character through centuries. England, moreover, is the hive of very different passions and powers, and the point whether, in a long war, giving each side money enough, England or France would triumph, is reduced to the question whether the effervescent impulses and military enthusiasm of the Celtic blood are superior, as spiritual qualities, to the more slow and sullen force, the cautious but persistent resolution, and the tough obstinacy of resistance that make up the power of an Anglo-Saxon army. In the great campaigns of Wellington in Spain, and in the conduct of the struggle at Waterloo, this was the real strife, — a wrestle of certain spiritual qualities with each other. The charge of the

French under Ney or Murat, and beneath the eye
of Napoleon, was the gathering roll and swing of
the storm-waves ; whatever was movable must
fall before it ; but the mind and the resources of
Wellington and the temper of the men who served
him were the Saxon rock on which those magnificent Celtic surges swung their white wrath in vain.
Every charge of Ney's cavalry against Wellington's
central position at Waterloo was the beat of a fiery
sensibility against a stony patience.   The whole
scene was less a contest of military science than
a visible conflict of different passions and a thorough testing of their strength.   It was the old
hypothesis, in dramatic play, of an irresistible in
contact with an immovable.   The irresistible was
spent ; the immovable stood fast.

All fighting illustrates the same law.   In the
old Greek days Darius could oppose a hundred
spears to each one of Alexander's, and we wonder that the Persians were so easily beaten.   The
reason is that the fighting in the young Greek
general's army was done by spears plus brains,
courage, enthusiasm.   Discipline in a battalion is
of more consequence than numbers, because it
adds a spiritual force to that of muscles ; fervor
is often found superior to the most thorough discipline, for fervor is a higher spiritual force and
outweighs the weaker.   Bayonets are never so
sharp and terrible in the hands of an advancing
line, as when they are bayonets that think, as was
the case in our own Revolution ; and there are

no regiments so mighty and dangerous as those which Cromwell headed, where the highest spiritual qualities were drilled into the ranks, and the bayonets could not only think, but pray.

Thus, in all cases, a nation or an army, so far as its persons — all that we can see of it — are concerned, is only a show; the substance of it is the ideas, passions, genius, enthusiasm, that pervade it, and are not seen.

Our doctrine is illustrated, also, by the fact that the power of a nation is made up, in part, by the generations of past years, whose bodily forms long ago mouldered to dust. There is no more beautiful or impressive law of history than that by which the past genius, heroism, and patriotic devotedness are woven into the structure of a people, giving it character. The acts and spirit of a person's former years are not lost, but are represented in the face, the habits, the weakness, or the power of the person's mind and heart to-day. In the same way a state has a personality that endures through centuries; all its great men and bad men, its good laws and vile laws, its faithfulness and its crimes, contribute to its character; nothing dies; but what was fact and show in a living generation becomes force and substance when the actors have departed. Look at England, for instance. Is that which we call England composed simply of twenty millions of men and women that inhabit that island now? How truly do the statesmen, patriots, orators, poets, kings, cabinets, and parties of several hundred years, belong to our conception of what England is ! The witness of their activity is not only prominent in the literature and art, the castles and cathedrals, the palaces and towers, the liberties and laws, that are visible on the English land and in their society, but an incalculable force has been shed from this background of greatness and genius into the generation of to-day, and through the present will be transmitted into the future.   Let a hostile cabinet declare war against England, and try to tread out her spirit and influence, and they would find that a force is needed competent to crush twenty generations. For, though the merchants, traders, and laborers little think of it in time of peace, and perhaps care not half a fig for the men that walked through the streets they tread, two centuries ago, Sidney, Russell, Pym, and Hampden, Newton, and Shakespeare, and Chatham, the great dead of Westminster Abbey, and the honored names of Oxford and Cambridge, still stand in the background, and in an emergency would start forward and give the immense momentum of their spirit to an onset against an invading foe.   As the ghost of the hero Theseus appeared, according to the Athenians, on the field of Marathon, and inspirited their ranks against the Persians, the greatness which a nation has enshrined in its traditions is part of its deepest present life ; and it often happens that the shades of the fathers are a more substantial rampart for a land than the swords of the children.

See, too, how our revolutionary experience, genius, and fidelity are involved in the character of America. They are not dead facts written in mute annals; they are vital memories of the nation, as though the same men that are now on the stage had once performed them. We take the crèdit of that wisdom, persistence, and sacrifice partly to ourselves; we are proud of them; and in any crisis our arms would be the stronger, our wit the quicker, our fortitude the more heroic, because of the impulses that would thrill our veins from the beatings of that revolutionary heart. Strike out the idea of America and the hope of America from our people, and a great portion of the force and enthusiasm of our people would be annihilated. That period of our national fortunes is far more than a show in our history; it is part of our present substance. It was not a fact of the past merely; it is a force of our national character.

The most mournful sight in the case of any nation is the evident destitution of any great political sentiments and principles that have grown for centuries, and are rooted in its heads, habits, and hearts. What a sad thing that, on the intellectual and moral soil of France, — beautiful, enthusiastic France, whose genius has been refining for ages like the wine its own vineyards distil, — no ideas of rights and constitutional freedom have

grown, that could not be pulled up in a night
by a dissolute ruffian, wearing and polluting a
splendid name! Think you that in England or
here any cowardly conspirator could weave the
noose that in one night should drag down the
form and the sentiment of Liberty from its sacred
niche in the popular affections, and the next day
make the people themselves applaud that it was
done so well? A Bedouin robber might as well
try to lasso and uproot a hickory-tree that had
toughened its roots in the ground for a century.
Poor France was overgrown with the merest
weedy sentiments of liberty; for it is only weeds
that bayonets can scratch up.

If we reflect on the sources of national power
and prosperity, we shall soon see how its strength
rests on an invisible and ideal base, and is developed out of mental and moral resources. Little
Greece resisted the flood of Persian arms, and at
last conquered the East, because there was more
vitality — more courage, genius, enthusiasm — in
her people than in the swarming myriads which
the bulk of the Persian Empire enclosed. Rome,
too, rose to supreme sway by the despotic influence
of character, not of legions. When Rome fell she
had more troops and fortifications than in the
height of her republican supremacy, but she had
lost her real and invisible strength, that of temperance, hardihood, valor, moral soundness; internal dissension, luxury, and bad government had
unnerved her hands; and therefore her visible

defences of battalions and armaments were nothing but empty shell and show. The British dominion is supported now by the strong fibres of Saxon wisdom and pride that run through the whole extent of it. It is those that knit Calcutta and Australia, Gibraltar and Cape Town, to London and Liverpool and the Parliament House.

The most effectual way to paralyze the prosperity of our country at this moment would be to smite an ideal element that interpenetrates the land. The soil over half our area might be blighted, pestilence might decimate our laborers, tornadoes might scatter a great portion of our tonnage in ruins upon the sea, droughts might shrivel the rivers into thin and feeble rills; but all this would be less disastrous than to annihilate the system of credit that pervades the mercantile world. Destroy that impalpable thing, break down the confidence between city and country, the reliance which State feels upon State and East upon West, the trust which man reposes in his neighbor, and it is the same as if you arrest the pitch of waterfalls, and smother the breezes that ruffle the deep, and wilt the fierce energy of steam, and unstring the laborer's arm, and quench the furnace-fires, and stop the hum of wheels, and forbid emigrants to seek the West and cities to rise amid the silence of its woods. Our prosperity and our hopes lean back on that moral bond more than they do on nature or on capital ; shake it, and there is an earthquake of society ; restore it, and order, activity, happiness, and wealth return.

As a bond of union for our States, moreover, there is one element more substantial than even the wisdom of our Constitution, the interlocked geographical unity of our territory, and the power of our central government. It is our common memories of a great history, and the one language that is spoken in all our zones and over all the breadth of the lines of longitude, that mark the leagues from the Atlantic to the Pacific shores. It is hardly possible that any wisdom of political structure or administration could hold so many States together against such diversities of social customs, intelligence, and interest, if the different districts of our empire spoke different languages. But our unity of speech, — the common way in which we articulate our breath and write our thoughts, enabling the farthest backwoodsman to feel kindred with the culture of the East, making all commercial correspondence simple and easy, allowing us to read the same books, to read the same speeches with common delight in a common eloquence, — this is like a soul breathed through all the limbs of our confederacy, giving it a stronger unity than its geological skeleton or its political muscles can.   Destroy this community of language, give a distinct tongue to each great division of our land, introduce confusion of dialects into our capital, and we could have no more permanent unity than the mechanical one which Nebuchadnezzar's image had, with its head of gold, its breast of silver, its thighs of brass, its legs of iron, and its feet of clay. Its parts might be dislodged from each other. There would not be invisible unity to mould into vital permanence its unity of show.

The politicians every now and then get up their schemes of division, but the common mother tongue drowns them before they swim far. As long as the free soil and the Hunker speeches in Congress are made in the same dialect the danger of their antagonism is greatly abated. Only the old mother tongue does try to tell us, through the dictionaries, that the word "slave" is not Saxon. It came into our speech by foreign immigration ; it cannot show any naturalization papers, the Constitution rejected it, and so certainly, according to the present tendencies of party, it ought not to be allowed to gain power and office over the good native American noun " freedom."

I have several times used the word "civilization" in connection with the subject we are considering. Let us see now what light the meaning of that word sheds upon our theme. There are a vast number of things that make up civilization. They are invisible, but they are among the most substantial and potent realities connected with our globe.

Besides the men and women, the houses and wealth, that exist in Christendom, there is such a thing as civilization, which has been growing steadily, and which lives on while the generations die. There is government in the civilized world,

there are reverences, laws, manners and habits,
tastes and principles, and all these make up the
structure of society.   Just as the surface of the
globe is composed of various layers of clay, sand-
stone, slate, and granite, which successive geological epochs deposited, and the united strength of
which uphold our soil and support our steps, the
moral world is constructed of strata of laws, customs, opinions, truths, discoveries, sentiments,
which successive races and generations have deposited, and which our souls live upon now.   The
best life of the nations that are gone is still in our
civilization.   Influences from the Old Testament,
from Grecian literature and character, from Roman
heroism and law, are steadily poured into our
moral life from countless churches and colleges,
although the Hebrew State, the Greek Republics,
and the Roman Empire have been buried for centuries.   And so from the German barbarians of
the Northern forests, from the feudal customs,
from the Crusades, from the Catholic church in its
ripe power and glory, from the life of Socrates
and the intellect of Augustine, from the speech
of Paul on Mars Hill and the thinking of John
Huss, from what Bacon wrote and Shakespeare
imagined and Faust invented and Newton discovered and Fulton devised ; in short, from all the
victories of heroes and the blood-sealed fidelity
of martyrs and the holy achievements of saints
some contributions have been made to that progressive reality we call civilization, and they all

exist around us now as beneficent forces that ennoble our lives with privileges and a value which cannot be estimated. Your father may not have left you any legacy of houses and stock, but the whole past is your mental and moral father, and that leaves to every one of us an inheritance which it would be a miserable bargain for us to sell for a fortune of millions on condition of being disentangled from the civilized life of the race.

The poorest man in this neighborhood is immensely rich, so far as attaining the great objects of life is concerned, especially if he has a family, compared with what his poverty would be if he could own a hundred square miles of original nature, and must live on it alone with his family, cut off from all privileges of society and with the wealth of civilized influence forever cancelled from his brain and breast.

Thus we see that the substance of the past lives on and is vitally present with us now. All that is visible of a nation dies, but its soul survives ; the truth it discovered and illustrated is preserved ; its essence passes into civilization, improves society, and becomes the common property of after times.

In the old furniture-shops of Boston you can buy chairs and tables that came out of the Mayflower to an extent that would load a fleet. However much humbug there may be about this, thank Heaven the spiritual cargo that was packed into that little hull is not all unloaded yet. New Eng-

land liberty and thrift have been disembarked
from it ; half of New York and Ohio and Illinois
and Wisconsin have been heaved out of its hold
by invisible stevedores ; and there is enough left
yet to set up good Constitutions in the farther
slopes of the Rocky Mountains and make Kansas
free.

Think for a moment, too, of the order in a
great city, and how it is preserved. What passions are boiling in London and Boston and the
streets of New York ! And how is it that we are
kept from conspiracies and mobs and devastations
of license? How is it that the spirit of our social
life is higher in respect of peace than the aggre-
gate of individual lives, which is the splendid
mystery of civilization ? It is not by direct and
visible pressure of resisting force, but by the fine
network of interests, opinions, reverences, feelings
of honor and shame, fears and loves, disposed
over the community, which hold the brutal elements of our nature in check, as Gulliver was
made prisoner by the threads which the cunning
Lilliputians wove over his body, and one of which
they fastened to each of his hairs.

Does any man say that the laws, the courts
and sheriffs, uphold our order? Plainly the sanctity of the laws does not consist in their enact-
ments by legislatures, or their preservation in
sheep-skin binding (a style of binding, by the
way, which many of our laws had when they were
yet in the brains of their authors). Sentiments

and principles in the people, faith and loyalty, varnish the laws with their real majesty.

Once in a while a great officer of the law comes along, like the venerable Hays, so famous in Boston, who stands forth as a physical Napoleon of police. It is not by his personal finite genius that he wears such terror. But he is a good conductor of the respect for law which is latent in the community. His frame is electric with the potency of civil authority everywhere. We had a marshal in Boston lately that sometimes appeared on a Saturday night in a circle of gamblers, and though he was but one man among a score or two, he changed the game very quick, and he infused a sudden passion for a different shuffle and cut than any laid down in Hoyle. The play shifted by magic from whist and loo to leap-frog and all-fours, because a worthy embodiment of social law, invested with the moral force of civilization, appalled and scattered them. When the lightning strikes a tree there is a stream of electricity from the ground that conspires with the flame from heaven to complete the bolt, else it is harmless ; and so the law in the guilty men leaps out and combines with the electric flash from every great officer's form, to do the work of moral paralysis. There was great wisdom sententiously expressed in the exclamation of a little constable I heard of once who went to arrest a burly offender against the statutes, and was threatened with a shaking if he did not " clear out." If it had been a matter of

2

fists and muscles, the majesty of the law would have been miserably bruised. But the intrepid little officer responded : " Do it if you please ; only remember, if you shake me you shake the whole State of Massachusetts."

The substance of power is that which sways the minds and hearts of the people ; all else is the show of it. And so the highest badge of civic authority now is not the sceptre of a king, not the dress of a president, not the uniform of a general, but the pole of a constable. The English or Yankee policeman wears a badge which society spontaneously respects, which innocence and weakness instinctively rejoice in, which guilt and knavery instinctively fear. What is the authority of Nicholas the Czar, or Louis Napoleon in his rocking-chair of bayonets? (may every point of them prick the tanned hide of his conscience yet !) — what are they but imperial bullies with military bull-dogs to keep the wrath of the human race at bay ? Mr. Bumble the beadle sits on the throne of civil power ; to him the human race goes down with honest awe upon its knees.

Surely this nation could better afford to part with its armies and navy, its forts, guns, magazines, and military science, than to have an abatement of one per cent from the regard which the people have for the forms of a town-meeting, their deep reverence for the statutes, their quick submission to a writ, their dread of mobs, their love of home, and the awe that attends the hearing a sentence of death from a judge. In the first case the country would lose some visible facts which represent its strength, and which might be replenished by taxation ; in the latter case it would part with forces, inherited from past ages, which are its strength, and by which it is swung over the abyss of lawlessness, as the globe is hurried over the black depths of space by the threads of gravitation that are more subtle than sunbeams.

Finally, character is one of the prominent substances of the world, that is, it is one of the things which do the most as causes to uphold society and quicken it. Character, in the sense of great personal energy, changes the face of nature, digs mines, builds railroads, levels mountains, founds cities, evokes factories, dwarfs the oceans to convenient ponds. And in higher senses, we cannot tell what impress one original soul like David's, so splendid in genius, so sensitive to every breath of circumstance, so sincere in his piety, his sin, and his terrible remorse, leaves on the fortunes of after generations. His great heart has been an electric battery to the bosoms of countless millions of whom he never dreamed. Who of us is acute enough to untwist the whole of our debt to the burly substance of Martin Luther's spirit ? Strike him out of the last three centuries, and you tear out the very spine of our liberties and mechanical arts ; our railroads and steamships, and most of the material forces of Protestant civilization are rent away with him, for they radiate from his rough generic thought. The Duke of Wellington assented to the estimate which somebody made, that the presence of Napoleon on the field was equal to forty thousand men. See, too, what the character of the Puritans is doing for New England at this moment. It gives it a firmer basis than its granite strata. It is the stamina of the present virtue of those States. It has built and reared their colleges and schools. It is the vigor of their intelligence and the sinew of their piety, and thus is a substantial benefit after the bodily forms that once housed it are crumbled. And advert, for a moment, to what the character of Washington has done, and will yet do, for America and freedom. Better for our country in the crisis of its history to have lost its collected treasures, to have parted with half its territory and half its citizens, than to have been robbed of the heart of Washington. His soldiers derived courage, faith, and food from his serene and hopeful majesty, and during that terrible winter at Valley Forge the nourishment of future ages was in the continuance of the resources in that one breast. His character is part of this Western World forever, as much part of it as our forests and our rocks.

So there is an ascending series of creative and substantial forces, beginning with mechanical energies and running up through chemical affinities, vital powers, perception, will, ideas, to personality. We often use the expression with regard to a person in society, that " he is a man of substance." Generally this phrase conveys the idea that a man has acquired some property. It would be very applicable if it stood for the "real estate" which a man has amassed, — that is, for his personal estate of great qualities, forces of genius, learning, truth, moral power, and influence. For it happens that, in the supreme realm of which we are citizens, and where the eternal laws tax and weigh us, our personal estate, that is, what we are, is our real estate. How absurd to use the word "substance" of a man, and make it signify a house, bank-stock, a heap of guineas, a store full of merchandise ; things that do not touch his humanity at all. He is the man of substance that has the noble qualities which belong to human nature packed into him, and that can stand up, strong and solid, if all the accidents, such as fame, position, money, worldly consideration, are stripped away. It would be just as sensible to take a man in the last stages of consumption, — a weak and wasted frame of bones, — and after getting a tailor to dress him up and pad him out large with batting, to call him a man of physical substance, as to use that phrase of persons that only have a market control over some dollars, and are destitute of the forces and resources that belong to a mind, heart, and soul. Your Herschel and Newton are men of intellectual substance, Fénelon and Wesley of spiritual substance, Wilberforce of moral substance, Luther of heroic substance, Howard of affectional substance ; and if we are lean in these qualities, we are shadows, and all the bricks and mortar, land-deeds, certificates, and doubloons, in London cannot redeem us from being thinner than mush, — a body-load of mist and fog.

Character is the culminating substance of nature ; and we may say here that a man may be what he pleases to be.   The forms of our activity are prescribed for us by nature, but circumstances do not make the real, central man.   Circumstances often determine how much show a man shall make. To be famous depends on some fortuities ; to be a president depends on the acute smellers of a few politicians and a mysterious set of wires ; to be rich depends on birth or luck ; to be intellectually eminent may depend on the appointment of Providence ; but to be a man, in the sense of substance, depends solely on one's own noble ambition and determination to live in contact with God's open atmosphere of truth and right, from which all true manliness is inspired and fed.   We often talk about ghosts, and wonder, sometimes, at our winter firesides whether any ghost has ever returned from the regions of the dead.   For one, I am content to leave that question of revisits to be decided by Mrs. Crowe's " Night Side of Nature " and the vast and increasing crowd of spiritual rappers, who are able to make any luckless spirit beat a tattoo on smooth walnut or mahogany.

Now, the answer we should give if anybody should ask us if we had ever seen a ghost will depend wholly on our standard of what a ghost is. Some men would not be satisfied unless they could shoot a bullet through him without injuring any intestines. Another would want to strike a club at him, and have it pass through as though it were six feet of moonshine. In Dickens's "Christmas Carol" the old miser was satisfied he beheld his dead partner's ghost, when he looked right through his stomach and saw the buttons on the back of his coat. Any test which would prove that an unfortunate being had no body would satisfy most persons of its claim to ghostship. By any such standards we must probably give up the honor of having seen a ghost. And yet the world is plentifully spotted with apparitions ; they are all about us, in the streets and the stalls and the stores ; they are in the Congress rooms, and editors' chairs, and pulpits, transacting a great deal of the business of the world, — not revisitants of the earth, because they have never left it, but shows of people, human haze and ghastliness, without the substance of energy, virtue, truth, to fill out the plain promise of their clothes. For our popular definition of a ghost is just the reverse of the truth ; it makes one consist of a soul without a body, while really a spectre, an illusion, a humbug of the eyesight and the touch, is a human body not vitalized through and through with a soul.

When a person has only money to support his claim to substance, his highest nature is made up of mortgages and rent-rolls, notes and titles, — a man of bank paper, not of realities, — and a commercial revolution would tear him up. Some men's claim to substance depends on a large stock of calicoes ; and a fall in the thermometer of trade reduces them to zero. Where station is the sole basis of that claim, the person's soul is a great bladder blown up by popular breath, and a pin-hole of accident will make him collapse. But of all those classes which the world puts forward as its darlings, the dandy is the most removed from the domain of real qualities and takes first rank as a ghost, since he is "a whiskered essence and an organized perfume."

The climax of my purpose in this address will be gained if it will lead any of you to see that the stuff a great soul is made of is the most real and unwasting material of the universe, — something which moth and rust cannot corrupt, nor death with the tooth of its savage chemistry impair. As men walk the streets they seem about alike ; the differences they show seem to be the difference of height, weight, complexion, and clothes. But it is not so. As you stand at a little distance from this metropolis, upon a hill that commands its avenues and circuit, you see of what various buildings, differing widely in cost and splendor, its beautiful panorama is composed. And so would its human inhabitants seem, if you could stand on some spiritual eminence and see the realities which their fleshly tenement conceal. . . . . Thence would we see the churches of our spiritual city ; and over them, kindred but superior, with more intricate grace and capacious measure, the cathedral spirits, like such as Channing, whose voices are bells that call to worship, and whose thoughts, like spires, are always lifted above the world, conversing with light and God, rebuking the vanity of the earth, and shedding over all below the promise of immortality.

1851.

2*   C

II.

THE LAWS OF DISORDER.

UNTIL a more accurate and luminous formula suggests itself, I must announce the address which it is my privilege to offer you, under the paradoxical and vague title of " The Laws of Disorder." Let me hope that the illustrations to be brought forward will sufficiently interpret the fundamental purpose of the lecture, — which is to show how laws wind into regions of nature and society that we never conceive of as subject to a plan and a purpose, but rather as chaotic, or, at any rate, at loose ends.

If a die should be thrown a million times, it would turn out that aces, trays, sixes, would appear in about equal proportions. The result of each throw would be uncertain enough, but a man might stake his estate on the ratio of deuces or sixes in the million casts with less risk of loss than most of the lines of business are attended with. This fact, drawn from the logic of chances, furnishes the keynote of my lecture. The order which nature loves and weaves is not a stiff and laborious regularity, but an easy and beautiful play with materials that seem to the senses huddled and anarchical, — a harmony soaring, at last, out of independent, interlaced, and often tangled forces.

We often say, for instance, that the order of the solar system is made up of two great forces, the centrifugal tendency of the planets and the gravitating energy of the sun. But this statement gives one no idea of the intricacy and complexity of the plan in which we live. If we could stand outside of any one of the planets in our family, we should not find it cutting a regular path in space in obedience to two simple forces, but beating this way and that, now swinging out towards its neighbor next beyond, and then reeling the other way to hail its fellow-orb whose path is next within, and so oscillating and whirling through all its months until it accomplishes its round. We should imagine, could we see them very near, that the planets were let loose, to cut up capers in space, rather than to measure a marvellous harmony. The earth never travels the same track any two successive years, and yet it never fails to be punctual to the minute, and the fraction of a minute, when its revolutions should be accomplished, but keeps time, in spite of its roving, more accurately than any machine of human invention can be made to do. The forces that whip and curb the planets suffer them to dally and prance and curvet on the great race-course of the ecliptic, but are sure to bring them in swift and punctual to a second at the goal; so that the order of the solar system is not the poise of two forces merely, but the balance of constant and countless perturbations of that poise. As though it were not enough to bring our globe around true to its second every year over a track of six hundred millions of miles, her path is changed every year, and still the time is kept exact; and if it were not for the jaggedness, the continual shifting, and the seeming disorder of her orbit, the accuracy of her obedience and the stability of our harmony would be ruined.

So the regularity of the mean temperature of any district is a striking instance of the secret play of law in a most frolicsome way. The wind is our type of inconstancy; but a physical atlas of the globe will show us that its currents are about as well defined as the outlines of the continents. What is more uncertain than the weather a day or two from now, what more capricious than the changes of the weather during a week? Yet the powers of vegetation are so nicely fitted to a certain average temperature, that trees and plants would die if in the whole year, or in a succession of two or three years, the mean warmth should fall five degrees. Such a variation never takes place. Irregular as our winters are, and uncertain as the summer heat is, we get the needed result with wonderful precision when the temperatures of our three hundred and sixty-five days are shuffled together and brought to an average. Of course, the electrical laws, the evaporating forces, the disturbances that generate winds, the way in which the earth turns to the sun every month and the swiftness of its rotatory motion, the laws of heat with respect to the earth, the water, and the air, are all balanced to each other as the condition of this order ; and the mean temperature is the beautiful figure which these shuttles that fly criss-cross and hap-hazard from all quarters of the universe weave patiently, as a witness of providential order, into the warp of time.

We find, too, that the minutest organizations on the earth's surface are so related to the largest and wildest forces of nature as to show wonderful delicacy and subtlety of law. When we see common plants and shrubs growing so easily, we have no idea how the general order of the globe and sky is toned to their necessities. With regard to a common wild-flower, we may see that the force of gravitation which holds its fibres in the earth and strengthens its stalk is graduated so that, while it supports a constellation, it shall not prevent the juices from rising through its cells to carry life to the leaves. So the bulk and heat of the sun, the constitution of the air, the size of the sea, the swiftness of the earth's whirling and the diameter of its orbit, are determined with admirable relation to its need of heat and rain and wind, its alternations of light and gloom, and the changes of seasons from spring to winter. An alteration even of a slight percentage in the mixture and partnership of these great forces would destroy the possibility of the daisy's life.   But these brawny and furious powers are ordered to bend themselves carefully to the needs of the most delicate structures ; and every flower is so nice an index of the adjustment between the forces of the universe, that one might believe, looking at it exclusively, the globe and the solar system were built by the Almighty as a factory to turn out the violets which embroider the spring.

In the methods of atomic combinations, also, a striking instance of the same subtle presence of law is seen.   Everything we see in nature is a chemical compound, and an analyst can untwist its component elements and show them in their simplicity.   And various as the mixtures are, it is found that a splendid regularity rules over them. Separate the parts of water, for instance, and we get 8 parts oxygen to 1 part hydrogen.   Now, whenever oxygen and hydrogen combine in any substance, it will be in a ratio of which 8 is the basis.   There may be 16 parts oxygen to 1 hydrogen, or 24 parts to 1, or 40 to 1 ; but no instance can be found, no substance in all known nature, in which the ratio will be 9 to 1 or 7 to 1, or any other than strictly 8 or some multiple of 8. So we find that carbon will combine with other substances only in the ratio of which 6 is the key, nitrogen in a proportion of 14 or some of its multiples, iron by parts represented by 28, gold by 199, etc.   Thus it is plain that the invisible atoms of things are under strictest chemical drill, and, stir them together as we may, they will file by regular platoons, and only according to the original word of command, into steady combinations.

The science of botany has unfolded some very singular and beautiful facts which contribute richly to the illustration of our subject. Many of the most important plants and trees are dependent, as to their fruit-bearing, upon intermediate agencies that carry perhaps from a great distance the vegetable dust or pollen to the flower of the plant by which it is made productive. The whole date-harvest in some countries of the East, on which the sustenance of millions of men depends, is intrusted to the fidelity of the winds, which sweep the quickening seed-dust sometimes even across Sahara to the waiting germens of the fruit-bearing palm. Sometimes insects are the mediating agents between the different trees. The fig-trade of Smyrna, and the food of thousands of our race, is dependent on the yearly fidelity of the gall-fly, which carries in season the needed stimulant from tree to tree. So the Syrian silk-plant is made productive by the bees that, in search of nectar, carry on their waxen thighs the feathery principle of life from flower to flower. And so the increase of the Kamschatkan lily, by whose bulbs sometimes the whole population of Greenland is saved from starvation in a hard winter, is suspended on the regular theft of a kind of beetle which carries the quickening principle of growth to the plant, when it means only to steal its own support. Thus the one beneficent purpose of Providence is secured year by year through means that seem to be chances or accidents : what seems fluctuating disorder to the senses is the easy and joyous pulse of law.

Thus the great force and beauty of the argument against atheism, as constructed by modern science, lie in this, that so many independent laws conspire in producing the regularity and system of Nature. One might conceive that out of the tumultuous heavings of chaos for ages some general order might turn up at last ; but a mechanism so intricate as our globe displays, and yet so delicate, perfected by a thousand junctions and conspiracies of separate threads of design, the failure of any one of which would entangle the skein, — what length of ages seems sufficient to produce so many beneficent concurrences of accident, what calculus of probabilities is able to state the infinitesimal likelihood of such a system happening into existence ?

We may represent it in this way. A heap of types many millions in number might be tossed up so that every now and then they would fall into combinations of words. But can you conceive of a throw that should leave them in words grammatically joined, so that each independent sentence would be readable ? Now try to imagine what chance there is that a throw could happen in which the separate sensible sentences should make consecutive paragraphs? And when you have tried that calculation, think of a throw occurring in which the types should fall so that words fit into sentences, sentences into paragraphs, and these again into chapters, nay, perhaps rhymes or measured lines, paragraphs and chapters giving you a Waverley novel or a tragedy of Shakespeare or the Iliad of Homer, — not only connected grammatical sense, but characters drawn and related to each other, the finest strokes of genius visible in the subordinate portions, and all fitting into a subtle unity which the most cultivated critic studies with greatest marvel and delight ! There you have the problem of atheism partially presented in the light of science now. The unity and harmony of the natural world are analogous to the unity and symmetry of a printed work of genius ; and so the doctrine of *chances* ridicules the theory of *chance.*

A whole lecture might be devoted to the beautiful proofs from the physical world for the play of law amid seemingly chaotic and accidental facts ; but I must pass on and invite your attention to the most striking illustrations that may be drawn from society. The idea very seldom enters any mind that there is any organization of society at all except that which men deliberately produce by rules of laws or by military force. The general feeling is that outside these arbitrary arrangements social facts are casual and at loose ends. But the truth is, that the order which man makes in society

is very slight compared with that which secret forces
make, over which he has no control, and whose
processes human wisdom cannot fathom at all.

No statutes of human enactment, no progress
of the age, no increase of scientific, educational,
or mechanical advantages, nothing in the range
of human wisdom and power, is of such vital importance to the interests and growth of society as
that there should be in every generation a particular and stable proportion between the men and
women that inhabit the globe. The idea of setting a man to guess how many boys and how
many girls there are in each household of Boston
would seem ridiculous; and yet extend your survey to the State of Massachusetts or to New England, and a mathematician will tell you with surprising correctness, not only what the proportion
of boys to girls is now, but also what it will be in
the next generation. Looking over this civilized
world, we find that the ratio of births is always
one hundred and six males to one hundred females.
Various speculations have been entertained as to
the cause for this preference by Providence of a
slight excess of the sterner sex. Some have said
that it is to compensate for the wastes of war and
to furnish material for standing armies; others have
imagined that it is Nature's method of supplying
candidates for the Catholic priesthood ; again, it
has been suggested that civilization needs the
peculiar influence that is shed into society from
a certain number of old bachelors, the delicate

aroma and flavor they impart to civilization, like the drops of lemon in a punch, or mustard in a salad, and therefore that the constitution of things ordains that there must be four or five per cent at least of the masculine race for whom no partners are furnished in the waltz of life ; but perhaps the most philosophical and satisfactory reason is that which a lady gave me the other day, namely, that it is to insure an equilibrium of character, this inequality being Nature's subtle way of confessing that a hundred women amount to as much, any day, as one hundred and six men.

But whatever theory we adopt, here is the wonderful fact that this proportion continues century by century, upholding civilization by its mysterious constancy. If it should alter by any considerable percentage in favor of a large majority of males, civilization would be encircled by a ferocity as pleasant to contemplate as a circle of wolves belting the huts of settlers in the forest. If it should alter in favor of a large majority of women, the present discussions and movements in favor of women's rights would simply change the gender of their pronouns, and the position of Mrs. Abby Folsom in a public meeting now would be a type of masculine influence and heroism among the feminine autocrats and politicians.

Moreover, subordinate to this general law which fixes the proportions of births, we may see a singular and unfailing order in the boundless diversity of expression produced out of the general likeness of features among people. It is very difficult for an artist to conceive and chisel a new face out of the proportions of the Greek outline, or any strong national type. Yet out of the millions living in any large country, out of the hundreds of millions on the globe, nay, out of the myriads of millions since Adam, scarcely any two could be mistaken for each other. And all this is effected by dissimilarities so slight, when measured by the compass, as to seem of no consequence when mathematically stated. Nature distinguishes the red-haired people from each other as easily as the brown and black heads; pug noses are discriminated most happily; dark complexions do not confuse the individualities of countenance ; no two pairs of blue or hazel eyes are steeped with the same gentleness or brilliancy ; and even the Chinese, who look certainly to an uneducated eye like a monotonous nation of universal twins, no doubt seem to their own visual organs broken up into distinguishable personalities.

Now, we need not reflect long to discover the various and indispensable benefits of this beautiful law. How apparent it is that the subtlest pleasures of social intercourse, the possibilities of friendship, the interesting arts and the delicate joys of courtship, and even the solemn interests of justice, hang upon these fine distinctions in the faces of people. Of how trifling avail would laws be, if men could hide their guilty personalities under a mask of universal resemblance, so that the rogue need only say in the court-room, where fifty copies of himself perhaps surrounded the bench, " Thou canst not say I did it." In case of marriage, too, the only question for a person to decide would be what age he or she would prefer for husband or wife, taking the first that offers ; the only sure way of proving identity would be for persons to wear tickets with proper labels, attested by the minister or court, "This may certify that I am Henry Johnson's wife," or " This is proof that I have married Sarah Jones " ; while the ludicrous experiences of the two Dromios in Shakespeare would be the keynote of daily life, and society would be a magnificent " Comedy of Errors." The illustration may be light, but is not the fact suggestive and sublime, that hidden laws altogether beyond human will provide for this diversity of expression on which the glory of society depends, and do it all so easily and within such moderate limits that nature seldom strays into a monstrosity, seldom offends us with Albinas and bearded women, Aztec children and Siamese twins?

Some of the statistics concerning the physical development of man are quite interesting. Thus it is a law of nature that the pulse shall vary by regular gradation by the increase of years. The hearts of the infants on the planet six months old are tiny time-keepers, beating one hundred and thirty-seven strokes a minute, at a year old one hundred and twenty-six beats a minute, at two years old one hundred and twenty, and so by regular decrease till in maturity it is from seventy-five to eighty, and in old age from sixty to sixty-five. Those, therefore, who complain of the restless activity of children might as well complain that the minute hand of a watch moves faster than the hour hand.   Stop the fever in their veins, and you may stop their mischief, their disquiet, and their glee. By these swift and constant pulses through their arteries Nature tells us that she will have all the children alike in the quickness of their motion, the agility and spirit of their intellect, the keenness of their sensibility, and calls on all parents and teachers to graduate the laws of their home and the customs of the school to the motion of blood that is faster than the fever-speed.

So in regard to growth there is law.   All the children of the world gain nearly eight inches in height the first year of their existence, gaining two fifths from their birth to that period ; during the second year, the gain is one seventh ; during the third, one eleventh ; and so on in regular gradations till increasing height terminates, which in man is a little after twenty-five and in woman about twenty.   Those who live in affluence are generally taller than those who do not; those who live in town at the age of nineteen are taller than those who live in the country.   The stature we reach is about three and a fourth times greater than our measurement at birth, and our weight almost twenty times as much.   At twelve years old, the two sexes weigh about the same.   Man attains the maximum of his weight at about forty, and woman at about fifty.

As to mortality, the statistical tables all bear witness to secret and constant laws. We talk of the uncertainty of life ; and with regard to the duration of any particular person's existence, nothing can seem to be more uncertain. But take a city or state into account, and we can prophecy with singular accuracy how many of any ten thousand infants will live to be a year old ; how many will pass on to two, three, and five years ; how many will weather the diseases and dangers of youth ; — in a word, what number will be sifted out by each year into the grave, and how few will be left at eighty, ninety, and one hundred to tell of a generation that has gone down into the dust. It is impossible to designate, or calculate, the particular individuals that will fulfil this law ; but the law itself will hold as rigidly as the rule of three. We may even foretell what proportions of those that die will be males and what females ; what diseases will carry them off ; how many will die of brain, of liver, of lung, or stomach disorders ; what months will be most disastrous ; what professions and trades will send the largest percentage to the tomb ; and among what classes of occupation those who live the longest will be distributed. We may mention here what an aged clergyman said, not long ago, of bronchitis, which does so much to swell the profits of transatlantic navigation : " Seems to me, I never heard of bronchitis till they began to talk about the independence of the pulpit." The law of the statistics of any ten or twenty years is the law for the statistics of the next ten and the next twenty ; except when there has been increase of cleanliness and of sanitary fidelity on the part of governments, — for this care reaches directly into the census-tables, and reduces at once the percentage of mortality. We know with what confidence life-insurance offices rely upon the stability of law with regard to the duration of existence. They may lose on Mr. A. or Mr. B., but they lay their premiums so that on ten thousand lives they are sure of the result, and can foretell the profit they will make. Life-insurance, dealing in risks and staking on accidents, stands in the front rank of those lines of business in which there is no uncertainty.

In the more literal sense of the term, the disorders of the world obey some law. For the diseases to which the human body is subject have their order. The variety of them, the regularity of the symptoms, the methodical stages of their progress, the spiritual uses they serve, show that the same providence which is manifested in our health and the symmetry of our organs is hidden in the disorders that afflict us. All measles have the same stamp. Fevers are classified, and train in companies with uniform. Contributions to natural theology as rich and conclusive can be made from the laws of malady as from the healthful action of our frames. A distinguished physician of Dublin pulished, two or three years ago, a very interesting work called "God in Disease," to illustrate the subtle plan and under-current of beneficence in the sickness of mankind. Nature is no Vandal in destroying our health : she does not attack the frame usually with a lawless battering-ram, but takes down the pillars and ornaments and roofing of our bodily temple very carefully and systematically, as though she was packing up the parts for shipment to another clime.

Even crime is not incalculable. The lawless elements in human nature, the anarchy in a state, obeys a law. The moral darkness, the social neglects, and the inward depravities of a state or nation, reveal themselves steadily in a remarkably constant proportion of criminals and of the kinds of criminals. So that the problem would not be at all insoluble, How many forgers, burglars, murderers, and counterfeiters will New England turn out next year ? It could more easily be ciphered than the number of bales of manufactured goods which our factories will supply could be forecast. The scamp element is less subject to fluctuation in society than the cotton element ; and in regard to cotton, its moral influence upon the politics and feelings of New England would be a question admitting of surer prophecy than the amount of money to be made on it.

Thus we find it continues true that about one man in every six hundred and fifty in France is a

3   D

criminal (beginning with the Emperor). And a moral map of the country has been drawn, showing definitely shaded districts within which crimes against persons or crimes against property are shown to be predominant, — steady moral causes lying underneath which reveal themselves in these different disturbances of order. So the number taken in charge by the police in London and other great cities for drunkenness and disorder keeps, week by week, the same percentage, except where the Maine Liquor Law jumps with a constable's pole into the arena ; then the number is very sensibly reduced.

It is discovered that the number of suicides observes a constant proportion to the number of people. A statistician can tell how many persons will take their life in Paris during the next two or three years ; the proportion of these that will hang, drown, poison, and shoot themselves, and also between what hours most of such deaths will occur. For it is a fact that between six and eight in the morning is the most fatal time, and that while suicides between twenty and thirty years old prefer to die by the bullet, those between fifty and sixty, which furnish the largest number, select the rope.

It is singular how the most out-of-the-way facts, when rigidly inspected, betray a curious order. Thus it is found in the post-offices of large cities that mistakes and oversights of direction, and the number of letters mailed without addresses, is,

year by year, proportionately the same. And a
" Guaranty Society " was formed a few years ago
in London to insure the integrity of clerks, secre-
taries, and collectors. The instances of dishon-
esty were so regular, that by clubbing all the
clerks and taxing each one a slight sum, they
could be security for each other on the principle
of fire or life insurance. So railroad and steam-
ship accidents keep a sufficiently steady ratio to
indicate some law and order in their confusion.
As to shipwrecks, it is said the average is one to
every tide, — the storm spirit levying that tax
upon the world's commerce to offset the general
safety of the sea. It was the " London Punch,"
I believe, that made a mathematical demonstration, a few months ago, of the folly of ever ex-
pecting to go to the moon by railroad. (No matter, it said, if a track should be laid and the
trains start regularly from this planet, and the
passengers get ticketed through, the case is hopeless. Scientific calculations show, it said, that
one hundred and eighty thousand miles is the utmost limit that any train could travel without a
perfect smash-up, by series of disasters, axle-break-
ings, collisions, explosions, open draws, snake-
heads, spreading of tracks, snow-storms, etc. ;
and as the distance to the moon is two hundred
and forty thousand miles, it follows, by arithmetic,
that every train would be demolished and all the
passengers used up by the time they had gone
three quarters of the distance.) It is affirmed,

also, now, as a settled truth, that the number of
those who draw any tolerable prizes in lotteries is
about the same as the number of those who are
struck by lightning. So that a man has only to
ask himself, when about to try that species of
gambling, what he is willing to pay for the likelihood of a visit from a thunderbolt, and offer his
cash as a conductor. So it is reported that of the
five hundred and thirty-seven young ladies who
fainted the last year, it is quite remarkable that
only two fell upon the floor. Somewhere, too, I
have seen it stated that if on a public road you
meet a party of four women, it is at least fifty to
one that they are all laughing ; whereas, if you
meet an equal party of my own unhappy sex, you
may wager, safely, that they are talking gravely,
and that one of them is uttering the word "money."
Mr. Beecher has lately, I believe, discovered that
the proportion of ministers' sons who turn out
rascals is two and a half per cent, thus deducting
ninety-seven and a half per cent from the truth
of the maxim that "ministers' sons are the devil's
grandsons." Thus the survey of the tables of
birth and death in all their minuteness, and of
other eccentric statistics, justifies the remark of an
essayist, that if you find one man in fifty, in any
community, who eats his shoes and marries his
grandmother, you may be sure that all over the
world it will turn out that one man in fifty eats his
shoes and marries his grandmother.

Perhaps I have delayed too long an allusion to

the curious columns which the records of marriage offer as contributions to our subject. Not only the proportion of marriages is generally the same, but the ages of the parties maintain regular relations. Moreover, statistics are continually forcing upon our notice a fixed percentage of repentant old bachelors ; also of young bachelors that marry widows ; also of young women that marry old men and of widowers that renew their vows ; while the ratio of second, third, and fourth marriages is very constant. It is no more singular than true that eccentric unions are as regular as the more natural ones. Indeed, it has most profanely come to pass that, just as the stars are nothing but points of vast triangles and diagrams to a cold-blooded astronomer, so every unmarried woman in the community stands as an algebraic symbol to the eye of a social mathematician : if she is twenty years old, representing three quarters of a likelihood that she will change her name ; if twenty-five, standing for one quarter of the same possibility ; if thirty, reduced to a fraction of one divided by ten ; and then decreasing in a geometrical ratio which it would hardly be polite to put into figures here. On the contrary, a man of twenty-five represents the fraction one-half as to the probabilities of marriage, which is so vulgar a fraction that most young men of that period strive ardently to annihilate it by finding the other and better half which restores their integrity.

This last point suggests the fact that even love —

indefinable, capricious, romantic, as we often think
it—is most delicately restricted within bounds of
law. No doubt every young lady in her early dreams
is very particular as to the looks and quality of the
youth that shall gain her heart. He must be the
very flower of the human race. And every young
man is equally dainty in his reveries concerning
his ideal partner. She must be the very flower
of the human race. But the stock of Adam does
not bear flowers enough to supply this wide demand of perfection ; so that if we should compare
the dreams which are in the hearts of youths of
both sexes, nothing would seem so hopeless as to
match the world in the long contra-dance of marriage. Plato, in one of his dialogues, worked out
a sportive fancy that the human race was originally
created so that each was complete, — the proper
partner of each soul being joined to it from birth.
But as the race was altogether too happy and independent thus, Jupiter cut the blissful couples in
two, as quinces are divided before they are preserved, and then dispersed them over the planet.
So, he said, that each person is the counterpart of
another human creature, and goes about seeking
its complement. The happiness of every marriage, he maintained, depends on finding the real
half that belongs to the soul ; all unhappy ones
are false assortments, — the man sometimes not
being a fair match for the woman, and very often
the woman being an overmatch for the man. Now
if the difficulties of mating people happily were

as great as they should seem beforehand, — if there were not a large probability that those exquisite feminine dreams should embody themselves in the young man that really offered his hand, transforming him into the Adonis ; or if the celestial ideal of the youth did not, after a while, almost surely interfuse itself into the form and glorify the face of some young lady not far from his own terrestrial latitude and longitude, — what a miserable world we should have of it ! Sentimental Raphaels pensive and melancholy over the mocking beauty of their reveries, a world lovesick for ghosts ! But Providence has ordained that love shall wear the gossamer harness of law ; and so the race falls into line, two and two, by marriages that are generally happy, as naturally and regularly as the animals walked two and two into the ark.

Indeed, as we take the moral world more strictly into the domain of our urvey, the results are more marvellous. Society is an immense organization, intellectually and morally, as well as politically and by statute. As to conservative and radical tendencies, it has a structure as defined as the relation between nerves and bones in the physical frame. In every community there are enough of those restless by constitution, and reformatory by vision, to prevent society from sinking into stupid lethargy ; while the majority are made to be reverent of the past, content with the present, and needing great stimulant and the pressure of great wrong to provoke them into attitudes of resistance or the countenance of revolutionary schemes. This is a matter of birth and temperament, resulting from the infusion of different classes of sentiment into the original structure of souls ; and thus permanent basis is provided for the strong and solid growth of civilization. In fact, it is a decree of our organization that the reformer himself shall grow conservative after he is forty or forty-five, while the shell of the natural Hunker hardens on him then like the case of the crocodile. If a generation should be born in which no fiery souls with burning democratic instincts and hopes, impatient for the future, should appear, society would be like a long train of cars without an engine. And if, for once, all the individuals of a race should grow up scornful of past wisdom and rabid for advance, — social Jehus, — what a moral stampede would be exhibited ! A general rush on all sides for no particular object except " the good time coming," making society like a long train of engines, each with the steam up, each crowding the one ahead, but with no train attached, no passengers or freight, everybody an engineer or fireman, and bound for no place in particular, only for progress as long as the track will hold out !

How beautiful, too, is the law that distributes multitudes of society into different occupations, thus insuring a full development of social good ! Different callings are provided for by inborn tastes. Nature predestines some of our race to be sailors. They are baptized to be agents and expressmen of the world's commerce by the spray of the sea. Their fancy in childhood is busy with the restless waves ; their hearts are cradled in young dreams upon the maternal swell of the deep, and the " Pirate's Own Book " only adds the charm of danger to the other invitations away from the comforts of a settled life which the billows whisper to them.

So the classes of farmers and mechanics, of merchants, surveyors, and engineers, have natures among them predestined by their aptitudes to be eminent and successful. Many have an inborn passion for an adventurous life ; explorers, pioneers, settlers of states, frontiersmen, the first on the ground in Californias and Australias, burrowers after buried Ninevehs ; while there are others whom no temptations could induce to abandon the settled ways and regular comforts of home. Some, moreover, are foreordained to be mathematicians ; in childhood, Euclid is their story-book. A few are appointed to be poets ; they lisp in numbers, for the numbers come. Others are compelled to be artists ; while here and there a musician starts up in whose heart winged melodies nestle that by and by visit a thousand homes and charm the attention of a grateful world. Every profession, too, finds those that have its stamp upon them, marked by nature to be physicians or instructors, lawyers, legislators, or clergymen.

3 *

Each of the sciences has its predetermined vota-
ries; for there are eyes that turn spontaneously
to the sky; men like Kepler, Newton, Laplace,
Herschel, Le Verrier, — as much ordained to
track the stars as the stars are ordained to move
and shine; tastes, too, there are that find their
nutriment in chemistry, in botany, in optics and
statics, in geology and mineralogy; while the
bees find their poets, the birds impassioned Audubon, the animalcules their delighted analysts,
every tribe of animals its biographer and critic,
and every bone, nerve, and disorder of the human
frame its preordained anatomist and skilful benefactor.

With regard to the rarer manifestations of literary character and tastes some law seems to hold.
There are always enough with a delicate appetite
for old wisdom to give the best authors of the past
an appreciative audience, and continually renew
their dress in modern type. Critics do not fail,
who shall be nice tasters and appraisers of the
great creative and constructive minds. We find,
too, that every community is supplied with anti-
quarians, mousers of genealogies, rummagers of
old print-shops and pamphlet-baskets, autograph-
collectors, coin-fanciers, microscopic sceptics who
must have a focal blaze upon every received fact
of history; whitewashers of old rascalities who
find subtle reasons to reverse the judgment of
centuries, and to turn Catiline and Tiberius Cæsar, Richard III., Robespierre, and Napoleon into

unrecognized and injured saints. A fixed percentage also seems to limit the number of those who shall carry on the ultra-abolition meetings, and carry on in them. So the Women's Rights conventions, Fourier newspapers and plans, the Kossuth hats and Bloomer costume, Second Advent Miller, and the Mormon Bible are in pre-established harmony with a certain proportion of every civilized community that must be fed on excitements, extravagances, and vagaries. The social world has been compared to a vast board with all kinds of apertures in it, — square, three-cornered, queer, crooked, — and every generation to a set of plugs carved by Providence into shapes to fit the openings. But alas! on one point statistics begin to stand aghast ; percentage and proportions have rapidly risen till we begin to ask what limit shall be set to the number of mediums that can throw healthy chairs into fits and make a sober table tipsy, or the believers in the univer-cœlum who take the wrigglings of furniture for inspiration, and delight in the electric jigs of a ghost on smooth walnut and mahogany.

We all know with what beautiful accuracy the wastes of the human body are supplied with blood, — how the right proportion of nutriment is carried to every limb and organ and each particle of the skin. Thus the various limbs and organs of society are refreshed and restored by the new currents of population which feed its veins against the wastes of death. With regard to masculine

and feminine elements, it is plain and it is well
that the proportion does not fluctuate ; for society
depends not only upon the continued ratio between men and women, but also on the continuance of the manly and feminine type of character
underneath the wide diversities of individuals in
each sex.   The women's rights movement is wise
and wholesome to this extent, that it is bringing
into prominence the ministry and the worth of the
feminine side of the social organism.   The next
great movement in civilization, we may believe,
will be to bring this into equipoise with the energy
and strength of man, so that the finer and softer
qualities of the other sex, with all the wisdom that
may ripen upon them and all the influence that
must belong to them when perfected, shall become
of account in education and appear in the complexion of society.   The demands that women
shall have equal political authority with men, be
legislators, merchants, commodores, and generals,
are only the momentary contortions of a movement that has deep roots and immense importance, founded in the necessity, for the sake of
social health, that women should be more than
elegant autocrats of the kitchen, graceful ornaments of the parlor and ball-room, and walking
advertisements of lace-stores and bonnet-rooms ;
that they shall become sources of qualities which
shall make society refined as well as strong, cover
it with affections and sensibilities that enwrap
its vigor, and save it from standing to our imagi-

nation like a bony and slab-sided Yankee, hard, calculating, and shrewd, uncouth, irreverent, and clumsy. Let those who would be acquainted with the best sense upon this vexed and vexing question obtain the published lectures of Mr. Mann.

In further illustration of this organization in society, we may say that some men do for it the service of an eye ; others of a brain ; others again of the lungs ; some are its muscles, some its feet, some its hands. Historians stand for the faculty of memory in the large human nature of which we are a part ; poets and artists its imagination ; heroes its enthusiasm ; mechanics its constructiveness ; soldiers its brutal bumps behind the ears ; believers its reverence ; saints its love and hope. These, and all the functions essential to the grand man, are supplied steadily to the character of society by the new nutriment that bubbles up through the fresh comers into the world to restore the wastes of death. In some periods one faculty is developed more than another, and progress consists in the strong and equable development of the great organs, brain, heart, and lungs, which the prominent orders represent ; but society is never without all these organs in some degree of vigor. And we cannot reflect too reverently on the laws of this permanence established by Providence. If all the great men of one generation should be endowed, as some of them are, with despotic tendencies to one line of study, — if men were not made to be equally eminent in walks so wide apart as statesmanship, science, law, mechanical ingenuity, the pulpit, mercantile life, — if for a single half-century there should be a dead level of capacity in every line of power but one, how would civilization suffer ! To use the pertinent metaphor of St. Paul : " If the whole body were an eye, where were the hearing ? if the whole were hearing, where were the smelling ? " And the conclusion of St. Paul is the one we are brought to by considering the subtile provisions for the welfare of society : " But now hath God set the members every one of them in the body as it hath pleased him ; that there should be no schism, but that the members should have the same care one for another."

Just as every army has its grade of officers, from the corporal to the chief, society has its commissioned men, who prevent the race from falling into disorder and keep it in a regular march. With regard to labor we talk of a law of demand and supply which determines how many men shall be miners, iron-workers, factory-hands, shoemakers, carpenters, blacksmiths. But this law does not account for the great poets, discoverers, reformers, and constructive thinkers of history. They are born, not made by circumstances. And if every crisis seems to have its great man ready, if every great opportunity seems to be met by some man that fits it, it is not because the crisis or opportunity makes the man, but provokes him out, that he may show himself in his grand pro-

portions of power, as God made him. The needs
of the Hebrew people in their Egyptian slavery
were answered by a Moses ; but was it those
needs that wove the faculties of Moses into his
frame, fitting him to be their deliverer and law-
giver? Was it any set of circumstances that we
can comprehend which stretched the musical
nerves of David upon his body, or kindled in
another heart the enthusiastic fire of a Paul, that
has warmed the air of the world? Was it by the
coarse law of demand and supply that a Columbus was haunted by the ghost of a round planet,
at the time when the New World was needed
for the interests of civilization, or that a Luther
sprung up with a brain and energy competent
to organize a new movement for human liberty?
Can we tell why it was that a Shakespeare rose
from the crowd of boys which an English village
bore, or a Milton started up to refresh the religious sense with the sound of majestic music
and the sight of an athletic virtue? Was it the
necessities of our country that built the grand
architecture of Washington's patriotism? or, rather, was it not most fortunate for us that Providence did not suffer the crisis to come without
first fashioning a nature competent to be its representative and guide ? And, standing in the
shadow of our last great man's departure, should
we not consider whether it is by any wisdom that
we can understand, that such a stately intellect
was ordained to be the guest of that massive

brow, that such a stalwart understanding rose up by the side of the Constitution, ready, at the critical period, to be its interpreter and defence, and that the tongue which Nature gave him was made minister of an eloquence that echoes back to Demosthenes ?   No ! great men are made *for* us, and the law by which every generation supplies one or two of such in every line of human labor is a law which Providence has secretly established and which is sustained for our welfare, that truth may steadily advance, that the ranks of the race may always have their competent captains and generals, and that civilization shall not stagnate and waste away.

In regard to the tastes of people for food, there is singular uniformity of law supporting wide diversities of appetite.   Some persons would n't touch a cabbage ; to others an onion is an abomination ; with others a turnip is a kind of produce that produces a quality which the word represents upon the nose ; many will not look at condiments and spices ; and there are those to whom a goose, or a leg of venison, or a dish of eels, or a rabbit, or a mess of pork and greens, is perfectly repulsive. And yet, as a whole, the civilized stomach is very catholic ; and all the produce of the fields, from parsnips up to peaches, finds a ready welcome, and the diversity of the tastes keeps commerce busy, as the purveyor of appetite, and all the tribes of the earth and the sea that are eatable travel and swim towards the larder and the kitchen.

The different races have the bump of alimentive-
ness split up queerly and regularly between them ;
the Hibernian Celts, with a little assistance from
the Dutch, pay their respects to the cabbages ;
the Saxons attack the beef and mutton ; the
French celebrate the creative goodness that made
onions and frogs ; the Chinese pride themselves
on rats ; the Esquimaux attend to all the waste
whale-blubber ; Italians rejoice in macaroni ; and
the unsqueamish army of beggars devour what
they can get. Statisticians call for statistics. I
would respectfully suggest to them this :

> " Jack Sprat could eat no fat,
> His wife could eat no lean ;
> Betwixt them both they cleared the cloth,
> And licked the platter clean."

In any family of eight or ten we shall find that
tastes are related to the roast turkey as skilfully
as those of Mr. Sprat and his wife were balanced. There are so many that love white meat,
so many that can eat nothing but dark meat, two
that prefer a wing, two that lie in wait for the
drumsticks, and as surely as there is a wish-bone
will there be a demand at least equal to the
supply. Now, whether we conceive the turkey as
prefigured for the family, or the family tastes as
an after arrangement, the order is equally admirable, and bears ample witness to the prudence of
nature.

In riding in the stage-coaches also in New
Hampshire, among the mountains, I have been

E

compelled to notice the admirable distribution of characters in every load of twenty-five : how there are always sixteen that prefer the places for eight on the outside, and how of these two are always clergymen and one a doctor, one has travelled in the Alps and can give you comparative criticisms ; one is a grumbler and thinks the mountains humbugs, puffed up by hotel-keepers and stage-proprietors to gull the public ; one is a punster, and one a Southerner ; nine and a baby that could not ride anywhere but on the inside seats ; three of the nine that can ride backwards without discomfort ; and how regularly it happens that the baby is gifted with a taste for music, and shows its lineage from Adam by its *crying* sin.

Among the other steady relations I have spoken of as belonging to society, the fact may be mentioned that the idiots and the insane are in regular ratio to the whole population. The deaf and dumb, too, maintain a strict proportion to the bulk of society. According to the last census there were 9,717 deaf-mutes in the United States. A careful calculation will show that these are just about enough to furnish the proper number of legislators for the whole country. May we not guess that Providence intends that this unfortunate class should be educated to be our representatives and senators ? Then we should have deliberative assemblies. No speeches for Buncombe, no lobbying, and the most eloquent man would surely be he that should make the best motions. Our feminine reformers insist that things will not go right till ladies are elected partially to represent the nation, which would relieve us about as pouring oil on a fire would soothe a conflagration; but we think true patriotism will seriously consider whether the deaf and dumb are not born to be our lawmakers. There could be, it is true, no Speaker of the House, but we should not need one, for there would be no speakers in the House. Ruffianism of language would be avoided, for how absurd to call a man a liar by the fingers; and justice would be more likely to be done to the great interests of a nation, in the solemn silence of such a conclave, than it is now amid the general chatter which is intended, not to elucidate the subject, but to fetch an echo of applause from home.

If we reflect upon it carefully, we shall be struck also, I think, with the marvellous secret and constant action of the laws which superintend the growth of national life. In the case of every individual there is steady development of character and unity of experience from childhood to old age. All the powers, memory, sensation, reason, wit, imagination, conscience, are vitally welded together into one consciousness, so that often the sins of the past are punished in the present, and the rewards of goodness are received from the bright hopes which the blended fancy and conscience paint upon the future. Now, by a law of which this is only a miniature, every nation has a distinct character to which all its individuals contribute and which successive generations help to develop. Think what boundless personal peculiarities there are in the millions that make up a great kingdom ; and yet the national type is distinctly marked to a vivid imagination. The qualities of the Irish character remain the same through centuries ; the difference between a Frenchman to-day and a Gaul of two thousand years ago is a difference which the polytechnic school and the dancing-master make, that is, a difference of polish, not of substance ; and the Jew with his old clothes now is essentially the Jew of Herod's and Pilate's days. How easily we typify national qualities, and make our pictures of Brother Jonathan, John Bull, Johnny Crapeau, and the Russian Bear, thus proving that each empire is a grand man, and unites all the varieties of temperament and qualities in its citizens into a constant expression, as the different elements of character in a person run together into a distinct and constant countenance! A recent physiognomist has called attention to this fixity of national types, by showing, in an odd way, that different national faces have always a marked resemblance to certain animals. Thus, Prussians resemble cats, Germans look like lions (though the Hungarians seem, in our country at least, to turn most easily to lions), Chinamen favor hogs, Yankees humanize the physiognomy of bears, and Persians have the likeness of peacocks entailed upon them.

The beneficent results of this constancy of national character are very various. Without it there would be no stability to society, no moral order in civilization. If there was no certainty that the next generation in a country should possess essentially the same qualities with their fathers, if the Irish might produce a race of English temperaments, and France give birth to a colony of German or Italian heads and hearts, and America rear a race of stolid, quiet, ease-loving Chinamen or Turks, with no *go-ahead* infused into their blood, of course history would be like a succession of cross-readings of a newspaper. It would be exactly as if men might sleep away their characters and moral identity, — the honest man at night waking up a scamp in the morning, the coward shifted into a moral hero, the thrifty man into a loafer, the Hunker into a furious Abolitionist, and the cotton-planter transmuted into an enthusiastic patron of " Uncle Tom's Cabin."

This constancy of national temperament and character shows its beneficent influence in literature. There are national literatures, just as there are national languages and peculiarities of feature and expression. The English imagination and pathos, the French keenness and brilliancy, the Spanish romance, the German subtlety, and the Jewish reverence run through all their intellectual activity; and so the intellectual world has consistency and permanence, the literatures of nations being, for diversity and consequent charm, like the conversation of a circle of cultivated gentlemen, — one wise and sombre, one gay and witty, one filled with sprightly recollections and anecdote, one scientific, another poetic, this one religious, that one gloomy, here an artist and there a sage.

In respect of literature, as a general thing we may say that there are statistics of genius : the inventive powers come first to maturity, judgment ripens more slowly, and the highest dramatic and poetic capacities find their perfection, — the tragic from thirty-five to forty, and the comic, which demands clearer insight and a cooler poise of the brain, from forty to fifty.

There seems to be a law, too, which determines that great genius shall come in clusters upon the branches of national history. The culminating periods of intellectual life in Greece were the times of Pericles and Alexander. In Rome, the century of which Augustus was the centre bore the ripest shock of minds. And there are plenty of modern instances, besides the era of the great painters and the age of Shakespeare, to show that the intellectual soil nourishes rich growths and then lies fallow for an interval. But all this is only introductory to the fact that each nation has a literature of a distinct character.

The conclusions we should reach from this wide survey are very important. First, society is belted by law. The best definition of Providence is constant and beneficent law, and when we see how social statistics fall, as it were, into order and rhyme, we find that there is the same scientific proof of Providence in society that there is of an organizing and controlling hand in the balanced harmonies of the sky. Some persons have felt reluctance to dwell upon the facts which the statisticians have presented, from the fear that they indorse fatalism, showing that man is a tool and a puppet. But they do not add any important weight to the argument for fatalism which logic is able to frame without them. They only show that man has not such freedom of will as to make society perfectly lawless ; they show that the Deity will have some order in society in spite of sin, and that sin itself, as in the case of the regularity of crimes and of criminals at certain ages, will express itself in results by a constant and terrific arithmetic.

And so the most important sequence to which our survey points is this : that society is one compact, organic, living thing, that the laws of the world treat it as a whole, play with it as though it were a person morally responsible, and apportion its punishment or its good exactly in the ratio of its fidelity or its vice. The statistics of crime, ignorance, mortality by pestilence, blight of industry by war, degeneracy of physical power, point back to a certain proportion of evil in the heart of the nation. Does any man say it is a proof of fatalism that there are so many thousands of the perishing classes steadily rising up out of Boston and New York and London, keeping a fixed percentage every five or ten or twenty years? It is no more a proof of fatalism than the fact of individual experience is, that a carousal over night surely breeds a headache in the morning, or that the bite of a viper corrupts the blood and makes the limb swell. The great question is, Can the nation reduce or rid itself of the causes whose results are ciphered out with such permanent consistency? Introduce ten per cent more of clown-principle into Boston and New York, and see how the annals of Broad Street and the Five Points, and the reports of ignorance and crime, will acknowledge this new element. The fidelity of society as well as its infidelity will reach the statistician's tables at last. The great lesson of our subject is that we cannot escape law, and also that we can use law. Every community, every state, every empire, is in the coil of moral principles as surely as every man is, as surely as every constellation is played with by the law of gravity with as much certainty and ease as the pebble. Truth works on a large scale just as rigidly as on a small one, and the algebra of social order coldly demonstrates to the legislator and the statesman what the prophet chants in their ears, that wrong principles, false laws, popular Mammon worship, indifference to neighborly welfare, are terrible realities, and break out on the body politic in crimes, ignorance, jails, insane asylums, pest-houses, demoralization, and at last loss of liberty and death.

Men are generally and foolishly sceptical as to

the certain play of moral causes and the reality of moral laws. They imagine that the intellectual and ethical domain, everything that belongs to the unseen sphere of social character, is a region of chance and accidents, or that what forces work there work helter-skelter, without the possibility of foresight or control. But everything visible in society is the token of invisible essences, and the regularity of statistics only betrays the surety of spiritual as well as material agencies in their obedience to law, and thus the possibility of controlling them. Celtic institutions and statistics differ from the Saxon because the qualities of character differ. Whether the price of grain rise in a community of poorly paid labor, or the opportunities of education be reduced, whether a material or a moral spring be touched, the effect is equally certain and calculable : crime will increase and public suffering will ensue. There is no more uncertainty about moral causes than about physical ones. The man who can put up a new school house where one was not may be as sure that he benefits his race and abates the percentage of crime as if he could directly alter the character of a town by a word, or erase with his pen some of the statistics of guilt. The statesman of commanding influence who utters a base sentiment in the Senate-House, or publishes it from the Cabinet, may be as sure that he contributes to the disorganization of his country as if his pen had immediately added to the arithmetic of public disease. The

4

laws of moral gravitation and moral chemistry have
no more caprice, and may be relied on as serenely,
as the forces of the firmament and the crucible.

And so we are told with all the precision and
coolness of science that, a nation being one living
and responsible thing, having its roots in the past
and its hopes in the future, its character is the
most important element in relation to its strength
and permanence.   As there is a character housed
in every human frame, so there is a character
enshrined in every nation, to which its rising generations contribute.   Its nobility and greatness
depend no more on its prosperity, wealth, and
strength than the nobility of a man depends on
the size of his body, the acres he owns, and the
gold he has at command.   A ruffian may have
such claims to greatness as these ; and a nation
having these, and yet guided by no feelings of
honor and love of right, may be only a majestic,
rich, and titled savage.   It is character that gives
nobleness; and only as a nation is pervaded by
the moral elements which make up worthy character will its statistics show progress towards
permanent power, and history draw its portrait
as a benefactor of civilization.

Ah ! how impressive and grand does history
seem when we think that every country is a mighty
pedestal lifting up a national figure symbolic of
the character, the prospects, and the perils of the
people that dwell on its domain !   The surface of
the world, to the imaginative eye, is dotted with

these representative forms. See the genius of old Rome stand on the eminence of an all-shadowy throne, with grim and cruel eyes, and traces of the vices that rotted its sinewy heart. See Egypt on its pyramid, with the massive voluptuousness in its visage, incarnating the scourge and doom of its millions ; Assyria, nodding in sottishness on the high and hasty platform of its power, and dropping its flashy sceptre from bloated and nerveless hands; Greece, lifting the enervated beauty of its face, as of some shameless and profligate Apollo, from its sculptured eminence over-looking the Ægean sea ; swarthy Hindostan, lost in sodden reveries over the vast volume of its cosmogonies ; China, with the swinish cunning of her eyes, showing off, from her broad plateau, the un-tattered robe of her customs ; Arabia, overlooking her deserts with a face ploughed by the passions, long since spent, that once ravaged the civilized world ; decrepit Spain, with the old fire of her romance gleaming out, now and then, over her impoverished and seedy dress ; brilliant France, with sparkling eye, blending into one expression the intellectual vivacity of her Laplaces and Racines, and the volatile, graceful levity of dancing-masters and grisettes ; Italy, lifting from the ancient throne of the Cæsars her manacled, delicate hands that once left the Madonna upon canvas, and " rounded Peter's dome " ; Austria, rooted on a pedestal that crushes noble nations, and insulting the sky with the depraved duplicity of her tyranny

and arrogance ; the magnetic North, gazing from
her throne of snow, bound about the brows with
the grotesque and frosty mythology of Iceland ;
dignified and stately England, with haughty brow
and stubborn breast and manly mind, wearing a
look that interweaves the genius of Newton, Watt,
and Shakespeare, but with a heart not softened yet
enough towards the chronic miseries of her subjects, — look at these figures with their various
visages and various lessons, and then raise the
question to your fancy, In what guise shall the
incarnate genius of our own land stand before the
centuries, on the structure that represents the latitudes from Aroostook to the Golden Coast, and
the zones from Lake Superior to the Gulf of
Mexico ?

Shall her policy and public spirit be such that
she shall stand out on that eminence with a shrewd,
cold eye, bespeaking idolatrous quest of money,
and a robber's avarice for another's land, with a
chain in her left hand that fetters three millions
of hopeless bondmen, and her right pointing continually to that dark spot in a vast bond which
promises to return the fugitive ?   There is danger
of such a destiny for the soul of our country ; and
what a maturity were that for the infant form that
was born on Plymouth Rock, baptized to freedom
by the cold ocean spray, and cradled in reverence
and prayers !

Should she not rather rise on her pedestal
among the nations, as a glorious statue with the

unrolled declaration of Independence expressing
her steady enthusiasm for liberty, and her interdict
of bondage for her unstained soil, — a chart that
has on it a dotted home and welcome for every
wanderer from beyond the sea, and a countenance
fresh as the airs of her North, a heart warm as the
sunshine of her South, an ambition for good vast
as the enterprise of her East, and a hope broad and
generous as the prairies of her West ? Is not this
the representative character we desire for our
blessed land ? He is the statesmen, they are the
patriots, who strive to have it realized, and who
believe that the laws which defeat disorder and
prevent decay are the laws of righteousness and
liberty.

1852.

III.

SOCRATES.

THE subject of my discourse is Socrates. Though his name is familiar to human lips as the representative of the highest spirit of duty, yet little is generally known of his life and character. His spiritual physiognomy is not clearly seen amid the cloudy sanctity which envelops him in the reverential regard of men. It is known or believed that he was a preacher of pure morals, and a man of invincible purity of life, — a light walking in darkness, — perhaps the clearest light that brightened the ante-Christian years ; still the man is but feebly perceived by most of those who revere him as an ethical teacher.

Socrates was born in Athens in the year 468 B.C., twelve years after the battle of Salamis. His parents were poor, his father an ordinary sculptor named Sophroniscus. Nothing more than the common training of an Athenian lad was given to him in early life. This, however, was not all his education. We must not forget that his years fell in the period when the intellect of his countrymen was in the very bloom of its first enthusiasm, and

rejoiced in the fulness of creative life ; for it was
when the tragedies of Æschylus and Sophocles
were frightening and fascinating their first auditors, and the chisel of Phidias cut the white rock
from Pentelicus as though it were snow, and Pericles was fashioning the Athenian will to his purposes by his eloquence. Athens, through its arts,
was fast becoming a sort of play-ground of Apollo,
and Socrates, amid the general worship of beauty,
was apprenticed as a sculptor. We know nothing of him except that he worked at his profession till he was about thirty-five, when we find
that he deliberately threw down his tools, and
determined to be the moral schoolmaster of the
most intellectual city of the world.

Socrates is classed among philosophers ; yet
his first movement in the mental world was a pro-
test against all that was called philosophy in his
time. He had read all that the masters of Grecian thought before his day had written, and found
it profitless. He found their pages busy with
theories about the origin of the world, the way in
which it had grown to its present form, and the
nature of God. One said the earth came up from
a waste of water. Another maintained that everything solid is compressed air. A third contended
that it is plain enough the globe is an animal,
that the stars are its gills through which it takes
in and puffs out its breath, while the tides measure the heave and fall of its huge chest. Again
it was guessed that mud was the basis of all being,

which was quickened by the sun's heat to produce plants, animals, and men. Parmenides affirmed that the world is a proportional mixture of light and darkness. Democritus showed that all the differences of form and function were caused by different assortments of the imperceptible atoms of which everything is made ; and Heraclitus asserted that fire is the primal life element, that anything is good in proportion to its dryness. In proportion to a man's goodness his soul became dry. He contended that a dissipated man had a moist soul, so that our popular saying that a drunkard is "a soaker," may be a bowlder from the old Greek philosophy.

What was called philosophy in Greece before Socrates was most tedious and fruitless stuff, — a continent of speculation and fantastically changing mist-clouds, having no basis, guided by no law, leading to no result. Socrates saw it, and said so. He marvelled that none of the great thinkers had taken up the question which the soul of man suggests. The great region of inquiry and interest is not the world of nature, but human nature. What is man here for ? What is the law of happiness ? Where is the path of nobleness and peace ? What is the foundation of the law of duty ? These themes Socrates did not find treated in the books of the schools, and, at about the maturity of his manhood, he determined to impress upon his countrymen the importance of one sentence, " Know thyself."

And here we are arrested by the fact that Socrates was far in advance of our own time as well as of his contemporaries in his conviction that it is better to study our own nature than to be turned from all interest in it by ambition to know the laws of the physical universe. He contended that men could arrive at more certain as well as more valuable knowledge by studying their own experience and powers than by investigating the world of matter. "It is all guess-work," he said, "these conclusions about what the earth is made of, and how it was produced. You may speculate about the floor of the firmament, and what the stars are, and how the winds blow, and whether the globe is like a colossal turtle and paddles around the ether, but you cannot *know* anything about it. But about ourselves we can learn something. We can know what virtue is, where peace may be found, whether there is such a thing as justice, as truth, and whether man was made for a higher walk and destiny than a beaver and a goat."

Very few of us really believe that now. Few acknowledge that thoughts are as substantial as things, that a feeling is as real as a paving-stone, that the soul is a congeries of actual forces as truly as the body is, that a moral principle is as persistent and fatal a thing as a chemical agent, and that, in the deeps of the mind and in society, laws are ever at work as constant and stern as those which spin the planets and heave the sea and poise the firmaments. The majority of think-

4 *   F

ing men still practically believe that the track of
certain knowledge is in the visible and solid world.
The stars, the rivers, the rocks, they think afford
material of science, but the soul is a region of haze
and moonbeams, the law of right is a matter which
none of us can be sure about, and conscience a
bodiless echo of the passions and desires which
cannot safely be relied upon.

If this is so, our bones are the noblest part of us,
and religion, not being a certainty, is " a mockery
and a horror." Its glories are the fancies of a
dream, its terrors the figments of a nightmare.
Socrates came to the conclusion that it was not
so. He felt assured that the mystery in which
the world floats is more real than the earth's ribs ;
that the stone which his chisel chipped was less
substantial than the soul in every human form; and
that the beauty which his cunning carved into the
block was less charming and permanent than the
beauty of truth, temperance, and holiness, which
faith and culture could leave upon the invisible
essence of every man. He therefore resolved to
abandon the lower for the higher art of sculpture,
and instead of being an artist in marble to be a
fashioner of men.

From an obscure workman he suddenly became
a missionary. We must not think of him as in
any technical and stately sense a philosopher.
He never wrote a book ; he spent little time in
abstract thought ; he was not a student. He was
a home-missionary. His interest was in men,

their occupation, trials, and character. His method of instruction and influence was conversation, and the street, the shop, the market-place, or the exchange was his school. He meant to be to his townsmen, as he himself said, "like a gadfly to a strong and sluggish horse," buzzing about him continually, and stinging him from his laziness to a brisk and healthy trot.

As he was not a philosopher by occupation and methods, neither was he so in the character of his mind, and still less in his appearance. Take him as a whole, in essence and appearance, Socrates was a compound of mystic, logician, and buffoon.

A spirit fellow with the Quakers and Soofes inhabited that grotesque frame. In this respect also he was not a philosopher, but a seer and a saint. He did not spend his time in investigating truth ; he believed it by the assurance of an inward witness ; he saw it and worshipped it. When he left the sculptor's shop he took up his new employment with the consciousness of a heavenly call ; he boasted of a divine commission, and relied on spiritual help. "This duty," said he, "has been enjoined me by the Deity through oracles and dreams, and in every mode by which any Divine decree has ever enjoined anything to man to do."

He believed in supernatural influences, in answers to prayer, in visions, and in divination. He always insisted that from boyhood he had been conscious of Divine warnings in his own nature, —

a sort of Rochester rappings in his bosom,—which he revered, and obeyed without hesitation. They dissuaded him, he said, when a course would be very wrong, but gave no positive counsels. If a youth desired to study under his guidance, if a journey was contemplated, if a thought was about to be expressed, and the inward tick was felt, he forbade the youth to approach him, he relinquished the journey, he smothered the thought. Sometimes he was led to utter prophecies, which his friends say never failed of fulfilment.

And yet, unlike other mystics, he was a logician. A man of severer methods never lived. He had a prophet's flaming heart, and he had a brain of ice. He laid gas-pipes as systematically as Calvin could for his Quaker light. Nothing could baffle or confuse him. As a contemporary said of him, he could track a principle in all its windings "like a Lyconian hound." He would hold a thought and inspect it as a mineralogist examines a crystal. The symmetry or inconsistency of a thing he would see as quickly and keenly as an artist appreciates the proportions of a statue. He would untwist the elements of a judgment as an expert strips off the layers of mica. Thoughts were things in his grasp.

Here lies the marvellous originality and power of his genius, that he was a saint in his own contact with truth, and a logician in his communication of it to others. He always conversed with men, tried to make them see the importance of thinking accurately, linked question to question, till he drew out from his interlocutor his fundamental faith, or, by the contradictions he led the poor man into, showed that he had no fundamental faith, and then advised him to acquire some principle of action that he could live by, that would stand the test of argument. He never harangued or grew eloquent, but analyzed, disputed, and discussed, — always with the view of getting down to some rocky certainty that would bear the weight of the understanding and afford a substratum for the life. The prophet's heated utterance he discarded, but put on the missionary robes to convince his fellows that virtue is truth, and that nothing else will stand the strain of inquiry and logic. Therefore be sure of the foundation of your life. Know why you live as you do. Be ready to give a reason for it. Do not, in such a matter as life, build on opinion or custom, or what you guess is true. Make it a matter of certainty and science. Do not one hour obey a virtuous impulse, and the next a caprice or a passion. Above all things, make your life consistent. If you know at any time that virtue is highest and true, enthrone it ever after ; follow it in all things. Else your conduct will be a miserable patchwork and discord.

And this was the principle he went by in dealing with men and instructing them. All truth is kindred, and so clear thinking is consistent with holiness and leads to it, while inaccurate thinking on any subject is morally dangerous, and an uncertainty or falsehood in the intellect might at last be found to be the " apex of hell." Therefore he determined to benefit the Athenians by testing their thought, by making them appreciate the moral truth which they partially believed, and showing them that, where the soul has no moral reverence and certainty, the life is based on quicksand and marsh.

He went into the Athenian streets as an inquirer after truth. So far from writing anything, or assuming to teach a system of truth, he pretended not to know anything, to be a thirsty seeker of the highest knowledge. All that he claimed ability for was to detect nonsense. " I create nothing," said he ; " I am only an accoucheur of the mind. If possible I will assist the birth of opinions in you, and choke them if they look monstrous, but do not ask me to teach anything directly ; I am a learner, and the humblest of all."

Most persons, however, found his ignorance more tough to deal with than the wisest man's knowledge. If he fell in with an atheist, his questions brought the argument from design into such splendid prominence and concentrated strength that we imagine it is Paley's pages we are reading, and not a heathen Greek, and the climax is reached in a query like this : " Seeing thou thyself, Aristodemus, a small and dependent part of the extended earth, art conscious of reason and intelligence, supposest thou there is no intelligence elsewhere in the universe ? "

If he found a man that did not worship, he began a conversation which rose to such a height that he assented to the conclusion of Socrates : " Piety alone fits the soul for the communication of Divine secrets ; and no others reach them but those who consult, adore, and obey the Deity."

If he met a voluptuary, his logic riddled the theory of pleasure, and set in clear relief the folly of tampering with the laws of spiritual health ; with the rich he unveiled the truth that the soul's growth is worth more than the wealth of Crœsus and the power of "the great king " ; talking with rulers, the conversation would lead at last to the fact, that to do injustice is worse than to suffer it ; and at feast-parties he would contrive to intersperse the fun and laughter with questions or stories about " spiritual love and eternal beauty."

It will be clearly seen, as we advance, that the grotesque appearance of Socrates was a symbol of the homeliness and ludicrous cast of his illustrations and imagery. Any facts that could be strung upon a moral law, or made to reveal or suggest a religious truth, however common or coarse, he would press into his service. To the mystic insight of Coleridge, and the burly understanding of Dr. Johnson, he joined the shrewd Yankee sense of Franklin. He could draw illustrations for his highest themes from the kitchen as well as from the Iliad and the religious myths. Skimmers and soup-pans were hieroglyphs of truth and holiness as well as poetic goddesses and fictions of Elysium.

It is chiefly as a pure religious thinker and a moral teacher that Socrates is known to the majority of persons now, and in the popular imagination he is conceived as a lofty, dignified personage, with a severe and majestic presence and a bearing solemn to the verge of being tragical. There is, probably, no great character of history from whom an accurate acquaintance chips so clean the mythic burr and halo of general report. He was truly no saint in appearance, and he had no clerical or prophetic method or demeanor, and made no impression upon the beholder of Athenian polish, politeness, or grace. His head was as round as a pumpkin; he was goggle-eyed, and was debtor to nature for that slight cast or inequality of axis known as an interesting squint. "Your eyes see only in a direct line," said he, "but I can look not only directly forward but sideways, too, the eyes being seated on a kind of ridge in my head, and starting out." His nose was short, flat, and snub, and the nostrils were wide and turned up, — being more useful on that account, as he said, since they were "able to receive smells that come from every part, both above and below." His mouth was wide and his lips thick, which he "thought might be envied by young men, since kisses, with such a liberal application, would, as he contended, be more luscious and sweet." He had a rich way, too, when he had hooked a man in argument, or was saying something rather sly, of holding his head still, and turning his eyes among the company, — a habit which his contemporaries compared to the way a bull glares around him with his head down. His form would have been more classic and befitting a philosopher, if his neck had not been quite so chunky, and if he had not manifested something above the canonical corpulence of an alderman. The most rigid temperance of diet and rigor of bodily discipline did not avail to reconcile his moral temperament and his physique. He even danced at home in private, with the hope to disenchant his frame of its fleshy encumbrance ; but to little purpose. Nature had determined to intimate in his constitution a cross between a Brahmin and a Satyr.

The information is preserved for us that he had one pair of dress-shoes that lasted him for life, — a story we may well believe, since history has recorded no instance of his wearing them. Winter and summer, his custom was to go barefooted, and it was, moreover, with a slouching gait and a very seedy dress that the son of Sophroniscus roamed about Athens in his tabernacle of clay. He has improved a little in respect of dress during the last two thousand years, though his style is still somewhat eccentric, for in some of the spiritual communications with which our times are so favored, Socrates has revealed himself as a tall, middle-aged man, dressed with striped coarse trousers, very loose at the top and tight near the feet, and a kind of frock open in the front and without sleeves.

But though he was not a model Greek in outward symmetry, he was a perfect athlete in bodily vigor and power of endurance.   Underneath
his dissolute-looking flesh were thews of brass,
muscles of oak, and sinews of steel.   He inured
himself to hardships as a duty, in order to perfect
his body as a gift of Providence and an instrument of the mind.   Sleep he never needed if
good conversation was to be had.   Report goes,
that during the terrible plague of Athens, although
he never left the city, he was the only inhabitant
that wholly escaped infection.   Twice the toughness of his frame was proved in the hardships
of the camp and the fatigues of battle.   When
about forty, he was drafted for a winter campaign
in Thrace.   The army, at one time, was short
of provisions, but hunger did n't trouble him.
Plenty returned, but he escaped dyspepsia.   Total abstinence societies had not then been
formed, and even philosophers were not expected
to be Washingtonians.   On one or two occasions,
when compelled by good-fellowship to drink with
his young comrades, who were very fond of him,
so tough was his brain he might have used the
words of Lady Macbeth, as he surveyed the result, — " that which hath made them drunk, hath
made me bold."

To the Athenian frame a Thracian winter would
be something like the pleasure which a Carolinian
planter would enjoy among a camping party in
the Penobscot lumber-lands during January.   But

while his companions just ventured from their tents, wrapped carefully, with hair-skins around their legs and fleeced sandals on their feet, they would get a hearty hail from the dialectic corporal, scantily covered with his single threadbare summer robe, and walking barefooted on the ice. It was on the expedition to Potidara, also, that he surprised the camp by standing for twenty-four hours motionless, in a sort of meditative trance. He was as unwelcome a foe to a Thracian boor with his javelin as to an Athenian demagogue with his lasso of logic. In the battle of Potidara he was the most valiant fighter in the troop, and saved the life and weapons of the first young man of Athens by his persistent valor. And afterwards, on the field of Delium, when the ranks were routed, he walked away steadily with the general, perhaps discussing the nature of courage or the mode of life in Hades, as they kept military step, but, at any rate, with such a "majestic composure," as Alcibiades says, who saw him, "that the pursuers concluded to try other game."

The comical antithesis of his appearance and his spirit of course made him one of the most interesting objects to the citizens of Athens. He was always "before the people," was passionately attached to his native streets and soil, and even the beauty of nature could rarely tempt him beyond the walls. "From fields and trees," said he, "I can learn nothing, but I can from the men in town." Now and then some young enthusiast could ensnare him to the bank of the Ilissus, with the bait of an oration by Lysias folded in his bosom. "By holding out written speeches before me, you could lead me about all Attica, and wherever else you please, as shepherds lead their hungry flocks by shaking leaves or fruit before them." And melted by the youth's reading, while they reclined in the shade of the plane-trees and the flowering agnus-castus, their feet dabbling in a fountain that bubbled near, the old man would indulge in some rich and dreamy talk on religious traditions and the beauty of goodness. But his instincts usually kept him to the crooked streets and dingy shops of Athens.

He knew, probably, almost every individual of its fourteen thousand free male dwellers, his business, his prospects, his abilities, his wealth, and habits of life. He considered the city as his parish, and could not reconcile it with his conscience that the highest or lowest of his flock should slip the benefits of being catechised occasionally. There were no newspapers in Athens ; but Socrates seemed to be a strolling and scattering London " Punch " among the citizens. Follow in his wake for a day or two, to the walking-grounds in the early morning, into the forum before noon, through little squads of talkers later in the day, and to some party of poets, politicians, and mustachioed gallants in the evening, and one will hear the strangest medley of clear-thinking, ac-

curate statement, sublime principles, queer analogies, keen and merciless satire, drollery, eloquence,
and witty nonsense, as though the tongue of some
crazy genius was bewitched. As to the forms
and methods of dealing with his company, he
would be as flexible and compliant as a Jesuit,
but in his aims he was as serious as Fénelon. At
one time he is splitting the seemingly simple proposition of some enthusiastic philosopher into its
various elements as expertly and smoothly as an
adept will tear apart the laminæ of a thin plate
of mica. In a few minutes he is lashing the
licentiousness of a talented man through some
gorgeous fable, and cross-questions him about
what is most desirable in life, till his victim con-
demns himself before a crowd of eager listeners.
Some forenoon he may be found in the bridle-
cutter's shop that stood near the Athenian forum.
The young, rich, and handsome Euthydemus is
there with a circle of admiring cronies, — a lad
who has a fine collection of the poets, and boasts
that he will yet govern Athens by his 'sweet voice
and fluent speech. Socrates feels moved to let a
little light into his mind upon the qualifications
of a statesman. He proposes some meek inquiries about Athenian history, diplomacy, commerce, and law, and finds that his knowledge is
very shallow. He probes him with some test questions on justice, wisdom, prudence, and law, and
shows that his conceptions are feeble and hazy,
and then gravely informs the bystanders that the

political ambition of the stripling somehow seems
to him like the advertisement of a doctor running
thus : " It is true, gentlemen, I never thought of
making physic my study, and did not even wish
to have the reputation of it ; but be so kind as to
choose me your physician, and I will soon gain
knowledge by making experiments upon you." It
is pleasant to know that one more interview like
this converted Euthydemus into a friend of Socrates and a sober, studious man.   One cannot
help thinking what a profitable bargain it would
be if our own government could have a Socrates
every winter at the price of his second-hand toga,
soup, and shoes, to dog and drill the experimental
politicians of Congress on the avenue or in the
lobbies.   On one occasion a person could hear
Socrates reproving the quarrels of brothers, convin-
cing them of the beauty of fraternal love by induction, and reconciling them by syllogism.   Soon he
is convicting a military teacher of ignorance of his
profession ; in a little while he is in the studio of
Parrhasius, and thence to the shop of Clito, the
statuary, drawing out of them, by his corkscrew
inquiries, the confession that art is never so well
employed as when put to the service of what is
noble, modest, virtuous, and amiable.   His pleasantry would show itself in his enigmatical way of
introducing or enforcing a lofty proposition.   With
a mixed company around him, he would quote
and urge the line of Hesiod, —

" Employ thyself in anything rather than be idle."

Then what delight it gave him to see the group
look somewhat sceptical as to its morality, until
some captious or very common-sense man asked
whether employment in gambling, stealing, and
debauchery is better than doing nothing! How
would he define and examine and make the doctrine blaze before their minds that gambling and
all vice were not employment, but the most corrupt and infamous idleness! At a feast, once,
where the company were called upon, each by
another, to state what they chiefly valued themselves upon, Socrates rose in his turn and with
the greatest gravity said that he valued himself
on being a pander and procurer. The guests
were astounded, and most of them roared. Afterwards he went to show, in no joking way, how
earnestly it was his aim to make perfect souls
that should be desirable and useful to the state,
and to bring together those who should love each
other for the best qualities, and be improved by
each other's company. What a fine union of
sense and fun in his criticism upon a volume of
Heraclitus which Euripides loaned him : " That
which I understand of it is excellent ; I believe
that also to be excellent which I do not understand, but it would take a Delian diver to reach
the sense." At such parties he might often be
heard to preface a tough dialogue with a young
man by sallies like this : " My young friend Cal-
lias here went to a noted instructor to learn mne-
monics, and succeeded well ; for if he sees a toler-

ably handsome woman he can never forget her, so perfectly has he learned the art of memory." It does n't need sophists to teach young men that art now. The young gallant might be quite proud of the pleasantry for a moment, but if he had a weak spot in his character let him tremble, for the humorous remark is only a coating of sugar for the stringent medicine that is to follow soon.

At times one might find him in friendly chat with a priest of the dominant religion, and when he had warmed and flattered the clerical man sufficiently to the temper of good-fellowship, the modest query might be heard from the lips of Socrates, " Can you tell me what is holy and what impious ? " " O, yes," is the patronizing response ; " that which is pleasing to the gods is holy, and what is not pleasing to them is impious." " Admirably answered ; but, my excellent friend, do not the gods quarrel, and is it not said that there are enmities among them, and jealousies one of another, so that what is pleasing to Jupiter would be very uncomfortable to Saturn ; and what would make Vulcan clap his hands would make Juno bite her lips with vexation ? " " It is, truly, so said." " So, then, you see, if what is pleasing to the gods be holy, the same thing would be at once holy and unholy, since it is pleasing to some gods and displeasing to others." Here is a dilemma, indeed, but it is at last relieved by this new and broader definition that " what all the gods hate is impious, and what

they all love is holy; but that what some love
and others hate is neither or both." "But, my
dear Euthyphro," resumes Socrates, "is not that
which is loved one thing, and that which loves
another?" "Certainly." "And all the gods love
holiness, according to your statement?" "Yes."
"But, since the gods are one thing and holiness
another, is holiness holy because they love it, or
do they love it because it is holy?" That question
should have made every temple shake on the
Acropolis. Thus does he suggest to the dormant
mind of the priest that polytheism is a blunder of
induction, — that there is something intrinsically
and eternally pure and excellent which hangs
and flames like a zenith star above the world of
spirits, above all theologies and creeds, and beneath which the mythical Olympus is but a miserable, dirty ant-hill which the foot may kick into
dust.

A man that could talk thus would, no doubt,
be a treasure to the delighted intellectual listeners,
but would not be especially welcome to the gentleman he felt a divine impulse to enlighten, or
hold up spitted upon his barbed dialectics.

We may realize his relations to Athens if we
fancy some subtle professor of moral philosophy,
some acute and tough-brained Father Lamson,
some courteous and imperturbable Mr. Brownson,
inflamed with the idea that he must improve the
Bostonians in clear and proper thinking, and assume the mission of reforming loafer about town.

And so he happens in upon the broker's board at eleven, with the gracious but astounding salutation, "Well, my friends, suppose we dismiss the topic of 'Sullivan' bonds, and the 'Old Colony' stock, and the prospects of the 'Vermont and Massachusetts,' and discourse a while on the chief end of man." At twelve he is disputing pitilessly with a great criminal lawyer, just hurrying to the bar, whether it is kind and friendly to save even a relative from the just punishment of a crime, and holds him by the button till he has impressed on his fancy that there will be no eminent counsel for villains at the last assize, but that every scarred and bloated soul shall be put to the penal discipline that looks to health. At half past one he saunters into the rotunda of the Exchange, and before they know it is exercising a group of merchant princes on the nature of the beautiful and the true riches of the soul. At two find him at "Parker's," where he draws his chair beside some well-known epicure, and with an air of the most tender interest opens this proposition: "Eating is not a desirable occupation, and not an appetite to be pampered by a wise man. It is merely, you see, the gratification of a want, thus restoring the system to equilibrium. The part of wisdom is to keep as free as possible from the want and the necessity of serving it. The satisfaction of the finest dinner is like the satisfaction of rubbing an itching skin, and a clean soul would as soon aspire after the erysipelas for

the delight of scratching, as rejoice in a clamorous stomach for the sake of smoothing it down
with venison and turtle-steak. The temperate
man's soul is a sound cask well filled with honey
and milk, and giving no trouble to the owner;
while the life of the epicure is like a barrel full
of shot-holes, which he is compelled to fill continually with liquors that are hard to obtain, or
suffer exquisite agony. If you go on in this way,
my brother, you will be doomed in Hades to fill
a colander by bailing into it with a sieve." At
four he is dissecting before a patriot the relations
of conscience and the constitution. He drops in
to tea with an eminent clergyman, whose brain
is laboring with the Sunday sermon, and cools
his mental fever by a challenge to prove to him
that virtue can be taught, and what is the sanction of duty. Perhaps at eight he is at the
museum gauging the moral influence of " Cinder-
ella" (and if he finds it bad, let Warren look out
for him the next day), and at ten appears, barefoot,
unshaved, and self-invited, among a supper-party
on Beacon Street, which he entertains by his wit
and the ample resources of a disciplined reason
till, just before the close, he silences all mirth, and
through a most eloquent allegory or myth lets a
stream of dazzling radiance upon the point that
the only true life is one of rigid temperance,
piety, and devotion to the highest duty. And
when we add that he extends his parochial visitations to every tinman's, carpenter's, and hatter's,

to every cobbler's shop and bookstore and
bakery, to editors' sanctums, to the market-stalls,
to the reading-rooms, to oyster-saloons and watch-
houses, with his testing questions, and that terrible
spiritual proof-glass which brings up before a
man's own eyes the very sediment of his soul, we
know what Socrates was to Athens, and how he
would be welcomed here.

But the setting in which Socrates is generally
placed by historians of philosophy is in contrast
with Grecian sophists. These were a class of instructors — often itinerant — in rhetoric, eloquence,
gesture, correct use of language, and the general
knowledge which would be a good outfit for an
Athenian man of the world, and which was essential to polished bearing and practical success.
The Athenian lads delighted in talk. Extempore fertility of invention, acuteness and supple-
ness in debate, apt poetic allusions, sweetness of
diction, and happy artifices of arrangement were
to them like the voice of Jenny Lind to a soft-
nerved amateur. It was part of the business of
their lives to speak in the assemblies of the people,
and no youth might hope to attain eminence in the
state unless he could bait the ear or captivate the
heads or rule the hearts of the acute, vacillating,
and "fierce democracie" by the honey of his
phrases, the agile sophistries of his tongue, or the
graceful heat and rhythmical intensity of his passion. Any teachers, therefore, who could impart
a dialectic or rhetorical skill were sure of busi-

ness and of enthusiastic welcome in the great Grecian cities. And the chief sophists did not lose any scholars through an excessive modesty of pretension.

Nowadays we have printed sophists which tell us, " German made easy " ; " Italian taught in ten short lessons " ; " History crowded into a chart." Then the golden promise was, " Reading, speaking, and fluency taught here ; universal science imparted in six free conversations ; philosophers manufactured in five sittings ; orators and archons polished for use at the shortest notice. Price to rich men's sons fifty dollars a lesson."

To tell the truth, most of the distinguished sophists made an attractive appearance. They were versed in the general natural science of their time. They were thoroughly acquainted with the great works of the poets. The mnemonic art they had mastered, and could pour out by the hour the great events, and even the driest details, of history. One of them boasted to Socrates that he could repeat fifty proper names after merely reading them once. They composed allegories on the virtues, the gods, and the origin of things, which were at their tongues' ends. Many subtle word-puzzles were stored away in their memory for frequent use. Generally they boasted that there was no theme on which they could not speak melodiously at a moment's warning, and their hearers were challenged to put them to the test. At times they would entertain a company with an

oration about a bee, and a polished disquisition
on so unpromising a topic as salt. The bearing,
too, of a prominent travelling sophist was most
dignified. He knew how to guard his person with
a magic circle of nice proprieties, and to make
himself attractive by a most polite reserve. And
on important occasions he knew how to dazzle his
assembly by his magnificent attire, — "his purple
robes, embroidered sandals, and fingers sparkling
with gold and gems." On such occasions every
curve was exactly the line of beauty, every motion
artistic, and, whatever the topic, the tropes and
metaphors sparkled in the gush of his speech like
the brilliant spray from the fountain's throat. The
sophists amassed immense sums by their vocation,
and one of them is said to have made ten times
as much by his profession as Phidias could gain.

When one of the most celebrated of these
men visited Athens, the young men among the
upper-ten were half wild with delight. For then,
as a few centuries after, it was true that "the
Athenians spent their time in nothing else but
either to tell or to hear some new thing." The
doors of the great stranger's dwelling-place were
beseiged before daybreak, and we don't know but
that there were crowds in the Bowdoin Squares of
Athens to watch his outgoings and return. It was
a marked day in the calendar when the lordly
sophist had a reception. Socrates would be very
likely to pay his respects, wish him the freedom
of the city, and offer him a greeting of welcome.

But his reverence and affection for a sophist were those of a weasel for a rat. They offended his principles and his practice at every point. They made large pretensions to knowledge; he continually protested that he knew nothing more than the best methods of acquiring knowledge. They taught for gain; he would take no pay for his instructions. It was often pressed upon him, but never touched. He thought it was as really prostitution to sell wisdom as love for money. In his view education was a serious and arduous matter, and he thoroughly hated any methods which made it seem easy. It was not that the sophists openly taught immoral doctrines that Socrates objected to them, but that they did not teach anything scientifically; did not ground their pupils on the fundamental principles of certainty. They diverted ambition from a patient and slow mastery of these, turned their scholars from a steady mining for the diamonds of wisdom to a scramble for the spangles of a surface information. And so, whatever might be their excellences, Socrates saw that, in the light of his stern theory of training, the sophists were vitiating the mental principles of the young. Instead of inspiring a method they imparted a knack. Their aims were wholly practical, and therefore low. He would make men thorough, earnest, and reverent thinkers; they would make them acute debaters, ready tacticians, accomplished orators. They would fit them for eminence in the forums of Greece ; he would make them wrestlers with ideas in the gymnasium of science. They did not pursue nor inculcate wisdom for its own sake, but only for the sake of one's private interest and political success ; and so in the sight of Socrates the sophists had no mental modesty or humility, and were but flaunting courtesans of knowledge.

It was worth one's while to see a meeting before the best youth of Athens between these ornate professors and the buffoon-prophet, the cool and comic enthusiast, the pug-nosed and chuckle-headed saint. To his fellow-citizens Socrates was a gad-fly, but to them a vampire, sticking with the gripe of a centipede, and sucking the conceit out of them with glee. He was so glad to see the great Protagoras, the sharp-eyed Prodicus, the all-accomplished Gorgias, or the celebrated Evenus of Paros ; what a blessing to Athens that they had condescended to come ; now, surely, he could learn about the supreme good, or the essence of wisdom, or the most fitting life, or what the just may be   And although he had not a fourpence to pay for instruction, he would beg a little talk in charity.   Then how would he prick their brilliant parachutes and let out the gas ; how would he rub down their definitions to sand on the grater of his dialectics ; how nicely would he put his tweezers on the head of a fallacy and " snake " it out of its artistic nest ; how would he inquire and inquire, and tire the brain of his courtly antagonist by leading him through the mazes of his own disorderly system ; and split some pompous axiom into a forked contradiction before his eyes, and thus teach the bystanders how to think and discuss, and force the baffled professor to exclaim, " I am sure, Socrates, that with five minutes' leisure I could answer you clearly, but just now I am tired and cannot collect my thoughts."

But what offended the dainty ears of the sophists most was the homeliness of his allusions and figures. He would reduce a general idea to its lowest denomination, and examine it in vulgar fractions. If one of them, in the full sail of declamation, advanced to his auditors the general and somewhat slippery principle that the wise ought to have more in society than the worthless, Socrates would try to get at his precise meaning in this way : " Then you would say, I take it, that the most skilful weaver ought to wear the largest robe and have the most clothes ; that the best cobbler ought to walk the streets in the widest shoes, or with many pairs on his feet ; and that the wisest doctor should be stuffed with the most meats." He got no light on the original proposition of the sophist, but he got the retort : " By the gods, Socrates, you never cease talking about shoemakers, cobblers, fullers, and cooks, as if our discourse was about them ! "

Or the learned Hippias agrees to instruct him about beauty, and shows him that " finely shaped

5 *

girls and noble horses and a well-proportioned lyre and golden ornaments and precious stones are beautiful."

"But suppose a hard-headed friend asks me if a fine porridge-pot isn't beautiful, and if a sycamore spoon for pea-soup, being more convenient and fitting, isn't more beautiful than a golden one; for he might say, too, that if you stir the soup in the tureen with a gold spoon you run the risk of breaking the dish and thus spoil a good dinner, while a wooden spoon, if made of an aromatic tree, would be safer, and would give the soup a better flavor. What must I say if my friend speaks thus, O Hippias?" "But who would dare use terms so coarse on a subject so noble?" replied the sophist. "Although such things are fine in their place and when well proportioned, yet their beauty isn't to be spoken of, compared with a fine horse or handsome girl or other splendid things." "Ah, a little patience, good Hippias: if we compare girls with goddesses, doesn't the same thing happen as when we compare porridge-pots with girls? And must we forget what Heraclitus said, that the wisest man will seem only like a monkey, when contemplated in contrast with God, for wisdom, beauty, and all such qualities?" Thus does he compel the dandy sophist to take off his mental kids and handle rough-looking realities, at the same time forcing him to widen his definition of the beautiful, and hinting to him the Divine loveliness which infolds all other beauty as the air embosoms the myriad glories of the world.

How fine was the simile of Alcibiades at an Athenian feast, to express the nature of Socrates ! " He is," said he, "exactly like those Silenuses that sit in the sculptors' shops, and which are carved holding flutes or pipes, but which, when divided into two, are found to contain the images of the gods. . . . . His discourses are like them, too ; the phrases and expressions he employs fold around his exterior, as it were, the skin of a rude and wanton Satyr. He is always talking about great market-apes and brass-founders and leather-cutters and skin-dressers, so that any dull and unobservant person might easily laugh at his discourse. But if ever one should see it opened and get within the sense of his words, he would find that they alone, of all that enters into the mind of man to utter, had a profound and persuasive meaning, presented innumerable images of every excellence, and were most divine."

It is, perhaps, superfluous to say that Socrates was not appreciated at his value by his fellow-citizens. Many despised him because he was poor, ill-dressed, and had no laudable employment. Some of refined taste were repelled by his ludicrous ugliness. Many feared the homely honesty of his talk and the precision of his probe. And not a few saw with alarm that his severe speculations were prying up the foundations of the state polytheism, unsettling faith in the thunders of Zeus and the trident of Poseidon. The comedians found him rich game. In the " Clouds," a comic play of Aristophanes, brought out when Socrates was forty-five, his house is called the "subtlety-shop," where students are taught the cause of rain and thunder, and exercised in measuring the leap of a flea, — the furniture of the house affording ample material for conducting the last experiment, since the couches almost jump of themselves from excess of life. Socrates himself is represented lying flat in meditation on a high shelf, that his mind, as he expresses it, may be hung up above material things, and his subtle soul be mixed with liberal air. Some of the scholars are disposed about the rooms, in the comedy, on their hands and feet, with their noses to the ground, looking like kangaroos on all fours. Socrates is portrayed instructing his pupils in precision of speech, and the take-off of his love of accurate classification is admirable, where the poet represents him as warning his pupils not to confuse réalities even so far as to call a male and female turkey by the same name ; but by all means to speak of the male as a turk*er*, and the female as a turkey*ess*. He promises also, in the play, to instruct any youth how, by proper subtleties, to make an unjust cause triumph over the right, — an art in which many subtlety-shops in modern times have perfected the visitants. An old gentleman oppressed with debt and a riotous son, tries to learn the mysterious secret sophistries of the thinking-shop, in order to dodge his bills, but finds them too abstruse for his soggy brain, and at last sends the son himself to be a pupil. The youth catches the art of making the worse appear the better reason, but he learns too much, loses his small remnant of filial reverence, and beats his father, soon after he graduates, because he had not good taste in poetry. The old gentleman naturally demurs, but the youth catches him fairly on the logic of the thing, as thus : —

> " Now, here's a mild
> And candid question for you,
> Pray, did you beat me when a child?"
> " Yes, for the love I bore you."
> " Then ought not I, too, to embrace
> The shortest means of proving
> My love for you, and beat you, as
> This beating's merely loving?
> Children are thrashed ; must fathers go
> Unthrashed and unadmonished?
> You'll say it is the law, I know,
> For children to be punished.
> But I'll reply that an old man
> Is in his second childhood,
> And if he's thrashed more fiercely than
> A youth, it can't be styled odd.
>
> .   .   .   .   .
>
> Just look how cocks chastise their dads ;
> Yet wherein do their natures
> Differ from us Athenian lads,
> Save that they're no debaters?"

The play closes with the dismantling of Socrates' house by the enraged old gentleman and his slaves.

It is not strange that Socrates should have been made fun of in a farce. But many critics

have racked their brains to explain how, if Socrates was a lofty teacher, he could be so vilified,
— his tenets so grossly libelled before his countrymen upon the stage. How should he, whose
morality was so stern, be scourged as a miserable sophist, a sapper and miner of domestic order
and filial ties? How should he, whose delight it
was to spear the loose thinkers of his time, be
selected as the type of the worst class of them?
It is as if some modern novelist or stage poet
should dare to dramatize Dr. Channing inciting a
riot, or Deacon Grant and John Augustus entic-
ing young men into gambling shops and inviting
them to take a social glass. We must make
great allowances, however, for the wild license
of Athenian comedy. We know that the farce-
writers did not care at all for truth in their repre-
sentations. Men who could, without impunity,
hold up Pericles himself to ridicule, in the summit of his power, would not bridle their fancy
about a poor, pale-faced, itinerant disputer of the
streets. Besides, Socrates was considered an in-
novator on the popular faith. The poet who
satirized him was a rigid pagan conservative, and
would not have the basis of a single altar weakened or questioned. And who does not know
what strange doctrines are associated, by the un-
thinking, with the name of every man whose
intellect throws off the swaddling-clothes of tradition and creed? The friends of the pagan order
knew that Socrates dealt with abstractions; and

so they called him a trifler, not inquiring into
the quality of the abstractions. It was enough
that he was a philosopher ; and they believed that
every kind of philosophy tended to poison ancient
morals and cripple the ancient faith. Blind conservatives never stop to make accurate classifica-
tions of their opponents. They make no account
of the various moods and spirit in which dissent
is made, and the frequent affirmations that accom-
pany denials. One man's denial is a *yes* he says
to something better which he loves ; another's is
merely a *no* to something which cramps his intellect, and restrains his will, and which he hates.
But the conservatives divide mankind into two
parties, the friends of establishments and the
malcontents. There are besiegers at the gates,
and the garrison of the fortress call them all foes,
not caring to ask who are seeking to enter in
order to repair and enlarge the old, dilapidated
castle, and to distinguish them from the mob
who would batter down the turrets for the sake
of sack and murder. Consider what a motley
crowd are lumped together to be laughed at under
the title " Transcendentalists " ; men without faith
and men of the deepest faith, conceited shallow-
pates and lynx-eyed seers, nebulous poets and
genius with its pen of adamant and tongue of
gold, flaccid pantheists and those whose loyal
lives adorn the eternal laws, are hooped about
and bundled into fellowship by that elastic word.
Shall a Catholic bishop stop to analyze and

parcel out the various grades of minds included in that category, when they can be conveniently anathematized in the gross?

Is not the term "neologist" in theology made to span the space between a Fox and a Martineau, a De Wette and a Strauss? Does not the title "Socialist" cover with equal reproach the Christian whose imagination revels in the pictured fulfilment of the prayer, "Thy kingdom come," and the Red Republican whose heart is fierce with hate, and the sensual enthusiast, like Henri Heine, who would lift from the race the restraint of principle and the "incubus of worship," and build the temple of license on the ruins of the home?

Let a man be heard to question the literal inspiration of "Chronicles," or to speak of the fragmentary nature of the Gospels, or to hint of any mistakes of the Apostles, and is he not called infidel and a foe of Christ? Socrates was called to pay the inevitable price of dissent and of a higher insight, by a total misconception of his views. The ultra-conservatives of Athens feared that the state would fall if the throne of Zeus was undermined, and that virtue would have no backer if the flames of Tartarus were treated to the wet blankets of dialectics. They could not see, and cared not to see, that the *no* of Socrates to the traditions was a higher religious *yes*. They would not look at the infinite sweep of Providence which, in his teachings, displaced the

sceptre of the thunder-god. They could not discern that native " beauty of holiness " which, in
his sight, was the only thing in the universe to be
desired. They could not comprehend the terrors
of that intrinsic spiritual retribution for sin which
he would substitute for the red surges of Phlege-
thon, and so the shortest way was to oppose and
satirize him as an atheist and a mental libertine.

To these causes of dissatisfaction we must add
the hostility of most of the demagogues, and even
of the statesmen, of Athens. He believed in the
application of science to public affairs as well as
to speculative questions. He believed that those
only had the right to govern who knew how to
govern. "The sceptre," said he, "cannot make a
king, and none are rulers who are ignorant of the
art of government." The whole of Mr. Carlyle's
famous doctrine on this point, in his " Latter-day
Pamphlets," is found in Socrates' conversations.
He was fond of picturing the qualities that are
essential to successful statesmanship ; and in this
way was holding up an ideal in the workshops
and before the youth of Athens, which threw too
much light upon politics for the comfort of the
politicians.

Once he did appear on the stage as a practical
dealer in public business. He was more than
sixty years old. Some victorious navy-generals
were on trial for their life upon the charge of
neglecting to save some of the sailors of their
own fleet whose ships had been sunk in the

engagement. The Athenian voters were exasperated against them. A motion was made in the assembly of the people, — a general concourse in their Faneuil Hall, — to take summary action upon the case of the generals without a special trial. It was plainly illegal, a proceeding of Judge Lynch, and the magistrates declared it so, and hesitated to put the motion. Amid great excitement another motion was made, " that whoever interrupted the free votes of the assembly should be involved in the same sentence with the commanders." A tumultuous shout greeted the proposition, but the presidents still refused. A demagogue arose and formally accused them, and the multitude demanded with clamors that they be called to account. It was no boy's play, this bearding the Athenian panther when his eyes were kindling, his claws starting from their cushions, and he had begun to growl. Socrates was by law the chief magistrate of the day. The rest of the board faltered before the fury of the populace; but the hard-headed old philosopher would not budge an inch. The leading men tried to terrify him, the voters threatened to impeach him, there was a tempest about him ; but he said that every action is open to a higher and searching inspection, and he insisted that he would not do an act which was contrary to law. The generals were condemned, but Socrates somehow escaped being mobbed, and lived to see the instigators of the affair impeached, imprisoned, and despised.

We cannot be certain to which law, the human or the higher statute, Socrates referred, when he said he would do nothing contrary to it. For, a year or two afterwards, the ruling oligarchy summoned him to the marshal's office, and ordered him to go with four others and seize a man named Leon, of Salamis, a fugitive. We do not know the crime of Leon, and cannot positively tell whether he was white or black. But Socrates thought he was entitled to his liberty, and was not attracted to kidnapping, for these are his words : "That government, strong as it was, did not so overawe me as to make me commit an unjust action ; but when we came out from the public office the four went to Salamis and brought back Leon, but I went away home ; and perhaps for this I should have been put to death, if that government had not speedily been broken up."

A picture of Socrates would be very incomplete that did not include a sketch of his domestic relations. He was a great admirer of human beauty, and there are many passages of his conversations that betray a noble and generous estimate of the nature of woman. He was above the prejudices of his age, and judged human beings by qualities of soul, and not by sex. Perhaps if now among us his voice would have been heard at the Worcester Women's Rights Convention ; for he said publicly at a supper-party in Athens, what was a heresy in Greece, "I have long held the opinion that the female sex are nothing inferior to ours, excepting only in strength of body and perhaps steadiness of judgment." And Xenophon, who was his devoted friend, in a fictitious dialogue puts into his mouth the words, — which show his estimate of female character, — " It is far more delightful to hear the virtue of a good woman described, than if the famous painter Zeuxis was to show me the portrait of the fairest woman in the world."

It has been well remarked by another, as a singular fact, that " the majority of those men, who, from Homer downwards, have done most to exalt woman into a divinity, have either been bachelors or unfortunate husbands." There is no disputing the fact that Xantippe, the wife of Socrates, was a tartar, or, as Aristophanes would say, a tartaress. She tried the temper of the sage in every way. She railed at him and stormed against him ; she disturbed his meditations with the mop ; she doused him with dirty water (clean water, it is said, would not always have been a misfortune); she trampled presents that were sent to him under her feet ; she knocked the tables over when he expected a philosophical friend to a frugal supper ; she tore off her husband's cloak in the middle of the street, which, as it was probably his only garment, must have been annoying. The children complained bitterly about her, and declared to the old gentleman that her tongue was worse than the claws of a wild beast. But the sage was never ruffled. The visitations of dirty water, he

said, were the rain that followed the thunder of
his good wife's tongue. He exercised the boys in
dialectics, and proved that they ought to ask pardon of the gods for their impiety, and all his own
perils he tried to turn to moral benefit.

"If you think so highly of female nature," said
a captious friend to him, "how comes it you do
not instruct Xantippe, who is, beyond dispute, the
most insupportable woman that is, has been, or
ever will be?" Pretty plain talk to a man's face
about his wife. "But, my friend," said Socrates, "those who would learn horsemanship do
not choose tame horses, but the highest-mettled
and hardest-mouthed. I design to converse with
all sorts of people, and I believed I should find
nothing to disturb me in their conversation or
manners, being once accustomed to bear the unhappy tongue of Xantippe."

So, in early church history, we read of a Christian lady who desired of St. Athanasius to pro-
cure for her, out of the widows fed from the
ecclesiastical fund, an old woman, morose, peevish, and impatient, that she might, by the society
of so ungentle a person, have often occasion
to exercise her patience, her forgiveness, and
charity.

That Socrates showed great genius in selecting
the toughest trial possible to the soul of man, and
that he breasted it heroically, is beyond question ;
yet there is something to be said for the much
berated wife. What was Socrates as a husband ?

He was so poor, by his own confession, that he was never master of all the proper implements of housekeeping. All the property under his roof would not have brought forty dollars at auction. He would not take pay for his teachings, but his teachings could not purchase fire-wood, and he would not do any other work. All the morning he would have a glorious philosophical lounge in Simon the leather-dresser's shop, and then go home to dinner, forgetting that Xantippe had not been furnished with a sixpence to trade with the fishman at the door. Husbands may be transcendental, but wives who must cook and bake have a curious way of looking upon life from the point of material interests. Socrates was always talking about how little a man could live on, but he did not earn that little. He was delighted that poor men in Athens could buy four measures of flour for an obolus; but where, O Socrates, is your obolus? His soul was revelling, no doubt, in the great ideas, and pointing out the everlasting distinction between the agreeable and the just; but his wife, all this while, was living among the empty stewpans and rickety chairs, and meditating how a good dinner would be both agreeable and just, and feeling the everlasting and infinite distinction between mutton and hunger, penury and household comfort, dependence on charity and an honest livelihood. Socrates was thinking over the benefits society derives from virtue and good teachers, while she mused on the greater ease with which the little Soccies could be clothed if the sage would stick to chiselling statues instead of sculpturing souls. Moreover, if the good woman ever discovered the motive of the sage in marrying her, can we blame her if she determined to assist his moral development by exercising her peculiar genius to the top of its bent? It was a Divine call, I know, that made Socrates a bad provider for his family. He would, perhaps, have violated the highest principle, and been a worse provider for the world, if he had fulfilled the ordinary obligations, and worked to have his parlor furnished and the larder stocked. But we must also remember that, to have domestic tranquillity in his circumstances, he should have had a female Socrates for a wife, and that only supernatural grace could have kept any ordinary woman from being a termagant and trial.

The family of Socrates was the circle of his friends. To understand him, we must comprehend his influence over persons, persons of great genius and of the most diverse temperaments, tastes, and gifts. There have been few such immense and tyrannical personalities known. The men whom he confuted in debate called him a cramp-fish that benumbed the wits of his opponents. And he attracted as powerfully as he paralyzed. Among those who valued him as the apple of their eye, and revered him as almost more than mortal, were some of the greatest names of Athens. The wealthy Crito was his steady adherent from boyhood till death, and would have rejoiced to turn his purse upside down for him, if Socrates would have permitted such a profanation of attachment. The acute and vigorous Antisthenes, founder of the sect of Cynics, was early captivated by him, and walked from his home six miles every day and back again to hear him talk. He despised all luxuries and show, and, though able to dress better, wore a threadbare cloak and ragged clothes. Socrates was the only being on earth he loved, but friendship did not save him from the remark, "Why so ostentatious? Through your rags I see your vanity."

With equal ardor the luxurious, oily-tempered, polished sensualist, Aristippus, was devoted to him, — a man who realized perfectly the formula that has been given for Goethe's nature, that "he succeeded in subjecting all irregular impulses to a course of disciplined self-indulgence." *Mihi res, non me rebus subjungere.* The society of Socrates was as indispensable to him as lazy leisure, wine, and bodily indulgence. But the terms of the intercourse reflect no dishonor on Socrates himself. He contested inch by inch with him the theory of pleasure, and forced him to confess before others its nonsense and inconsistency.

The virtuous and simple-hearted Xenophon was his pupil, and, as a child to him more than twenty years, believed him to be inspired, and wrote out his recollections of him to vindicate his character.

Euripides, "the stage philosopher," though older, was for some time his intimate companion.

The insolent and subtle Euclid of Megara, afterwards founder of a sect, was a constant satellite. So necessary was the society of Socrates to him, that when his native city was at war with Athens, and a decree forbade any dweller in Megara on pain of death to be seen in the Athenian streets, Euclid dressed in female attire and walked twenty miles by night to the house of Socrates, to have a few hours' talk.

And a host of others — Cebes and Simmias, who left their native country for his sake ; Phœdon of Elis, once a slave in Athens, but redeemed by Socrates' influence, who repaid the favor by the growth of his mind and his ardent affection ; the beautiful Charmides ; the young Aristides, who said he gained strength by being in the room with Socrates ; Aristodemus, Apollodorus, Critobulus — testified to the personal sway of the slouchy ambassador of reason.

The two sides of Socrates' nature were represented in his friends. He had his Boswell always near him, who consulted oracles about him, and was continually in a quarrel with somebody in regard to him, and who hardly dared to pronounce his name aloud, — the little, dark, shrivelled, dirty, fussy Chæropho, whom the comic poets delighted to hit off under the nickname of "Socrates' bat."

And there was Æschines, son of a sausage-maker, who took a notion for the linked thought rather than the linked meats, — a poor and unthrifty fellow, whom Socrates once advised in his distress to borrow money of himself by reducing his wants. After the death of his master he failed in the perfume business, and took to publishing Socratic dialogues for a living.

Two characters, however, appear in the circle of his associates who eclipse all these. The first was Alcibiades, a man who in his character united the distinguishing traits of Lord Peterborough, King Charles II., and Voltaire. He bore the most aristocratic blood of Athens. His wealth was enormous, and his face the handsomest in Greece. He began responsible life at eighteen, with a natural temper which education could scarcely tame, and amid circumstance that would peril not only the finest disposition but the firmest principles. He was proud, chivalrous, and munificent. He had a passion for all games, cock-fights, and horse-races, and an equally intense delight in literature. He kept the most costly stud and chariots, carried pet quails in his bosom, and owned a most valuable dog, whose tail he cut off close, that Athens might talk about it, and so not talk of worse things. He was self-confident, lawless, and dissolute, and indulged the wildest caprices of temper. The people petted him as one would pet a complacent lion's whelp. The women, of course, all loved him.

He struck a schoolmaster who did not happen

to have a copy of Homer in his house. He struck
one of the worthiest citizens of Athens on a wager,
and the next day went and stripped himself before
him, begging to be beaten for the insult. He
openly destroyed the public record of a charge
against one of his friends. He carried his wife by
force away from the magistrate to whom she was
applying for a divorce. He would reel drunk,
late in the evening, into supper-parties, where he
was invited, or would stand at the door while his
slaves went in and stole the goblets from the table,
which he would coolly give away as charity to the
poor. He shocked all Athens by breaking the
sacred busts of Mercury in the streets in a night
scrape. The Mysteries were caricatured in his
house ; and a comic poet who dared to spear
him on the stage disappeared suddenly by making, as was supposed, an unexpected midnight
acquaintance with the sea.

The dates of all these excesses are not known ;
but it is certain that at one time he was devot-
edly attached to Socrates, and was beloved by
him. They walked together, wrestled with each
other, occupied and slept in the same tent in the
camp. He went to learn the art of accurate
thought and speech, — he learned more. The
philosopher talked with him on his danger and
duties, made him cry over his follies, and drew
from him the confession that such society seemed
to be a heavenly provision for his redemption.
" When I hear him," he is reported to have said,

" my heart leaps up far more than the hearts of those who celebrate the Corybantic mysteries. He alone inspires me with remorse and awe. I stop my ears, therefore, as from the sirens, and flee away as fast as possible, that I may not sit down beside him and grow old listening to his talk." Better for him if he had thus listened ; for then he would not in his checkered fortune have typified the history of all lawless ambition and dissolute license ; he would not have had the mortification of failing to reach what he aspired after ; he would have been saved the disgrace of injuring his country almost fatally ; he would not have died in banishment and shame, and by the arrows of midnight assassins.

If we may credit a story of Apuleius, Socrates once had a remarkable dream, in which he seemed to see a swan fly from a sacred altar in the Academy to his breast, which afterwards extended its wings towards the heavens and allured the ears of men and gods by its harmonious voice. While he was relating the dream, Aristo brought in his son, a finely shaped and handsome youth, to be a pupil. As soon as Socrates saw him, and knew, by his outward form, what his mind was, he exclaimed, " This, O friend, was the swan I saw."

Socrates might well have had such a dream, for it was the boy Plato that came to him ; and if no other record remained to us of his greatness than the bent he gave and the spirit he breathed into the genius of Plato, his fame would be secure.

Ex ungue leonem. The indication would be as certain as that the discovery of an original and huge footstep in one alabaster slab would give a new mammoth to the lists of zoölogy, or that the finding of a majestic and faultless statue among the ruins of Etruria would furnish Phidias a mate in the realm of art. From twenty to thirty Plato was in the society of Socrates, then passing from his sixtieth to his seventieth year. He was gently turned by Socrates from politics and pleasure and a frivolous Athenian ambition to a life of study and thought. What the sage could not do for Alcibiades he did for Plato. Never was the service of education acknowledged with more ardent gratitude, never was it repaid with such delicate reverence. The lapse of fifty years, which made Plato the hater and bitter satirist of almost every prominent man and institution of society, did not weaken his memory and love of his master. He clung to him in thought as the one true, solid, and symmetrical man amid a crowd of phantasms, traitors, and dwarfs. Plato wrote no eulogy of Socrates, but wherever he has gone into the palaces of the aristocracy of letters, with his courtly mien and purple drapery, he has introduced his old slouchy, unshod master, as if saying, with elegant haughtiness, "If you would be honored with my company, make him also welcome who has made me what I am." His greatest works are cast in dialogues, in which the writer himself never appears, but where Socrates is the chief speaker and hero, as though the highest thoughts would be profaned in coming through other lips ; and thus, arm in arm, the stately duke and the democrat of philosophy walked down the lists of fame.

That sweet and mystic swan-song, — the liquid fusion of poetry and science, — with which the genius of Plato has filled the cloisters and oratories of the chief scholars of our race, has embroidered forever the name of the chaste and monastical Silenus with the melodious chants to " the first pure, first holy, and first fair."

From this point, where his greatest personal influence is visible, it will perhaps be most fitting to review the career and sum up the qualities of Socrates. It is plain enough that he was one of the men whose office it is to give a fresh intellectual impulse by shedding the light of new methods, and whose work, like that of Bacon and Descartes, is seen in the new products of thought that spring from the soil which they had ploughed. Milton has finely expressed his mission thus : —

> " Philosophy
> From heaven descended to the low-rooft house
> Of Socrates : see there his tenement
> Whom well inspired the oracle pronounced
> Wisest of men ; from whose mouth issued forth
> Mellifluous streams that watered all the schools
> Of Academics old and new, with those
> Surnamed Peripatetics, and the sect
> Epicurean and the stoic severe."

Had we time for it, it would be pleasant and profitable to follow his influence upon the fortunes of philosophy in Greece. He was the father of a new method of study. His thoughts were the seed-corn of systems. His pupils were the teachers of centuries. The great works of the leading names in ancient speculation were slips from the mind of Socrates. Each bump of his brain was the nucleus of a philosophical school. He held in his large reconciling intellect principles which separated when less massive thinkers tried to handle them, and were developed by rival parties as hostile elements. For a thousand years he held sway over the processes of the human mind ; and ancient heathen literature, when it sought an example of a noble self-sacrificing life of thought, spontaneously sought an illustration in some act or saying of Socrates.

His life is the dividing-point between the barren and the healthy periods of Grecian philosophy. His mind, so capacious and healthy, could be split up into various schools. Hardly had he left the world, than the strong and simple light he shed was scattered in various hues by the prismatic minds that had surrounded him or that succeeded him ; but in almost every case, — as happens when the strands of the solar beam are brilliantly dishevelled, — the vivifying principle, the actinic ray, was lost.

The Cynic system was an exaggeration of the personal habits of Socrates, his poverty, temperance, and contempt of wealth erected into a theory, but devoid of that absorbing reverence

for the right which made him forget the eccen-
tricity of his habits in the joy of his higher loyalty.
The Cynic intruded his tub and his dirt upon the
notice of the passer, as if to say, " See my estimate
of higher things by my comfortless indecency."
Socrates showed an adoration for the supreme
things that was genial, and tried to make others
recognize their beauty and worth; he did not boast
of his penury and cheerless home, but silently
paid that price for the privilege of leisure to
revel in his mission.   The hair-splitting Megarian
school was a caricature of his merciless dialectics,
lacking the buttress of his Franklin-like common-
sense to save it from caving into the abyss of
abstract and fathomless foolishness.   The Cyre-
naic theory was a Silenic parody on his principle
that happiness is the aim of man, and that every
soul should make circumstances subject to its
own control.   It was like abusing the principle,
" sufficient unto the day is the evil thereof," into
a warrant for intemperance and a free commission
to live as a Sadducee.

Indeed, we are not to suppose that his poverty
and the contempt of so many of his fellow-citizens
were at all delightful to him.   He felt his isola-
tion.   Xenophon, in a fictitious dialogue, makes
Socrates say in reply to a man who begged him
to correct any errors the sage might see in him :
" How can I correct you when you are already
possessed of the character of a good and honest
man ? and especially when I am taken for the

greatest trifler, who employs himself in nothing but measuring the air? or, which is a far worse character, that I am a poor man, which is a token of the greatest folly? This, indeed, might have been a trouble to me, if I had not met the other day a horse belonging to Nicias, with a crowd of people about him admiring his good qualities, and talking abundance in praise of his strength and spirit. This made me ask the question of the master of the horse, whether his horse was very rich? But he stared upon me, and laughed at me, as if I had been a madman, and only gave me this short answer, How should a horse have any money? When I heard this, I went away contented that it was lawful for a poor horse to be good on account of his free and generous spirit; and therefore I conclude it is likewise possible for a poor man to be good."*

This must be derived from a real saying of Socrates, for it does not seem possible that Xenophon could have had wit enough to invent its quaintness and pervade it so delicately with such sweet, pathetic humor.

The Platonic methods and speculations were the rigorous application of his mental principles and the coloring of his more practical and homely ideal faiths with the purple and gold of a gorgeous fancy. Stoicism was the apotheosis of his moral hardihood and self-poise, while the Aristotelian ambition to scour the kingdom of nature and

* Xen. Good Husbandry, 663.

label all the parcelled facts of the universe caught its impulse from his delight in the homeliest details which indicated or enforced a law, and his strenuous attempts after accurate classification. Nothing is more singular in the history of philosophy than the fact that a man so endowed with the analytic faculty should have guarded it religiously from roaming and rioting in unwholesome fields, and wasting itself in curious speculative exercises, or grubbing in miserable researches for the sanction of our primitive faiths, but should have devoted it to the work of elucidating moral truth, and made it steadily subservient to practical ends.

And here the singular dualism of his nature attracts attention. A radical distinction between men is often indicated by saying that some are intuitive and others logical in their processes of reaching truth. "The Arabs speak of a conference between a mystic and a philosopher. On parting, the philosopher said, 'All that he sees I know,' and the mystic said, 'All that he knows I see.'" Socrates was a seer and a knower. By his dreams, trances, and abstractions, his inward suggestions and Divine call, he is fellow with the Brahmins and Soofees, George Fox, Bœhmen, and Swedenborg. By his scientific methods and prying scrutinies and impatience of inaccurate statement he belongs to the thinkers and provers, and stands in close affinity with the Aristotles, Bacons, Hamiltons, Herschels, and Stuart Mills. He was a man of faith, and he insisted on knowledge.

He meditated logically. No prophet ever felt more thrillingly the supreme worth of virtue and the holy ; but he discarded the prophet's heat of utterance, and put on the missionary robes to convince his fellows by earnest conversation that virtue is truth, that there is no such dreadful thing as the insult men offer truth by not founding their behavior on it, and that what cannot be proved is certainly too dangerous to be lived.

His soul was doubly furnished, for it had strong wings and sturdy feet. With Plotinus he could take "the flight of the alone to the alone," and he could travel with any pedestrian rationalist and climb with him all day the rugged steeps of induction, and make no misstep in gaining the peak where the lower landscape is comprehensively surveyed.

This dualism is manifested in him at every point. We cannot sufficiently admire the fine proportions of his intellect, its majestic, planet-like poise. Mysticism never betrayed him into fanaticism, nor obscured by its luminous diffusive haze the clear boundaries between demonstrative and speculative truth. He would revel in volatile abstractions and practical details with equal delight. Let him get pitted against some subtle head from abroad, and he would never tire of leading or following for hours through all the intricacies of speculation about the relations of courage, temperance, knowledge, and piety ; and when his

poor opponent's brain was completely fagged out,
Socrates would take him to the best and cheapest
cobbler's stall, show him the miller's establishment where a poor man could buy a large quan-
tity of fine flour for a penny, walk with him to
the oil-man's where a chœnex of olives cost two
farthings, and then hasten to the slop-shop where
a jerkin without sleeves could be had for ten
drachmas ; and from these facts the foreigner,
who had seen him untwist the constitution of
knowledge, listened to a discourse on the felicity of Athens. Socrates was a transcendental
Cobden. He was a cool and comic enthusiast.
He was a compromise of Pythagoras and Punch.
He trod the mother earth with bare feet, and
stared into the spiritual universe with his lobster
eyes.

Some religious men regard sin chiefly in the light
of God's mercy, and see it as the deepest and
blackest ingratitude ; others conceive it in contrast
with Divine Sovereignty, and regard it as deliber-
ate rebellion ; others are absorbed with the feeling
of the immense wrong it does the soul, like the
scorching of a nerve by flame, and dwell on its
intrinsic evil ; others, again, forecast by their imagination the terrible results it is storing up, and
tremble before the glare of the future circumstan-
tial hells into which it will one day slide the spirit.
But Socrates saw chiefly the intense and towering
nonsense of sin. Evil-doing of every sort is hostile to nature, and is therefore idiocy. All hope

of gaining anything by it is like the expectation of bending the law of gravity from its customs for private advantage, or wrestling with the electric stream. No Gentile intellect has ever seen more clearly the leading vital laws. And what he saw he worshipped. A law once seen was as a gospel. He asked no other sanction for a principle than that it is a reality. The ordinary method with men is to ask, not whether a principle is true, but " What if we do not follow it ? " " What advantage is there in acceptance and obedience ? What jails, dungeons, stocks, and whipping-posts lie behind the statute, and enforce it with an eloquence which our nerves and self-interest can appreciate?" But Socrates did not slyly gauge the police force, nor count the sheriffs, which a law could muster before he concluded to be loyal. If Nature indicated that a clean tongue was proper, no pepper and artistic cookery went into his stomach. If she said that a firm muscle lay in her order, a bed of lamb's-wool would not be soft to him, and luxury was despicable. If Nature hinted the supremacy of justice and the good, all glory, material magnificence, pomp, wealth, and power were as nothing but playthings, and not to be accepted if they could not follow the path of entire consecration to what is best.

Virtue in his view was truth, and vice practical nonsense ; and since, in his belief, the parts of truth must be harmonious, he maintained that all clear and correct thinking is consistent with holiness and leads to it, while every dark spot of confusion or uncertainty in the intellect might turn out to be the "apex of hell." Hence the earnestness with which he insisted on accurate thinking; hence, too, his aversion to positive magisterial instruction. All truths are kindred, and truth enough he believed lay in every soul to save it, or at least to condemn its impurity, if the mind could be made to appreciate it. Consistency was his watchword and his sanative for the sin in the world. Whatever is worth considering is worth knowing thoroughly, and if any fundamental point is known scientifically all needed practical knowledge will come. "Enthrone," said he to men, "what you occasionally recognize as supreme. Do not make your conduct a practical falsehood. Be consistent. Give me one fundamental element of your belief, and if it is real I will get a purchase on it for my lever that will wrench your false soul out of joint; if it is unreal I will show you how your character is, or soon will be, as soft as mush." Thus he held up realities, preached intellectual morality, and belabored every unfaithful man with his own admissions. There was no invective in his private sermons. The terribleness of his method was its calmness and scientific coldness. By his leisurely conversations he made men judge themselves, brought the most hardened men up by the strain of his logic to see that their careers were founded on falsehood as deliberately and as surely as a bull is drawn by a windlass to the slaughter-house. " If you will live stupidly, like sots, it shall not be my fault. I will make you ashamed of it at least. You shall know that you are ninnies, and if the weapon I am commissioned to wield does not reach your heart it shall not be because it does not spike your intellect, — strike down through and through your brain." It was not his forte or aim to frighten people or to reach their affections, but to convince and convict ; and when, as in the case of Alcibiades, he did stir the feelings, it was probably by the suction-pump of his logic that he moved the fountain of tears.

We cannot estimate too highly the unfeverishness of soul exhibited by Socrates. It is better to be fanactical in the cause of righteousness than to freeze in self-love. But nothing is so grand and majestic in the universe as the sustained, healthy, and vigorous conviction in a strong nature that nothing is good or worth living for but what is holy. The play of Socrates' moral life, though so stern and uncompromising, was not forced or hard. As Montaigne finely said, " He made his soul move a natural and common motion, and raised himself, not by starts but by complexion, to the highest pitch of vigor." It is comparatively easy to pay the respect of being solemn and sad before the Infinite Justice and Goodness, but to see them steadily and be cheerful is a deeper worship. It is common to acknowledge them as law and adore them, but it is only by the rarest spirits that they are seen as life and accepted as the soul's treasure and joy. Socrates did not feel that a man should lie in the embrace of the spiritual laws as on a bed of bull-briers, but that the soul should feel secure, protected, and at home in them, as if cushioned in a nest of down.

And he was able to make practical religious themes subjects of easy and honest conversation. We imagine that they are for set, stately, or heated address, for preaching, not for talk. Generally, if the purest saintly man starts such topics with a friend, alone or in the house, the ledger is closed, or the book is shut ; the wife stops knitting ; the children sit stiff, and the soul takes a prim and rigid posture. There is no communion ; the tones of the speaker have no fresh inflections ; the dialect spoken is not that of the poem, the exchange, and the press, but the language has a musty, sepulchral smell. Socrates, however, talked with men about these things as a physician converses on symptoms and prescriptions, the unhealthly diet that has been indulged, and what the patient must do to regain vigor. Begin to talk with him on painting or housekeeping, wrestling, rhetoric, or poetry, and soon you are on the smooth and pleasant slope that slides you so gracefully into the depths of moral life. The tones are calm, the illustrations clear, various, and lively, and the talker finds that the law of duty is as entertaining a theme as the law of symmetry, and needs no more take the lustre from the eye

than a discourse of botany or music. The intense earnestness of Socrates was lubricated and
made genial by his humor. His life was as loyal
as the still tidal currents of the seas, and the
upper waves might frolic and foam without detri-
ment to his health or to the spiritual landscape
of the world.

We might speak here, too, at some length of
his love of men. He worshipped truth and right,
and he loved men because of their capacity to
know and serve what is best in the universe. The
greatness and priceless worth of a soul was his
frequent theme. Never was there a sterner spiritual republican. Titles and place were dim to
his eye before the faculty of comprehending the
just and living for what is good. This faculty he
saw in the artisan as in the blood aristocrat, the
wealthy merchant, and the lordly sophist. His
missionary sincerity and love of men were seen
in this, that discussion with a cook or a slave in
Athens was as delightful to him, if it was honest
and earnest, and could lift the mind an inch above
its ordinary plane, as banquet disquisitions and conference with the greatest men of Greece. Simon
the bridle-cutter published a set of conversations held by Socrates in his shop with the stray
visitants, of all degrees of social standing, that
happened in. Such is a slight sketch of the
mental qualities of a man who seemed to be a
compound of Wilkes, Franklin, Johnson, and
Coleridge. He had the ludicrous homeliness

and entertaining wit of the first, the shrewd sense and practical wisdom of the second, the burly understanding, social royalty, and conversational methods and resources of the third, and the analytic subtlety, entrancing eloquence, and mystical insight of the last.

We come now to the closing experiences of his career. The people began to tire of him, and to fear him, towards the close of his life. During the sway of the thirty tyrants — the reign of terror in Athens — a law was passed that no one should talk philosophy in the city. Socrates had used some striking imagery, a little while before, on the unskilfulness of a cowherd who should lose part of the drove every day, and see the rest growing sick and weak under his management. The gentlemen of the directory, who were confiscating property and murdering their townsmen, did not like such bucolic meditations, and one of them, a depraved wretch, the Greek Marat, could recall a conversation in which Socrates had enlightened him in company on the spiritual dignity and worthiness of a pig. No sooner had Socrates heard of the law than he waited upon the rulers, to have a little conversation by which his uncertainty as to the meaning of the decree might be removed. "Pray tell me," said he, "whether you take philosophy, as stated in the statute, to consist in reasoning right or reasoning wrong, since, if you mean the first, we must beware how we reason right; if the latter, the consequence is

plain we must mend our reasoning." The impudence was sublime ; it was like a Frenchman
joking Tinville with the guillotine before his eyes ;
and one of the board, choking with rage, replied :
" We will give you terms easy to be understood ;
refrain altogether from talking with young men."
Here was a chance for definitions. " Suppose,"
said Socrates, " I want to buy something of a merchant, must n't I ask the price if the man is under thirty ? " " We don't prohibit that ; but keep
a proper distance from carpenters, smiths, and
shoemakers, and let us have no more examples
from them." " Then I am not to concern myself
any longer with justice and piety, and the rules
of right and wrong ? " " By Jove, you must not ;
and, Socrates, don't trouble yourself any further
with the herdsmen, lest you occasion the loss
of more cattle." Those miscreants did not hold
power long enough after this to kill him, but, a
year or two following, his case was brought before
the tribunal of the people, three accusers appearing against him, with an indictment that held
three counts, — that Socrates did not believe the
gods whom the city held sacred ; that he designed
to introduce new deities ; that he corrupted the
youth.

It was one of the most singular and most interesting trials recorded in history. Socrates was
seventy years old, and was really arraigned before
his five hundred judges for being a universal cen-
sor and intolerable bore. A crowd of his friends

attended him, among them Plato. After the opening of the case by Melitus, Socrates was permitted
to speak in his own behalf. Fearing that his
bearing would not be most conciliatory to the
benches, the rhetorician Lysias had been induced
to prepare an artistic and elaborate defence, which
Socrates was urged to read, with the assurance
that it must produce acquittal. The inward voice,
however, opposed the plan. "Think you," said
he to his friend, "I have not spent my whole life
in preparing for this very thing?" Finely has
Montaigne said : "Should a suppliant voice have
been heard out of the mouth of Socrates ; that
lofty virtue have struck sail in the very height of
its glory ; and his rich and powerful nature have
committed its defence to Art, and in her highest
proof have renounced truth and simplicity, the
ornaments of his speaking, to adorn and deck
itself with the embellishments of figures and the
equivocations of a premeditated speech?" He
did not renounce truth and simplicity. He cross-
questioned his chief accusers sufficiently to show
the falsity of the charges in their spirit, and then
his talk was an impeachment of Athens, not a
defence of his own career. "When your generals
at Pohdara and Delium assigned my place in the
battle, I remained there and faced the peril of
slaughter ; and strange would it be, if, when the
Deity has assigned my duty to pass my life in the
study of philosophy and the examination of others,
I should, through fear of death or anything else,

desert my post." His serene haughtiness and affectionate assertion of superiority surprised his enemies, and determined the judges to put his temper to the final strain. They voted, and out of the immense ballot a paltry majority of six condemned him. His accuser proposed the penalty of death. The defendant had one opportunity remaining to conciliate the judges by an humble confession, a petition for mercy, or a proposition of some different penalty. " I know not," said he, " whether death is an evil or no. I will not choose imprisonment, for I do not like it ; and why should I say exile? A fine life, at my age, to go out wandering, and driven from city to city ! If I award what I think I actually deserve, I should say a public maintenance in the Prytaneum. I am a poor man, and need leisure to be your benefactor, and it seems to me that I deserve such an honor more than one who has been victorious at the Olympic games in a horse-race. Perhaps, however, I could pay you a small fine ; about fifteen dollars is the top of my means. But Plato here, and Crito, offer to be surety for thirty times that sum. I therefore name that as my fine." Four hundred and fifty dollars was a cheap valuation of him even at seventy, but he had tossed his life away. The enraged judges pronounced sentence of death by a heavy vote. His friends were in great distress, but his calmness rose to majesty, and his playfulness to the highest eloquence. " If," said he in closing, " death is

a removal from hence to another place, and if all
the dead are there, what greater blessing can there
be than this, my judges? At what price would
you not estimate a conference with Orpheus and
Musæus, Hesiod and Homer? For me to so-
journ there would be admirable, when I should
meet with Palamedes, and Ajax the son of Tela-
mon, and others of the ancients who died by an
unjust sentence. At what price would not any
one estimate the opportunity of questioning him
who led that mighty army against Troy, or Ulysses,
or Sysiphus, or ten thousand others whom one
might mention, both men and women?" Heaven,
to his imagination, had always been an atmosphere of refined and vigorous talk. How fine
and fitting that the old man's fancy should even
then revel in the rich society and the glorious
discussions to which the friendly vengeance of
his foes would send him! He begged his judges
to punish his sons as they grew up, if they cared
more for riches than virtue; he assured his accusers that he bore no resentment to them; he
looked around for the last time upon the Athens
which he loved and the citizens it was his great
aim to serve, and left the agora amid his heart-
broken friends to sleep fettered in the prison.

The sentence could not legally take effect for
thirty days. During that time his rich friend,
Crito, through some bribery, made preparations for
his escape, and went to him one morning before
daybreak to perfect the plan. He was sleeping

quietly, and said, when awaked, " The time of my death draws near : for in my dream just now a beautiful and majestic woman arrayed in white seemed to approach me and to say, ' Socrates, three days and you will reach fertile Phthia ! ' " Crito told him he had come to save him, and take him to Thessaly, where he could be secure and happy. But the old prisoner calmly reasoned down all his entreaties, and pictured to him how the personified laws of Athens would reproach him for his ingratitude if he should violate them then, how droll it would seem for him to escape wrapped in a disguise of cloaks and skins, and how much better it was to suffer than to commit injustice. " These things boom in my ears," said he, " like the swelling music of flutes, and make me deaf, my dear friend Crito, to all you say." He stayed to meet his fate. During his confinement he versified the fables of Æsop, and composed a hymn to Apollo, in order, as he said, if possible, to obey and fulfil a dream which frequently warned him in life to apply himself to music.

The pages of Plato give us a full account of the last day's intercourse between himself and friends in prison. After taking leave of his wife, the most of the day was occupied with a long and thorough treatment of the question of immortality.

His friend Crito begged him not to talk earnestly and steadily, for the jailer had said that bodily heat would counteract the poison, and make his death more painful. " Then let them give it to me twice or thrice," he said, and went on with the discussion. The day wore away while that circle recounted the arguments, presentiments, and myths that justify to reason the expectation of another life. As the sunset drew on, and the talk must close, a friend timidly asked, " How shall we bury you?" " Just as you please," said he, with a smile, "if only you can catch me and I do not escape you." Here, as always, his pleasantry was the cool expression of his strongest faith. " Say that you bury my body, and do it as is pleasing to you and most agreeable to our laws." He bathed, bade farewell to his children, who were brought in, and then signified that he was ready to the executioner, who said, with flowing tears, that he was the most noble, meek, and excellent man that ever entered the prison. The sun was not quite set when the hemlock juice was brought to him in a cup. He inquired calmly what the symptoms would be, and when he might know that death was near; and, praying that his departure might be happy, drank it slowly, looking steadily at the jailer, without trembling or change of color. His friends till that moment had borne up stoically ; but then they yielded to their emotions, and one of them screamed wildly in his agony. But Socrates, still walking, rebuked and cheered them all, and at last lay down to die. " Crito," said he, " we owe a cock to Æsculapius ;

pay it; do not neglect it"; and his spirit fled.
Æsculapius was the god of medicine and health.
A pious Greek made offerings to him after being
cured of any serious disease. The last words of
Socrates were an enigmatical assurance to his
friends that by the death of his body the disease
of an earthly life was being cured, and his spirit
restored to its native health.

The judges of Socrates are forgotten; his
accusers are remembered with infamy by association with his name; his prison is one of the
sacred places in the memory of the race; while
his career is the strength of reformers now, and
preaches to all men the· majesty of self-sacrifice
and the glory of devotion; and the loyalty of his
life, the firmness of his principles, and the seren-
ity of his bearing in his last hours fortify more
powerfully than his arguments our faith in immortality.

If his friends had had insight they might have
gone away from that cell where the body of Socrates lay motionless and cold, with a conviction,
a sense of certainty, that such a spirit was not extinguished. His temper and impregnable faith,
when death was approaching to take him by the
hand and lead him into the shadow, are demonstration to our moral instincts that it came as a
friend to bear him up to a more congenial sphere,
and bid him live more intensely and usefully in
other scenes.

Why, not a rigid bone of his lifeless body, not

a hardening muscle or useless nerve of the stiff frame that once obeyed his will, was to be annihilated. God's economical laws took care of them, dissolved them, mingled them with dust and air, and turned them to new uses. They are living somewhere yet. Not a particle of his frame has perished in the great treasury of matter. And has that mind dissolved, that robust spiritual greatness, that muscular, invincible holiness, that inward eye which saw the light of eternal truth as the steady flame of a zenith star? Is there no world of spirits to receive such realities as these? Must not such a nature have been a precious jewel of God while it lived and served him here? And is the Almighty so penurious of matter, and so wasteful of the wealth of perfect virtue, that he saves carefully each ounce of saintly servants' bodies, and permits their souls to be extinguished forever by a gill of poison, or shrivelled by a fever, or consumed in a wreath of flame? We had better not believe that until we have emptied the universe of all that is divine. The life, the moral greatness, of Socrates, is an argument for immortality such as his logic could not frame, nor scepticism destroy; and thus his prison is a bright spot in human history, for it is a buttress of the soul's immortal hope.

The most remarkable saying, perhaps, that has been reported of Socrates is this : " That in respect to these great questions we ought to take the best of human reasonings, that which is most

difficult to be confuted, and embark on it as on a
raft, so to sail through life amid its storms, unless
we could be carried more safely in a surer convey-
ance furnished in some Divine instruction." Down
the River of Life, by its Athenian banks, he had
floated upon his raft of reason serene, in cloudy as
in smiling weather, for seventy years. And now
the night is rushing down, and he has reached the
mouth of the stream, and the great ocean is before him, dim heaving in the dusk. But he betrays
no fear. There is land ahead, he thought; eternal continents there are, that rise in constant light
beyond the gloom. He trusted still in the raft his
soul had built, and with a brave farewell to the
few true friends who stood by him on the shore
he put out into the darkness, a moral Columbus,
trusting in his haven on the faith of an idea.

1851.

IV.

SIGHT AND INSIGHT.

I ASK your attention to some thoughts that naturally range themselves under the formula, Sight and Insight.

Vision is the most glorious privilege of humanity. The eye is our royal endowment among the senses. Physically, we are insignificant specks on the earth's surface ; but, by reason of the marvellous and exquisite eye, the loveliness of the earth is portion of our furniture. We stand on less than a square foot of soil, and the horizon is the wall of our dwelling, the zenith the roof of our home. One of our most marked distinctions from animals is this, that their eyes are the instruments of instinct and the servants of greed, while the eye of man is a general organ, related to the universe as a vast, inspiring spectacle, and serving as the window of the mind and soul.

There is a doctrine that all our knowledge comes through the senses, and chiefly by the eye. This is false. Sight of itself takes in only the surface-coloring of nature. The senses supply no knowledge, for they convey only impressions,

never ideas. We must see in the first place that
the senses, which seem to furnish all our knowledge, are simply reporters. The all-important
question as to knowledge is, What is at the other
end of the sense, or nerve, to receive the report?
The eagle has a stronger eye than man. But set
the Apollo Belvedere before it, and it sees only the
articulated whiteness of a piece of stone. The
human mind, out of the same sensations, discerns a glorious statue. The stag has a better ear
than man. But let it listen to an orchestra and
it reports only a mob of tones, which, when they
break upon the human nerve, are disposed instantly
into a sonata or a symphony. Put a moss-rose
to the nostrils of a hound and see if it will awaken,
through his keen scent, any emotions of poetic
delight. The senses of an animal report all that
senses themselves can catch; but their owners
do not have the faculties to arrange and interpret
the sensations, — and so having eyes they see not,
and having ears they hear not. It is mind that
draws meaning out of the reports which the senses
make ; and so what they tell depends on the
grade of the faculty to which they tell.

All knowledge is, therefore, the result of insight, and education is a process of insight. How
immense the scale which the human being travels
in the training of his vision ! The infant begins
by seeing everything as on the eye itself. The
furniture of the chamber, and the parent's face,
toys, trees, and sky, are a confused mass of color,

and seem to belong somehow to the little stranger's personality. It must learn, at first, to push the world off from itself by attributing distance and size to the objects which the senses grasp; and at last it comes to be a Herschel, with the globe as the pedestal of its imperial eye, measuring the awful distance of the Pleiades, gazing at Orion sculptured in light on the black walls of space, with his star-hilted dagger and his club of knotted suns.

Let us take up the suggestion of this last statement, and learn what has been done, almost within a century, in laying out the scale of nature. How narrow, in contrast with ours, was the universe into which an old Greek gazed through the shadows of night; or David, when, looking up with nothing but eyesight as an instrument to help him, he chanted to the rude music of his harp the words, " The firmament showeth his handiwork " !   Can anything be more amazing than a simple statement of the triumph of thought in laying out the scale of nature ?   Think what a few astronomers have done.   Think of those dots of creamy light, that, in connection with our globe, are found to belong to our solar system. Our eyes can detect no apparent difference in their distance from us or from our sun.   But consider how the human intellect, represented in a few students that " outwatch the Bear " in lonely towers, keeping its greedy eye upon them, has seen them swell into majestic orbs floating and

waltzing in immensity; how it has spaced them
millions of miles apart, each cutting a circle
within the track of the other; how it has caught
the plane on which they move, seeing them as
they swing and sway, now dipping, now rising
in their ceaseless sweep; how it has measured
mountains upon them and discovered snows that,
on some of them, whiten the poles and melt in
summer-time; how it has weighed their mass,
telling how many myriads of tons each of those
little dots includes, that we write poetry to as the
morning or evening star, as if it had a Titan
scale to put them in, with a beam poised at the
zenith; how, not content with running its line out
hundreds of millions of miles in constructing this
domestic solar system, it has stood on the spinning disk of a planet so far out in space as to be
invisible to the naked eye, and then cast the lasso
of its mathematics still beyond into the darkness
and reined up another globe, whose existence it
had guessed, and dragged it with its filial moons
into the light of science; how it has leaped upon
the parent orb, torn open the blazing vesture of
the sun, looked in upon his dark substance and
stupendous ribs, wound its measuring line around
his awful surface, and told his weight; how it has
followed the track of the comet fire-ships, reck-
oned the leagues they rush into the bleak, black
ether, and prophesied their return; and how, not
satisfied with all these trophies, its look has
broken the spangled roofing of the night into an

airy and immeasurable arch, within which the
solar system is a dot and its motions but a flicker;
how, after years of trial, it has found one of those
tremulous suns, against which it might lean its
ladder of spider threads and light, and then has
mounted on it into the gallery of our firmament,
probed through the ranks, five hundred deep, of
orbs that swing in its dome, — yes, lifted itself out
upon the roof of this star-tiled St. Peter's of
space, and gazed off thence upon the milky gleam
of the spires of other cathedral firmaments that
rise in the astral city of God !

This is the victory of the human mind over the
deception which the eye would practise upon it as
to the scale of nature. Modern astronomy is a
trophy of intellectual insight. When any of us
are tempted to distrust propositions and principles simply because they seem opposed to the
settled material order of society, and appear con-
tradictory to the instincts of selfishness, let us
reflect that we begin to live intellectually in nature only when we grasp a principle that pitches
the sun out of his path in the heavens, that dwin-
dles the earth to a little marble in space, and that
shrivels the visible wonders of the sky to motes
floating in a flood of luminous vitality.

All this grandeur of result has been made possible by the most careful and reverent scrutiny of
the most insignificant facts. The human intellect
was made to conquer nature by watching and
following the most delicate hints from facts which
everybody observes.

Every pebble, every stick, is an index pointing a hundred ways. There is a path from it out into chemistry, into statics, into the laws of heat and light, into forces of gravitation and electricity, into atomic and organic sympathies, — into the whole circle of the published wisdom of God.

The geologist can see no further into a millstone than any boor can. But he can see a great deal further into the solid world, though no more facts are presented to his eye. Both of them ride this globe as mere gnats on the back of a wild rhinoceros. Yet the first detects the depth and nature of the intestines of the creature that flies with him twenty miles a second ; follows the wrinkles and untwists the plaitings of its rocky hide, reads its age on its alpine warts ; writes its biography from its pulpy infancy till its bones had hardened, and up through the wild passions of its youth to its present maturity ; and is able to describe passages of its fortunes, a hundred thousand years ago, as clearly as he discerns the color of any district of its skin to-day.

The vast proportions of science are reared by the interlocking of ordinary facts through the allusions that invest them. And more than half the distance from ignorance to science is accomplished when a man learns to observe, to concentrate his mind into his vision, so that he shall see accurately and intensely what Nature has set before him. It is only when he sees the thing itself strongly, that he can detect the shadowy lines

7 *

around it of vaster and modest facts, like the
dusky thread that loops the space within the rim
of the new moon, hinting the whole orb while only
a segment is burnished with light.

There is an old proverb that "What is ever
seen is never seen." Science is now showing us
what undrainable meaning lurks in the minute
and common. Almost everything is told in anything, if the eye that looks through the sense is
patient. Cuvier learned how to build up the
whole animal from any single bone. And the
microscope now enables us to tell from a flake
of any bone what creature and what part of the
creature it belonged to, and at what age of the
world it lived. I was conversing, not a great
while ago, with the most celebrated chemist of
Massachusetts, and learned from him that a grain
of corn contains material enough to lecture about
for a month. Its structure is so complicated, its
secrets so intricate, its relations to the finest and
broadest forces of the universe so various and
minute, that it is inexhaustible in ministries of
instruction, wonder, and delight. Just as it is
said of some Western roads, which begin spacious
and grand, that they at last dwindle to a squir-
rel-track and run up a tree, — so we may say,
with sober truth, that forces which guard the
stateliest avenues of the universe run back, by
convergent lines, till they meet in the mystery of
a kernel of corn.

Agassiz asks only for one scale and will draw

you the form of the fish that wore it, tell every
fibre of its structure, the kind of waters it lives in,
and the nature of the food it takes. From a fossil scale he sketched the shape and size of a
fish unlike any in the catalogues of science, and
has seen his sagacity verified by the discovery in
another country of a petrified swimmer in pre-
adamite seas precisely like his drawing.

To understand anything thoroughly, we must
understand all its relations; and every highly
organized product in nature is related to the
universe. St. Augustine, fourteen hundred years
ago, ridiculed the dying polytheism of Rome,
which provided a separate deity for every process of
nature, by showing that, on such a theory, it would
require a hundred goddesses to weave a single
flower, so many energies are involved in the work.

A distinguished living geologist has published
a pamphlet on the geological wonders that some
pebbles hold. Taking his hint, suppose that we
follow it into other fields, asking you if you understand a pebble. What, not understand a common piece of stone that weighs an ounce or two!
Let us see. What is that you call its weight?
It is the pull of the earth upon it in your hand,
the relation between its mass and the earth's
mass. Why does the earth pull thus at it? It
is the action of what we call the force of gravitation. Why does it pull so hard? If the average
substance of the earth were no denser than the
ground directly beneath our feet it would not pull

so powerfully. That ounce or two of weight is, therefore, the sign and proof that the great globe is heavier as we descend, more weighty as a whole, than if it were all made of granite. Thus the intensity of its pull on the pebble opens into its relations to the mass of the sun and the mechanical structure of the solar system.

Why, too, is the pebble solid in your hand? Why is it not a mass of sand? The force of cohesion is the answer. But why, if you pulverize it, will it not unite so again? Why will not the whole pressure you can bring to bear upon it compress it as tight as before? What are the conditions and laws of that force? Answer that question and you know a great deal.

Break the pebble open, and you will doubtless find a sparkling piece of crystal in it. Explain that. A new force, not only of cohesion but of crystallization, appears. Tell how those particles were brought into that shining order, with angles and points as regular as a mathematician's diagram. The pebble grows more serious.

Melt it, you make it a liquid. Increase the heat, you reduce it to two or three gases. It was only gases knotted and clinched. How and why did they combine so as to make that quality of stone? The same gases appear in a thousand different kinds of matter. Why do slight variations in their proportions produce such widely different results? The mystery of atomic combination — the fundamental mystery of chemistry — starts out of the stone.

Again, the pebble is of a kind different from the stone in its neighborhood. It belongs to another stratum. How did it get out of that stratum upon the surface of the earth? Geology must come in with its proofs of central fires, convulsions, and mountain upheavals to explain it. Room for another science must be found on the pebble.

Its shape, too, how was that determined? There are scratches on it that icebergs caused, grinding over the face of the inhabited world. There are water-lines in it, telling that it has lain under seas which once rolled over the present land. Or there are fire-stains, that report earthquake eruptions ages ago. These forces must all be united into a system if you would comprehend the pebble.

Crack it and you will find a little fossil in it of a tribe of sea-creatures now extinct. It must have sunk into it when the pebble was fluid. How many ages ago? In what region of the earth? How was the creature fed, and what was its office?

Then the color of the pebble, what is that? Why are not all things of the same hue? The sun-ray holds several tints. How do they blend into colorless light, and what is the secret by which different surfaces reflect and absorb such unlike rays, thus suffusing the face of nature with countless tinges? You must answer this to explain the tint of the pebble.

The crystal beads, too, which it holds, have magnetic properties, — point to the mystery of electric and polar currents. There are some old manuscripts, called "palimpsests," from which you can rub off the writing and find another underneath, and still a third and fourth under that, — all of which by delicate art can be restored and read in turn. Thus some of Cicero's great works have been discovered under other and later writings.

Is not the pebble a marvellous palimpsest, holding convulsions of the earth and secrets of chemistry and astronomical forces written in it? The "sermon" in a common "stone" is woven of all the sciences. The man who understands it has insight into the physical system of the world.

In fact, the story of science in relation to nature is poetically symbolized in a story of the Middle Ages, which perhaps many of you are familiar with, — how a lady rescued her captured lover from the high tower in which he was imprisoned. His case seemed hopeless; at any rate, what could she, a feeble woman, do to release him? She caught a beetle, rubbed some honey on its nose, tied a long silk thread of the finest texture around its body, and placed the insect on the lowest round of the stony wall. Smelling the honey, and thinking it just ahead, the beetle climbed and climbed, trailing the delicate thread, till it reached the window of the captured knight. He caught the thread, pulled it in carefully, and lo! on the end of it was a twine, and gathering up the twine there was fastened upon that a rope, and pulling up the rope he secured it to the window bars and descended safely from his dungeon tower.

O, the wit of the women ! So the meanest fact has
a law fastened to it, which reason seizes by its insight, and at the end of that law another and still
back of that a nobler one, till at last the central
force is detected and the sense-bound thought is
free, and walks in the broad splendors of truth.

The chief difference between a very wise man
in natural science and an ignorant one is, not that
the first is acquainted with regions invisible to the
second, away from common sight and interest,
but that he understands the common things which
the second only sees.

If we appreciated such facts as these we should
be delivered from the danger of looking outwardly
into large and blazing wonders of space for peculiar revelations of the Creator. Some persons
dream that if they could be carried away from
what is so familiar around them on this planet,
and see the wonders of far-off skies or look at the
harmonies of a system of worlds, they would have
proofs of the Infinite One which are denied to
them now. But such revelry of sight would not
help them. It is insight they need. The Infinite
is not revealed in scale or splendors of space, but
in the wisdom that is manifest in facts whatever
be their scale. And nothing less than Infinite
Wisdom is expressed in a daisy. Whoever looks
beyond the life and growth of that, with an appetite for something more startling and stupendous
as a proof of God's existence, is in an atheistic
atmosphere now. His mind has divorced nature

from intellect, and no sight or external logic will
weld them for him.   If a daisy can live without
God a firmament can.   The true process is not
to wring out an Infinite Mind by twisting a nebula,
but to look with humility and gladness into each
fact of nature and see Him reflected as in the face
of a mirror there.

The primal distinction in eyes is that some see
facts, others see what facts stand for, and the degrees of this difference measure the whole distance
between a Bushman and Newton, between ignorance and knowledge.

The difference between sight and insight, and
the power of insight, are illustrated also in the
domain of beauty.   It is not the senses that discern the outside vesture of beauty upon the world.
You never surprise a dog, deer, or bear gazing
with satisfaction at the loveliness of the meadow,
the curve of a river, or the grandeur of a mountain.   They see all the facts as an inventory could
be taken of them, but not the charm of color,
grace, or motion into which the details blend.

The man is to be pitied who has no intellectual
insight into the truth of any district of nature ;
but it is a sadder thing to see a man on whom all
bloom is wasted, who carries an eye that shaves
the twinkle from every star, who disenchants
the light, and, wherever he moves, brushes the
halo from nature.   One of the vices of our American intellect in this age of mechanism is its
essentially mechanical conception of nature, — as

though the solar system runs by clock-work and the stars are whirled by bands, belts, and drums.

It was a typical Yankee who said once to a friend of mine at Niagara, before the roar of the English fall, "Well, I snum, I don't understand how it wallops over in that way. I'd like to see the whole consarn unscrewed for about five minutes and then put up agin." So it is that our universe is becoming one of carpentry, — lathed and plastered together with constellations clapboarded on the sky, — and not a swimming poem and mystery.

As to his humanity, a man would be an unspeakable loser to give up the power of enjoying a landscape, if he has it in any fine degree, for a legal title to all the land in New England ; for his soul would give up the birthright of a perpetual dividend of joy from the infinite art by which all matter is moulded.

The insight that discerns beauty is of a higher order than that which discerns mathematical truth. I would not look through the great Cambridge telescope at the present comet, if the sight thus of its boiling nucleus and its more voluminous trail should blunt, afterwards, the perception of its exquisite curve so tenderly shaded off into the gloom of the zenith, — a weird scimitar of light, fit for the hand of an archangel. Science is the prose and beauty the poetry of the visible world.

But one of the noblest triumphs of insight is gained when the truth of the world, as read by

K

science, is itself transmuted into beauty. One great value of scientific education is, that it enlarges immensely the area in which the mind lives, gives a boundless horizon and an immeasurable dome for our intellectual home, so that we can have the sense of grandeur for a resource and as a rich undertone in the whole life. And a still higher value is won, when the mind, through the revelations of science, feels itself surrounded and overarched by a more subtle beauty and charm than the outward aspects of nature supply.

Sometimes we hear lamentations of the decay of poetic fascination from nature by the banishment of all the exquisite fancies of elder ignorance and the myths of the classic theology. But we are richer in material of poetry to-day by reason of our spreading science than any age has been.

What a palace of splendors our cold explorers have been building with trowels of mathematics and the cement of law! What if they have worked like journeymen at their tasks, lifting the rough stones, item by item, without a sense of beauty, and putting in the oriel windows as glaziers, not as artists? Is it any the less a Cologne Cathedral they are erecting? And when their scaffoldings are knocked away, is it not beauty rather than masonry they have been rearing by their toil? Let any one read Lieutenant Maury's book on the Ocean, and ask if we have lost material of poetic inspiration and expression by the banishment of majestic Neptune, whose chariot-wheels scarce touched the glassy azure, and the Tritons with their shell-fish fingers and their porpoise fins. Mr. Campbell mourns that, —

> " When Science from Creation's face
> Enchantment's veil withdraws,
> Such lovely visions yield their place
> To cold material laws."

He said this of the rainbow, but it is Science that detects the enchantment in the light. Each pulse of it beats nearly two hundred thousand miles a second without jostling the air. It may blow never so hard, or it may be dead calm, and those vibrations fall equally serene. The most spiritual element in nature is the most stable. Eleven millions of miles a minute from the sun without any visible or conceivable chords of communication, every inch of the air a conductor, every ray of it stranded of seven hues, and an eighth element besides which slips through the prism and is the soul of all, never resting and never wasting in its journey of ages, — it rather dims the marvel and the poetry of the Atlantic cable.

And yet the relations of light and our eye are more astonishing still. To get the sensation of redness, our eyes are affected four hundred and eighty-two millions of millions of times in a second ; of yellowness, five hundred and forty-two millions of millions ; and of violet, seven hundred

and seven millions of millions of times.   I quote
from the careful Sir John Herschel, who says that
" they are conclusions to which any one may most
certainly arrive who will only be at the trouble of
examining the chain of reasoning by which they
have been obtained."   So that the seven-hued
rainbow, whose firm and subtle flame is reared
out of drops of water that are ever shifting, is the
result of a play upon the keys of the human eye
so astonishing that, though figures may state it,
the strongest mind staggers like an infant under
the awful revelation.

Think, too, of the marvels of vegetable growth :
how the oak draws almost nothing from the soil,
but is instituted air and rain ; how the chains of
mountains, as has recently been said, are made of
gases and rolling wind; how Nature, out of one
element of moisture, pours through the veins of
trees the juices of the peach, the pear, the apple,
and the plum, and conjures all the various nectar
of all climes out of dew, so that the mystery of
the miracle of Cana is repeated within the soft
vesture of the grape that distils wine, not, as in
some Boston cellars, out of vitriol and logwood,
but out of vapor and sunlight at the bidding of
God.

> " Truth is fair ; should we forego it ?
>   Can we sigh right for a wrong ?
> God himself is the best poet,
>   And the real is his song."

Perhaps the most fascinating picture which the
Greek mythology has transmitted to us is that of

delicate and resplendant Aphrodite, goddess of beauty, who rose out of the sea, as the fable ran, and hastened, with rosy feet, to the land, where grass and flowers spring up beneath her tread. Yet what is this exquisite picture, as a stimulant of the poetic sense, in comparison with the fulfilment of its dim suggestion in modern discoveries? What is it in contrast with the real Aphrodite of science whose substance is the misty exhalation of the ocean, and who wears the rainbow for a scarf?

All the verdure of nature is born from the foam of the sea. If every spring-time it should rise miraculously from the salt deeps,—if all trees, all grains, all flowers, should spring at once from the brine and be wafted by magic to adorn the land, — it would be only a sensuous exhibition of the fact which poetic insight discovers when it takes from science the truth that the sunbeams coax fresh vapor from the ocean's treasury; how the winds sweep them over the land, and how, dropping in dew and pouring in showers, they do robe the rocks with verdure interwoven with flowers, spread the face of nature with nodding loveliness, and so open to our conception a purer Aphrodite than the ancient one, — the daughter of God, her step on every blossoming patch of our soil, and her tunic brilliant with the representative flora of the globe!

The processes of nature, to the mind that penetrates to the springs of truth, supply richer beauty to thought than the visible bloom affords.

It may be thought that all this is very unpractical. But can there be any greater advantage to the mind from any study than to feel that it is pavilioned amid infinite poetry? Can there be anything more unpractical than to waste the opulence of creative thought, in whose mystic movement we are embosomed, and which the study of a few books would open?

If there were some process of mental cultivation that should produce the magical result of enlarging the house we live in, — widening its walls, lifting its stories higher, lining it with exquisite pictures, thrilling the air of it with music, so that the entrance into each room would awaken peculiar delight, — there would be little need of arguing for the practicalness of it to the most torpid miser. Insight widens, enriches, and emblazons the world, moving off the walls of the senses, bringing out the traceries and colors of the incessant imagination of the Creator. Wherever the body stays, the mind that will vitalize, through a few volumes that are level to an average comprehension by one winter's reading, the revelations of modern science, can live ideally, as passing from gallery to gallery of a magician's castle. Let a fool own a park and live in it, and he sees only the shell of some trees and the surface of some visible ground. Let Humboldt live in a porter's lodge by its gate, and he will feel that he is riding on a rolling wheel among the stars.

We come to a fresh and nobler field for the

illustration of our subject in turning from the natural to the social world, from matter to man. If we could find a person that has complete insight into a man, who could be said to know a single man thoroughly, we should find a person who comes as near to knowing everything as a finite creature can. All the inorganic forces of laws are told in the best crystal. All organic and vegetable truth culminates in the best plant. All wisdom of every degree, from every kingdom, rushes to a focus in any single human form.

The human being is the head of the animal creation. The lower orders of life, rising epoch after epoch and grade by grade, flower out in the proportions of his limbs and the implements of his frame. Nature struggled up through a myriad experiments and efforts to attain the perfected excellence of his eye, which commands all nature and catches the hints inwoven with the light with the subtlest truths of the universe. She spires up through the ears of the lower ranks of creatures to his ear, — the highway of all the music of nature and the exquisite melodies and harmonies of genius. She ripens the skill that buds in the fish's fin, the horse's hoof, and the lion's paw, in the twenty-nine bones of the human hand, so supple in their jointings, and clothed with such delicate sensibility, that all industry and cunning and art are prophesied in their mechanism.

In the Garden of Plants in Paris there is a building devoted to the progressive arrangement of the

bones of all creatures, living and fossil, that have
bones. The mind runs up the scale of vertebræ
till it comes to the human spine and its appen-
dages. The spine sits on the throne of matter. It
is not without subtle scientific propriety, therefore,
that we talk in the political world now about the
dignity and necessity of backbone. Life climbs
by spines. The skull and jaw we find now are
simply continuations and developments of the
back-bone. A man without backbone has no scientific right to skull or jaw. And if some men
should be obliged to take the shape that corre-
sponds to the dignity and stamina of their con-
victions, we should see them in Congress as
talking jelly-fishes or huge mollusks, rather soft
shelled than hard.

The physical man stands at the apex of the
pyramid of matter, — all the juices, flavors, and
fatness of the world converging to enrich his
blood and renew his flesh, and incarnate themselves in his organism ; all the forces of nature,
light, heat, atmosphere, electricities, chemical affinities, magnetisms, circulating around him and
refreshing his strength ; all the subtile arts of
matter playing in the secretions and the mysteries
of his moving laboratory of life. Your spirit steps
into your body to ride and wield the harnessed
forces of the world.

And now within the material home is the intellectual structure of a man, which mental phi-
losophies for ages have been trying to measure

and report in its large and graceful proportions of
reason, sentiment, passion, will. And interpene-
trating and towering over this is the beauty that
belongs to the human being ; not the mere physical beauty which hides and yet shines in the
fashioning of the limbs, and which glows in the
glorious marble of the Apollo, but the splendor
of intellectual strength that showers from the eye,
the calm that sleeps mysteriously upon a brow,
the majesty that enthrones itself over an eyebrow,
and lowers from the bony circle an inch or two
in sweep, built for an eye like Webster's, — a
majesty which, when Nature tries to intimate with
physical material, she splits a notch in the New
Hampshire mountains, and bars the awful walls
with a bare precipice of granite, — a pride of
power like that shed from the chest of Goethe, —
a commanding, all potent presence that swathed
the form of Washington.

And above all these insignia of meaning and
mystery are the spiritual forces that live and work
deeper and deeper in a human being, playing
even through his flesh as visibly as chemical processes leave their traces there. For, at the same
moment that the powers of the stomach are sending the flush of physical health to the cheek, a force
of Heaven is writing there, with delicate pencil
more subtle than a sunbeam, and more enduring
than a graver's steel, a line of expression, telling
of reward for some good deed or noble sacrifice.
And while the brandy a man takes immoderately

8

is publishing itself in the hue of his countenance,
a brush from the pit is reaching up to leave the
stain of a passion, or the coarse turn of a habit
and a sin.   Every power of this universe is at
work upon every man, — all the science, all the
beauty, all the forces of the realm of intellect, all
the pencils of the regions of heaven and hell.
Every sphere surrounds each human frame.   Our
feet are in the dust, but we rise through all climates, zones, kingdoms, and there is no one of us
whose base is not in the world of darkness, and
the summit of whose being does not pierce at
times to the secret heavens.

The compact of his spirit and his body, his
presence everywhere in it and invisible, the harmonies of his frame, the laws of its health and the
laws of its disease, the services of its interdepend-
ent members, the balance of voluntary and involun-
tary forces, the climbing grade of implements and
energies, — bone, muscle, vein, blood, and nerve, —
the equal need in it of gross and airy aliment, the
control in it of the chemical over the mineral processes, the vital over the chemical, the moral and
spiritual over the vital and intellectual, lifting him
as a series of kingdoms, with his feet in the dust
and his soul in the heavens, — these facts and relations of a human being tell you the manner in
which God pervades the universe ; tell you the
deepest laws of society, which is built on the pattern of the human form ; tell you about the unity
in the great ranks of service in a state ; tell you the

methods of public disease and the conditions of health; tell you the spirit that should be supreme in all government, collecting the finest forces of the skies to run invisibly into every limb and organ of the body politic.

You remember the old story how Menenius Agrippa quelled the insurrection of the Roman populace by his allegory of the belly and the members. They knocked under at once to that ventriloquism. The Apostle Paul set forth the propriety of different ranks of office in the church, and the equal need of all, in the argument, "If the whole body were an eye where were the hearing?" etc. He shows that its life is bound up into one stream by the assurance, "If one member suffer all the members suffer with it, and if one member rejoice all the members rejoice with it." This we feel to be not simply rhetoric, but reasoning from types. It was the same kind of logic that an old fellow used against the opposition to the protection of manufactures and other branches of American industry, on the ground that it was wrong to grant special privileges. "Don't you see," said he, "you can't fat your finger? Try to fat your middle finger, and you have to put flesh on your ribs and arms to do it." Society is yet a body diseased. We could draw its picture as a man staggering under maladies. Every vice and disorder in it answers to some cough, cramp, or canker of the human frame, — from the fever-and-ague of our traffic to the squint in our politics which prevents the eyes of the government from looking North. Whoever could bring a theory of social organization that would take up and fill out the analogies and orders of the human frame, would need no other logic to demonstrate its truth.

Shrewd Rochefoucauld said that " it is easier to know men in general than any man in particular." Complete insight into a man discloses not only these grand and subtile relations that hold in hieroglyphic the divine laws of society, but detects the personal structure and quality of character.

A physician can educate his eye so as to see in the hue of the skin the tone of the system and the amount of a man's abuse of the laws of health. Clairvoyant mediums have been known to tell from a hair sent them in a letter the disease the person is suffering. Each part of the body has the character of the whole body in it. There is no miracle in the most wonderful instance of these somnambulic readings, because the fact of every man's physical condition is in every flake of his skin, and a heightened power of perception catches it naturally.

So some persons have the faculty of insight into character. They see a man in a moment; read him, feel him, in an instant. Great noise has been made about phrenology, — whether, by laborious fingering in the valleys and over heights of the skull, one may concoct the character of the subject. But we ought to see that a man is scrawled all over with "ologies." Every nerve, every hair, every motion, every nail, is steeped in the essence of the person, and radiates it. We are published not only geographically in the skull, but by the whole configuration, and by effluence back of configuration and streaming through it. There is a tone-science; showing how character breathes in voice ; there is a tooth science, there is nose-ology, eye-ology, as well as phrenology. Each limb, organ, act, is a battery of the soul. Lavater, the great physiognomist, said that he could tell by the different ways in which fingers dropped money into the contribution-box of the church what their temperaments and controlling dispositions were. I suppose that the way a man's fingers don't drop it tells just as clearly.

Zschokke, a Swiss clergyman and novelist, had the singular power at times of seeing the history of persons that came into his presence. How, he knew not, but facts in a man's career would sometimes stand just as clearly before his mind as the outward man before his eye. He was a moral clairvoyant. The veil dropped from his vision that hides to most of us the substance of character.

All a man's experience is funded in him. We go about printing off proof-impressions of ourselves every minute in the spiritual air. And the finger-power which some natures have of detecting by subtle feeling the quality of others — the mesmeric power which feels from a letter the state of soul in which it was written — is perhaps only an intimation of the kind of world we are to live

in when the body drops away, and there can be
" nothing secret that shall not be made manifest,
neither anything hid that shall not be known and
come abroad."

The highest range of study in which the distance
between sight and insight is measured, and where
the triumphs of insight are more vivid, is that of
history. No man knows the science of nature
who simply catalogues all the facts that are patent
to his eye ; and so a man may commit to memory
every incident of mortal experience, the date of
every occurrence, the birth and death of every great
man of every kingdom, yes, of every inhabitant of
the globe, the arithmetic and fortunes of every battle that has been fought, and still not have advanced
an inch towards an acquaintance with the story
of humanity. It is when he begins to see the
ideal relations and harmonies and lessons of these
facts that insight into history begins.

Think what it is to know Europe as it exists
to-day ! There is the gazetteer's knowledge, — so
many acres, so many people, so many languages,
so many houses, offices, art-rooms, temples, ruins.
There is the politician's knowledge, estimating
the power, the material forces, the passions, the
attitudes, the purposes, of the states that checker
its surface. But higher than these, and including
them, the only real knowledge of Europe is that
of the philosopher, who knows how it came to be
what it is ; who knows the classic, barbaric, and
Christian elements that have interplayed and over-

shot each other in the web of its life ; what stocks
have intermixed to produce each people and determine its character ; how the art arose that gems
it ; from what deeps of sentiment its cathedral
spires have risen ; when the creative seasons of
its literature have dawned ; from what boiling
anarchies its now heavy and hoary despotisms
were cast up ; what cheering and disastrous forces
are at work in its life to-day ; and so what tendencies, according to the infallible laws of public
growth, are pointing to and fashioning its future.

All this knowledge streams out of Europe. It
is a perpetual exhalation from the visible facts to
the mind that has insight, or can feel the impalpable. Without it a man knows only the corpse
of the continent, not its life, its soul.

And thus it is that a man must study the
registers of ancient time. Niebuhr, Bunsen, Carlyle, Grote, have few other sources of knowledge
than old Rollin had. They cannot manufacture
a new fact. It is the sharper eye, the profounder
mind, the flaming moral sense, which makes the
difference between dates and facts as they lie
loose, and the same particulars as they knit themselves, upon their pages, into the anatomy, the
physiology, the expression, and the character of a
kingdom or an age.

The science of history has been making immense advances, of late, by the disclosure of new
material. The grave has been disgorging some
of its dead empires for our instruction. We have

heard the buried bones of old Nineveh rattle
under their desolate mound, and have seen its
cracked and half-calcined skeleton lift itself, at
the incantation of an English traveller, to glare
with blank eye-sockets upon the changes of three
thousand years.   But battered Sphinx and Aztec
masonry and unhearsed Babylon have not supplied such vivid and far-reaching knowledge of
the past as the keen scrutiny of the wrecks of
language has disclosed.   Little things in the fragments of literature and tradition tell great things,
as the scale of Agassiz conjures the spectre of
the fish that once wore it in the flesh.   Literature
is so steeped in the vitality of a nation that it
sheds the composite aroma of the national fortunes, — as it has been said by a great critic that
out of any one of Shakespeare's plays, the
most imaginative, the least historic, the essential
history and civilization of England, up to Shakespeare's time, could be unravelled.   Languages
tell more than ruins and external annals.   They
tell the story of migrations, relationships, collisions, and interfusions of race.   A word or two
in a vocabulary, the structure and inflections of a
verb, report the cousinship of widely sundered
peoples, — their original nearness in space and
kin.

Thus continually new and more important instruction is opening to us from the past.   As we
are carried further away from past generations
and the ancient world, we come closer to them

intellectually, and penetrate more deeply the truth their experience incarnated.

Many of you recall the little pamphlet, entitled " The Stars and the Earth," published a few years since, which contained some entertaining fancies founded on the laws of light. If one could be present now in some orb of the firmament to which the light from our globe would be a hundred years in travelling, he would, if he could by a miraculous vision gaze upon our earth, see what was going on here a hundred years ago. Let him remove still back in space to a point which light needs more than two thousand years to reach, and its beams would carry to him the picture of Socrates and his contemporaries ; and the farther back he should be removed the more ancient would be the people and the kingdoms that would be given, fresh and living, to his eye.

The historic glass does work this magic for us as we move off from the ancient world and time. We have men among us who know Greece to-day better than the average intellectual Greeks did. We can study now each great state of antiquity as a whole. We can perceive the working of law in organizing the state as one body in time, and study the secret, slow, and sublime play of providential forces in compacting its organism, and then unnerving its strength and paralyzing it for evil. Our insight seizes perspective, and detects symmetry, and puts each movement into relation with a persistent force or law.

8 *   L

And the lesson which the mind that has insight sees inwrought with history, striking through the story of every nation, and making every prominent page transparent for its rays, is that every nation is under the moral laws, veined by them and electric with them. The Infinite Justice gazes out of every historic chapter as out of paragraphs of Exodus and Jeremiah.   All " Books of the Kings " are serious and sacred.

Milton gives us the picture of Michael the archangel showing to Father Adam, from a high mountain, the flow of human fortunes.   He purged with euphrasy and rue the visual nerve which pierced even to the inmost seat of mental sight, and unveiled to him the procession of empires and the long, sad lineage of sufferings and wrongs.   The historic student looks back from such a height and with such a purged vision, and he sees that nothing is stable but justice. Empires shrivel and waste like ghosts because they import too little of the eternal substance to be adjusted to the tremendous forces of Providence.   Isaiah's insight is gained at once by cool-blooded science on that meditative height. Nations do not die from foreign blows, or from old age, or from too great weight of possessions, but from their meagre organization, their failure to distribute their classes by the principle of fraternity, their opposition, through ignorance or insolence, to that righteousness which is the inmost truth of things.   They break the law of

God, as they suppose, for their convenience and aggrandizement, and find instead that it has broken them.

Thus learn, insight into history is insight into to-day. All great problems are here. Just as Diomedes saw the gods in the battle, according to the Iliad, when Pallas Athene blew the mist from his eyes, every man who has had clear insight into history sees the antagonist gods, the powers divine and infernal, struggling amid the confusions and roar of our national experience, as clearly as in the days of Ahab and Elijah, Herod and the Baptist, Nero and Paul. In fact, if he has not been able to see them thus pitted against each other on the prairies of Kansas or in the literature of the Dred Scott decision, it is of no consequence what he sees in the story of Ahab or in his mummy New Testament.

The practical reading of this fact is that statesmanship is pre-eminently the science demanding insight. It is the highest trust, and asks the deepest wisdom. The grades of statesmanship are always determined by what the men see working in the nation. And that only is real statesmanship which guides itself by what history shows to be the enduring omnipotent forces, just as that is the only seamanship which guides by the eternal lights and the tested charts.

A demagogue would guide a state, not by insight or sight either. He sails in a fog and steers by the ear. An executive politician, the man whom we delight to call practical, shapes his course by a conception, perhaps, of the commercial and material greatness of his country. He counts himself one of the managers of a great business firm ; and his conceptions of the functions and duties of government would be filled out by putting over the National Capitol a huge sign : " South Carolina, New England, Ohio, & Co., dealers in negroes, cotton, hams, and hay." So long as he can keep the partners from quarrelling, and make the firm pay ten per cent under the parchment constitution, he considers his office discharged.

But the statesman knows, as clearly as he sees the sun in heaven, that the real constitution of every kingdom is an unwritten one. He knows that, according to forces that no pen can create and no votes can bar, — forces that play around and bend and magnetize all others, forces of character which after a while steal into the arithmetic of the nation's ledgers, ooze up from the soil and affect the harvests, travel with the colonists that seek the new land, distil through the breath of court-rooms, and so rot or rivet the invisible bolts of social union, — the nation is doomed to expansion and vigor or to barbarism and ruin. He knows how nations ought to live, because he sees how nations have died.

See how the imperial Roman oak of history died. Its religion perished first ; its hardihood sunk into effeminacy, so that it had no living con-

nection with the treasury of spiritual forces in the
soil and the air. And then the sap in its huge
veins began to dry ; the fibrous muscles which
centuries had toughened shrank; the leaves shrivelled from juiceless stems ; the bark softened ;
caterpillars and worms and bugs from all the
Eastern sinks made their home in it ; and, finally,
a howling storm of barbarism set it from the
Northeast, amid which, in its vigorous days, the
forest monarch would have stood erect, with hardly
the loss of a filial leaf, but which now whirled
branches and boughs before its gusts and left the
crippled trunk, a show of its greatness, to crumble
and rot into the soil of time. Trajan's Column,
the battered arch of Constantine the Great, the
ivied segment of the Colosseum walls, the crum-
bling colonnades of the Acropolis, are the letters
in cipher before a statesman's eye, rising over the
imperial cemeteries of history, hinting an important fact or two as to the constitution that knits
and governs a people really.

What sight so frightful, therefore, as to see a
great nation with a mighty future, guided, in its
critical season, by men who have no social insight, no moral enthusiasm warming their wisdom,
no faith in the superior permanence of moral over
commercial forces, — men who, it should seem,
must have read history with cataracts over their
eyes.

Goethe had a fancy that some men are educated into such large proportioned minds on this

globe that they become, when they die, the spirits
of planets, diffusing their energy through the substance of a world.   This is a good definition of
the capacities a great public man should have.
Very often the reverse is the case.   Pygmies contrive to perch themselves on Alps.   As a shrewd
farmer once said of one of our Presidents : " We
thought he was something of a man when we had
him in our State ; but come to spread him out
over the whole Union, he does average dreadful
thin."

The position given to some men on this earth,
with regard to a nation, is scarcely less sublime
than if we could see a mortal leap on a star to
steer through space.   If an astronomer should
follow such a voyager with his glass, he might admire the energy with which he should kindle furious fires beneath its granite boilers, whip it like a
top, and make it whirl swifter and swifter on its
axis ; but would he think that it showed any
celestial statesmanship to guide it contrary to the
law of gravitation?   Whoever should be at the
helm, would he not prophesy, with some surety,
that, by the constitution of the solar system, it
was whizzing towards a smash-up, to be beached
on chaos ?

Historical, political, and social insight discerns
the one deepest law which rules under the votes
of parliaments and senates just as surely as the
law of gravity upholds the capitols they sit in ;
and it bows to them with a reverence that would

seek to twist the certainties of the multiplication-
table for private benefit as soon as to doubt their
despotism.

Behind the facts of nature which the sunlight
kindles up is the order in which they play, and
which the studious intellect explores. Around the
facts, and diffused, also, through the order, is the
beauty which tempts and feeds another eye. And
now, deeper than order and beauty together, playing through both and using both, is the spiritual
meaning, the symbolism, of the facts which lie
before the senses. A finer insight, a more searching eye, is needed for this sphere, and richer
results reward it. Each thing in nature is a hieroglyphic. It has a structure which science draws, a
color which taste appreciates, a use of which skill
avails, and it stands for something, it holds and
hides a message which spiritual insight catches.
The world was not whittled into shape. God
could not create anything other than vitally, so
that it should be magnetized with all his attri-
butes and exhale them to faculties fine enough to
receive the effluence.

This is the reason every great writer utters his
thought in imagery. The world is his dictionary.
The processes of life all around him hurry to his
pen, eager to be the rhetoric of his ideas. No
sooner is a new science perfected and clinched
to the intellect by the calculus, than it dissolves
into a finer fluid for the inkstand of the poet and
the seer. It offers new and glowing symbols of
human life and the highest moral truth.

Set a golden statue by Phidias before a child, and it sees a mass of brilliant color ; before an avaricious eye, and it gloats over the stately embodiment of so much cash ; before a devotee of anatomy, and he finds a revelation of so much bodily proportion ; before a mineralogist, and he perceives so much chemical and mineral truth ; before an artist, and he gazes upon so much skill and beauty ; before a man of moral insight, and he discerns the grandeur of a God transfusing its substance, pouring over the brightness of its limbs, controlling its symmetry, breathing in undrainable suggestiveness from its face. Each eye lights upon a truth, but the last one pierces to the finest, highest, all-penetrating, all-dominating truth. So it is in the world. The senses simply stare at nature ; the mind looks, and finds law ; the taste combines, and enjoys art ; the soul reads, and gains the permeating wisdom.

Take a spear of growing wheat, and, after its chemical secrets and its beauty of structure are detected and appreciated, it turns to language, as when a religious writer illustrates humility by it in the figure. The mind that knows most is the most reverent, just as the ear of grain that is fullest bends over beneath the sky. A wisp of wheat has been carried to the noblest mill when a Christian poet extracts that flour from its grains. So the whole universe turns into a dictionary for the uses of the inseeing mind.

Christianity uses most freely the broad rich

facts of nature, in parables and allegories, to state its doctrines, putting its light within the ordinary facts that we see, and making them glow as transparencies of celestial truth.

The universe was created so as to serve the prophet's purposes, and be a sermon. All the dark facts in it dissolve into ink to write the folly and doom of evil ; all the winning and cheering facts in it melt into light to commend and eulogize what is good. When you have demonstrated the law of gravitation and have hidden its force in the dark substance of the sun, and shown it grasping thence the farthest planet that ploughs the chilly ether and balancing a family of worlds, have you not also shown how the justice of the Infinite Mind impalpably grapples all the spirits of the globe, however far they wander from him, and holds nations, as well as men, by the fine, awful tendrils of his law. And when you untwist the rays that leap unstinted and forever from the vesture of the sun, and find in each wave of them light and heat and all colors and vitality, and find them flooding the air of every planet as easily as they visit one, and present to every eye, kindling all nature for it, with no more labor than in doing it for one ; inflicting pain upon the diseased retina by the same beneficence that blesses the well one, and illumining a different world for each mind it visits according to its culture or its purity, — have you not found a finer, vaster solar astronomy by your analysis and research ? — found

a pictured statement of the interblending of
Infinite Mercy and Truth in the rays that stream
continually in upon the soul's world, how they
bless us and color us according to our faculty of
reception, and how they visit and rule every heart
and will as easily as they fall upon one?

In every department of nature " like a finer
light in light," the last word of any discovery,
the soul of the fact, is moral.

The earth

> " Is but the shadow of heaven and things therein
> Each to the other like, more than on earth is thought."

There may be a meadow farm among the mountains.   The heir to it gets a cabbage and a corn-
crop from it, suspecting no other latent fertility
and produce.   A man of science buys it, gets no
less cabbages and hay, but reaps a geology-crop
as well.   An artist buys it, and lo! a harvest of
beauty and delight, budding even when the grain
is garnered, dropping sweet into his eyes even
from arctic dawns and blazing snows.   A man
of deepest insight lives on it, and the laws of his
farm open to him the prudence and prodigality of
Providence.   In the way the grain grows, the
enemies it has, the friendships of all good forces
to its advance, in the chemistry of his farming, in
the peace that sleeps on the hills, in the gathering
and retreat of storms, in the soft approach of
spring, and the melancholy death he reads lessons
that become inmost wisdom.   He has a faculty
that is the sickle of more subtle crop-sheaves of
spiritual truth.

The different ways in which different temperaments and states of heart regard nature is very simply and sweetly stated in a little German poem of which I saw a translation yesterday. Two men had gone up from the city to visit the summit of one of the Alps. They returned, and their kindred pressed about them to know what visions they had enjoyed.

> " 'T was a buzz of questions on every side.
> ' And what have you seen ?   Do tell l' they cried.

> " The one with yawning made reply,
> ' What have we seen ?   Not much have I !
> Trees, mountains, meadows, groves, and streams,
> Blue sky, and clouds, and sunny gleams.'

> " The other, smiling, said the same ;
> But with face transfigured, and eye of flame :
> ' Trees, meadows, mountains, groves, and streams,
> Blue sky, and clouds, and sunny gleams.' "

Just as there are spelling-classes for the youngest scholars in our schools, in which the separate letters are the chief things they see, where the great problem is to combine them into words, and where the mental organs are not capable of configuring words into propositions, — so very few of us on the planet ever get able to handle the letters of nature easily, ever get beyond the power of spelling them into single words. Some are able to read off the aspects of creation into science. They can put the stars together into paragraphs that state laws and harmonies and grandeurs. Some go farther, and rhyme the mighty vocabulary of science into beauty ; but

few get such command of the language that they
see and rejoice in the highest, glorious truth
which the volume holds.

"What!" says friend Purblind Horneye, "do I
not see all there is around me? Are not my senses
as good as yours? What stuff to talk of more
realities right about me than the sunshine and
fields and streets and my office, my ledgers, my
bank-books, my horses, and my house!" "But how
is it, Brother Purblind, about studying the Iliad?
If you know all the Greek letters on all the pages,
do you master it? Are not the words to be
looked out? Is not their sense to be detected?
Are not the style and rhythm to be appreciated and
enjoyed? — the characters delineated there to be
known and discriminated? — the connections and
unities and poetic and moral laws to be felt and
comprehended? After your senses have seen all
that there is to be seen, have you done anything
more than reach the threshold of what there is
to see? What now, O materialistic Brother Horneye, if the universe, right about thee, is a sort
of Iliad of the Infinite Mind? What if each
fact in it, which thy superficial sense beholds, is
a letter of a Divine word or an adjective of a
mystic verse? And what if thy flippant estimate
of the meaning of nature is the child's slow
and stuttering spelling-out of Homer's syllables,
while the saint's vision of a life and glory all
around is the manly reading of the mighty poem
of the world?"

Insight, therefore, opens the intellectual world of law and harmony beneath the world of physical shows; within that, the world of beauty; within that again, the realm of spiritual language. In the human world it shows, deep behind deep, law working in society, controlling politics and shaping the destiny of nations; while, in the individual sphere, it unveils man as the epitome of the universe, clad continually in the electric vesture of his character.

Every man, as every animal, has sight; but just according to the scale of his insight is the world he lives in a deep one, an awful one, a mystic and glorious world. We see what *is*, only as we see into what *appears*.

Out of three roots grows the great tree of nature, — truth, beauty, good. The man of science follows up its mighty stem, measures it, and sees its branches in the silver-leaved boughs of the firmament. The poet delights in the symmetry of its strength, the grace of its arches, the flush of its fruit. Only to the man with finer eye than both is the secret glory of it unveiled; for his vision discerns how it is fed and in what air it thrives. To him it is only an expansion of the burning bush on Horeb, seen by the solemn prophet, glowing continually with the presence of Infinite Law and Love, yet standing forever unconsumed.

V.

HILDEBRAND.

THE career of the man who will engage our
attention admits us to the heart of the
eleventh century ; for his influence was felt powerfully in Europe from the year 1040 to 1085.
The proper background, therefore, for a knowledge
of his life is a conception of the state of civilization in the early part of the eleventh century, and
the relations of that period in the Middle Ages to
the centuries before. The "Dark Ages," as we call
them, commenced with the sixth century, when
Europe was completely disorganized by the settle-
ment of the barbarians over the domain of the
Roman Empire. There were more than four
hundred years of night. The darkness was deepest at the close of the tenth century, after the
empire of Charlemagne had dissolved. Indeed,
humanity seemed then in a hopeless condition.
A writer of the Middle Ages describes that time
as an age that ought to be called "iron," from its
fierceness, and "leaden," for its gross wickedness.
To understand the condition of Europe, as the
year 1000 of our era dawned upon it, you must

form a picture of society destitute of every feature, and seemingly of every force, that belongs
to what we consider civilization, — that can be
thought to make life a privilege, or even tolerable.
There was no such thing as education, for there
was no literature, no press, no books. There was
no science even for the highest classes. For
many centuries it had been rare for a layman of
whatever rank to know how to sign his name. It
was a striking exception when an emperor could
read. The Latin language, which held all the
treasures of learning, had died out of common use.
The ravages of pirates during the previous century had destroyed many of the libraries of the
church. All books were written then on parch-
ments, and they were so costly that only the most
princely fortunes could purchase them. And
most of them contained nothing more valuable
than legends of saints, or homilies, or works of
Jerome or Augustine, perhaps written over the
noblest treatises of Cicero or Plato. We read
that a certain princess in the tenth century, the
Countess of Anjou, gave two hundred sheep, a
load of wheat, a load of rye, and a load of millet,
with several skins of costly fur, for a copy of the
sermons of a German monk.

Nothing that we generally associate with the
Middle Ages as the glory of that period had appeared then in Europe. There were no grand
cathedrals, for Gothic architecture had not yet
germinated. There was no scholastic philosophy,

for Abelard was yet a hundred years in futurity.
There was no painting, no poetry, and no promise
of the Crusades.   There were no methods of quick
travel; few good roads from state to state, and
such as there were infested by robbers ; of course,
therefore, there could be no great commerce ; in
fact, there was scarcely any trade.   What we understand by government had no existence.   Feudal fortresses were rising as the prominent features
in every landscape, where nobles, who could not
spell their names and did not know a letter of the
alphabet, revelled in a brutal power, and looked
out over the dependent serfs in their miserable
huts ; and these barons were somehow aggregated
into what was called a kingdom, or an empire.
But there was no country then that was organized
socially, even so well as any district of Russia is
to-day ; and there is no mechanic's family in this
city that is not far more richly provided with what
we all esteem the comforts of life than the average
noblemen of Europe and their households were at
the close of the tenth century.   Europe, in the
earlier portions of the Dark Ages, was morally, to
use a geological figure, in the Silurian Epoch, —
everything insular and irregular, — chaotic patches
of the future continent swelling out of the sea of
barbarous passion, bearing only the lowest types
of life.

In the Middle Ages it had changed into the ter-
tiary period, showing larger organizations, enriched
with higher forms, and plainly promising the states,

the culture and the civilization of modern Europe. The eleventh century saw the transition to this latter epoch. And yet when it dawned there seemed to be no symptoms of any latent beneficent forces at work for the race. There seemed to be no reason why the wide-spread superstition might not be realized, — that the year 1000 would wind up human affairs on the planet, introduce the day of judgment, and inaugurate the millennium by vindictive and cleansing fire. The church, from which the only possible help, it should seem, could spring, appeared more deeply tainted than society itself.

We must not forget that both the doctrines and polity of the Roman Catholic Church were of slow growth. With the very commencement of the Dark Ages, we find the germ of a pretension sprouting in Rome, which found congenial soil for its roots in the decaying ancient civilization, and the precise nutriment it needed in the heavy air of barbarism. Century by century, while society and states dissolved, it stretched underground its fibres, and strengthened its stalk, and shot out leaf after leaf of doctrine, discipline, and ritual, — putting forth now its canon of the mass, and in another season its sanction for the worship of the Virgin and of images; budding next with its forged decretals and claim of the title of "sovereign pontiff" for its bishop; then with the doctrine of transubstantiation, and soon with its law for the canonization of saints and the system of

9   M

auricular confession ; letting no century slip by
without some large leafy sign of its slow and
secret energy, till we shall see it, when the Dark
Ages culminate, like a huge night-blooming cereus
ripen with its " consummate flower," — the pretension to universal authority over conscience and to
supremacy over kings.

It was in the middle of the eleventh century
that a vigorous attempt was made to purify the
ecclesiastical spirit and to complete and confirm
the ecclesiastical system of the Roman Catholic
Church.   That century, remarkable for so many
signs promising a greater future for the world,
streaked on its horizon with the gray pulsations
of a dawn, is chiefly distinguished by the movement within the church.   The introduction of cotton paper made from rags, which it inaugurated;
the commencement of the Gothic style of architecture, which it witnessed ; the Norman conquest
of England, changing the destiny of that island,
which belongs to its annals ; the invention of the
musical scale, which is one of its trophies ; the
birth of the scholastic philosophy, which dignifies
its records ; the building in England of Westminster Hall, which is one of its monuments, — none
of these, nor even the cheers of the Crusaders under Godfrey of Bouillon, pouring through the battered walls of Jerusalem in the year 1099, which
is its last and jubilant memorial, presents so striking a claim upon our notice and our study as the
efforts made for the cleansing of the morals, and

the widening of the power, of the Catholic Church through the genius of Hildebrand.

Hildebrand was born about the year 1013, in a Tuscan village in Italy, and was the son of a carpenter. He was educated in Rome, in one of its forty monasteries, — in an institution of which his uncle was abbot. Faithful in the stern discipline of the cloisters, he zealously sought by all its helps to chastise and subdue his passions ; and he felt his own pride in a monastic purity stimulated and justified by what he saw of the disorders and corruptions of Rome and even of the Church of Rome. Entering manhood, he betook himself to the monastery of Cluny, in France, celebrated then as the severest of all the ascetic schools. There he labored diligently for some years in the double work of perfecting his conquest over the flesh and of mastering the knowledge that was possible in that age. He was soon distinguished among the brethren for the severity of his mortification and the breadth of his learning, while for the power of his preaching he stood unrivalled, it was said, among the orators of the church. He studied and prayed to the Virgin, — he flogged himself and starved himself, till he drove the passions which nature had lodged in his blood into the arteries of his mind. His frame was diminutive, but his person seemed of intellect all compact. He moved among his fellow-monks, who cared chiefly for shelter from the ferocious world without and for personal purity,

electric with the majesty of great ideas, too broad
to be held within the walls of the abbot's rule.

His enemies in later years affirmed that he was
a sorcerer, and had perfected himself in the unholy arts through which a mortal has commerce
with Beelzebub. The foundation of this charge
was, possibly, some interest by Hildebrand in natural science, and a curiosity in a mind so strong
to track, by such experiments as could be made
in that rude age, some of the laws of nature. But
he was charged with owning a book of divination,
which would conjure the most frightful demons
for his service, — and it was generally believed
that he always possessed the power of shaking
his sleeves, and sprinkling sparks of fire from
them to awe people with the signs of his superior
sanctity. We shall see what sparks he shook from
his cowl, when the time came for the full play of
the ideas with which he had stored himself in his
monastic retreat. But the power of his genius
was most manifest in his terrible eye, which, it is
said, no enemy of Hildebrand, or traitor to the
church, could feel upon him without quailing and
submitting. Those who conversed with him said
that they felt that his eye read their secret
thoughts.

Among his brother-monks in Cluny, he meditated upon the future of the church he had sworn
to serve. He believed that it was the representative of Christ's authority upon the earth, and its
condition, as it lay beneath his gaze, appalled

him. The ecclesiastical world was more corrupt,
if possible, in the first half of the eleventh century,
than the civil world. The clergy were mostly
illiterate. In the year 1000 there was scarcely a
single person to be found in Rome who knew the
first elements of letters. The great·majority of
the priests in Italy were habitual drunkards. A
Catholic writer himself confesses that their function in those years "had contracted to the chant-
ing of psalms which they could not understand,
and to the mechanical performance of outward
ceremonies." An Italian bishop complains that
he could not prevail upon his clergy even to learn
the creeds, and that even his own flock were so
degraded as to be unable to conceive how God
could exist without a head. And one of Hildebrand's own friends, Peter Damiani, published a
book, showing up the awful depravity of the
priesthood, of which the title was "Gomorrhiana."

The records of the church during the hundred
years before his time were under Hildebrand's eye
in his monastery, and they offered a dreary commentary on the lordly high-church principles he
had espoused and matured. He believed that no
one had the right to hold an office in the ecclesiastical economy except by the call and consideration of its highest ministers ; and he saw how,
for generations, lords of the castle had been
giving away benefices of the church to their relations, or selling them to the highest bidders.
He read how a child five years old had been made

an archbishop, and how abbots were accounted
worthy, who did nothing worse than feast and
hunt to fill out their time.   He believed that the
incumbent of the papacy was really supreme over
kings ; and he saw that, not for a hundred and
fifty years, had any proud claim of spiritual
autocracy been made in Rome.   Nay, he read
the long and desolate story how the strength of
the church had been wasted in external and civil
quarrels, as well as drained by inward vice.   German emperors had set up popes to serve their
ends, and Italian counts, or the Roman rabble,
had pulled them down again.   Popes had been
exiled, as Germany or Italy conquered in the continual and vacillating strife.   Popes had been
strangled in Roman dungeons.   Popes had been
starved.   Laymen had openly bought the awful
office from brigands.   Popes had stolen the treasures of St. Peter, and run off to Constantinople.
Popes had ruled so outrageously that their bodies
were seized after death by an infuriated populace,
dragged through the streets, and transfixed with
lances.   More than twenty in a century had illustrated thus the anthology of crime, misery, and
degradation ; and at last, in Hildebrand's own
time, while he was studying those annals in
Cluny, a boy pope twelve years old was master of the spiritual sceptre, and was beginning
to lead a life so shameful, foul, and execrable, that
a subsequent pope has said he "shuddered to
describe it."

But the wider the darkness and the more frightful the degradation, the more intensely does the conviction possess the soul of Hildebrand that the church must be reformed. The evils of the times must be smitten at their root. The practice of the feudal lords, who were laymen, of selling the offices of the church, or of nominating to them at their own pleasure, must be prohibited. This evil was called "simony," from Simon Magus, who, the book of Acts tells us, tried to buy of St. Peter the power of working miracles, — supposing that the Holy Ghost was a purchasable commodity.

And second, the marriage of the clergy must be annulled, and their wives instantly put away. The laws of the church before the eleventh century had decreed that the clergy must be unmarried men. But they were not heeded. Throughout Europe, at the commencement of the eleventh century, the priests who had not wives and families were the exceptions. To strike with energy at two such customs, interwoven so variously and so minutely with the passions of the world, must task the stoutest statesmanship, and must wrench the framework of the whole Catholic organization.

But how shall Hildebrand be able to attempt it? In the year 1048, thirty-five years old, he is still a monk in Cluny. He had been concerned with one movement of reform in Rome, but it had fallen through, and he has returned to be

prior of the monastery. Filled with passion for
the purity and power of the church, what can he
do with his genius, his learning, his power as a
preacher, his terrible eye in his fleshless frame,
against the ruthless villanies and the chronic
vices that are disgracing and devastating Christendom ?

The opportunity for his service offered itself in
an unsuspected way.   In the year 1048 a new
pope had been appointed by the German emperor, who was to take the title of Leo the Ninth,
— a model of priestly purity and excellence.   On
his way to Rome, travelling with great pomp, as
some of the records run, he stopped for rest at
the monastery of Cluny. He met Hildebrand.
Their short interviews were long enough for the
mind of the monk to work its spell over the im-
pressible and feebler nature of Leo, and the Pope
invited him to join his retinue, and live with him
in Rome.   Hildebrand refused to go, unless the
pope would lay aside his pomp, travel as a pilgrim, and count himself unconfirmed in his great
office until the clergy and people of Rome should
have assented to the nomination of the emperor.
To consider himself as pope merely by virtue
of an imperial nomination, Hildebrand assured
the bishop, was to go to Rome as an apostate,
and not as an apostle.   Leo yielded to his terms.
The whole retinue left Cluny as pilgrim-travellers.
Hildebrand shut the door of that French monastery a second time behind him, turned his face,

in company with that cowled and barefoot band,
toward the Eternal City, and becomes the central
figure of the passions and polity of Europe in the
eleventh century, — the master-spirit in the history of the Holy Catholic Church. The legends
assure us that celestial music floated over that
party as they journeyed to Rome, and that miracles waited upon their steps, attesting the joy of
heaven and earth over the new era that had
dawned upon the church.

During the six years of Leo's pontificate, Hildebrand held complete sway over his policy and
mind. When Leo died, it was by the masterly
art of Hildebrand, foiling the emperor's wishes,
that a successor was chosen, best fitted of all living bishops to carry out his high-church views.
And when he died, another, and, beyond the
third, a fourth, was clothed with the papal office,
in accordance with his own wishes, till we come
to Alexander I., the fifth pope nominated through
the influence of Hildebrand, and pledged to his
principles of reform. Swiftly he rises from office
to office ; — he is cardinal-deacon, cardinal-arch-
deacon, legate to France, imperial legate, and, at
last, chancellor of the Holy See, — an office next
in rank to the papacy itself. There is continual
evidence through these years of a masterly, persistent, organizing mind in Rome, pledging the
power of the short-lived popes to a great constructive work. His messengers are flying from
kingdom to kingdom, spinning the web of his

9*

polity over every state. Edict after edict appears against the marriage of the clergy ; the sale of the church offices by laymen, and the purchase of place by the clergy, are visited with the anathema of Rome ; and, more important, perhaps, for the moment, than both, the power of appointing to the papacy is wrested from the emperor and lodged with the college of cardinals, — a revolution whose effects are visible in the order of papal elections now. He worked so fast that the enemies of his policy were confounded. One who felt his power, and who had no love for him, said : " The small sinewy tiger distances all arrows by his speed."

Hildebrand, however, during those years, is seldom prominent in the annals of the active stage, although we do see him, for once, as legate in France, presiding over a council to inquire into charges against bishops for purchasing their offices ; one scene of which is dramatic and striking. A bishop who was on trial before him, and who was known to have bought his dignity, had bribed his accusers over night, and then the next day proudly challenged in the court-room any evidence to his damage. There was silence. Hildebrand was confident of his guilt, and said to him, with an expression of sorrow, " Do you believe that the Holy Spirit is of the same substance as the Father and the Son ? " " I do," was the response. " Then," Hildebrand continued, fixing his eye upon him, " say the Gloria Patri."

The bishop commenced, but could not speak the words "the Holy Spirit," while that wintry eye was piercing him, though he tried three times. Then he cast himself at the feet of Hildebrand, confessed his crime, was degraded from his office, and immediately found the power to pronounce the words that had fettered his tongue.

But this personal magnetism of Hildebrand was, for the most part, used in Rome to control the nominal rulers of Christendom, and to dictate through them the policy of the church. For twenty-five years he was thus the power behind the throne, greater than the throne. Popes were his speaking-trumpets. The anathemas of councils were the language of his passion, and revolutionary decrees the wings of his ideas. He was called the "lord of the lord pope." While Alexander II. was in power one of Hildebrand's friends wrote to him, "You made him pope ; he made you a god." In these twenty-five years more had been done to detach the church, as an institution, from the state, and to knit its fibres as a permanent and progressive organization, than in the two preceding centuries.

In 1073 Alexander II., an easy, pleasure-loving, pompous man, the last of six popes who had been under the influence of Hildebrand, died. The monk of Cluny, who was thirty-five years old when he left the monastery, was now sixty. He was conducting the funeral service over the departed pontiff, in the Lateran church, when the solemnities were interrupted by the shouts of the people, — shouts which his enemies say he had paid for with gold, — " St. Peter chooses the archdeacon Hildebrand for pope." A cardinal sprang forward and exclaimed, "Ye know well, brethren, that since the days of Leo this tried and prudent archdeacon has exalted the Roman See, and delivered this city from many perils. Wherefore we the bishops and cardinals elect him now, with one mind, as the pastor and bishop of your souls." The speaker's voice was lost amid wild cries from the crowd, " It is the will of St. Peter ; Hildebrand is pope." The scarlet robe and the papal crown were brought out ; and the son of a Tuscan carpenter, the bowed and shrivelled monk of Cluny, the man whose head held a more audacious scheme of ecclesiastical authority than any pope had ever dreamed before, was led, as the story runs, reluctant and in tears, to St. Peter's chair, with the title " Gregory the Seventh."

We may well believe that he was reluctant to assume that mitre. His very consciousness of superior fitness for it, the breadth, austerity, and splendor of his conception of what the pope and the church should be, must have made him recoil from the obligations and labors which that robe and that crown would impose upon his mind. How, out of an ignorant clergy, a debased, corrupted, licentious clergy, — how, out of bishops, the majority of whom were tainted by having purchased their positions with gold, — how, against princes, kings, and emperors who denied the supremacy of the papacy over their thrones, and were held to spiritual allegiance to the church only by their fears, should he, bowed with labors and beginning to bend with years, be able to build up the great edifice of a church whose walls should enclose every kingdom of Europe, and before whose altar kings should kneel in reverence, to hear their disputes adjusted by authority, to be condemned for disobedience, and to receive their crowns? This was his vision; and if he steps into the papacy, he must turn, day after day, from his communion with this dazzling and august conception, to look at the barbarous and unjointed Europe, and the ignorant, lazy, and sensual church, which offer to him the only material for shaping out and perpetuating the dream! No wonder that he preferred to be the whispering counsellor in the ears of popes, doing something slowly thus for the great cause, rather than to feel the whole responsibility upon his shoulders, by taking in his own person the office of vicegerent of God!

He commended himself with great fervor to the help of St. Peter and the Virgin; spent a few months, with wily Italian caution, in intrenching his power; and then struck with frightful energy at the evils within the church that stood in his way.

First, at the marriage of the clergy. It had

been denounced before by the popes whom he controlled; but now it was as if for the first time the wrestle of a papal idea with a myriad-handed passion had really commenced. He determined to outroot the evil of a married ministry, and to lay the corner-stone of his great structure on a celibate priesthood. He forbade the people to attend mass where his edict was not obeyed, or to receive any service from any married priest. "Their prayer is sin," he said; "their blessing will be to you a curse." He allowed no time for dallying with the law. Men that were devoted to their families must instantly give them up. Marriages sanctified by the tenderest love and the sweetest domestic happiness were placed under the same ban with connections looser and impure.

In Italy, France, and Germany the bishops and priests were stirred almost to madness. Councils broke up in mobs, and the lives of legates were scarcely saved. The clergy quoted Scripture against the infallible head of the church. In many cases, doubtless, it was all the Scripture they were familiar with; just as now we find a very general acquaintance with the injunction to take a little wine for the stomach's sake among men who would be puzzled to know where to look for it, or to tell whether it was said by Moses, Job, or Judas. Peter, they said, was married; Paul did not forbid it to the clergy; Jesus left it optional. They howled in councils the charge to Timothy, "The bishop must be sober, the husband

of one wife." They insisted that they would renounce their priesthood sooner than their marriage vow. "If the pope is not satisfied with men
to serve the churches, let him turn us out," they
said, "and then find angels for his purposes."

His missionaries were frightened, and pressed
him to abate his rigor. But no expostulations
availed with the steel-handed prelate who ruled in
Rome. The miseries of the poor women, wives
of the priests, who were condemned by his decrees as infamous and abandoned, the tidings of
how they killed themselves as their homes were
invaded and broken up, did not move him. He
played for an idea, a system, a future. He knew
that he had a party in the church, though in the
minority, which was devoted to him as the hand
to the brain ; he believed that he could rely upon
the help of the people, by exciting them to spiritual rebellion against disobedient priests ; and he
determined to carry the measure through, though
Europe was in an uproar, and the church was
rocking. He was cruel, as a revolutionary intellect, when at work, is always cruel ; because its
ideas are not framed with any regard to the way
in which human affections are inwoven with an
imperfect social organization.

We will not ask the reader to consider the wisdom or the righteousness of this movement. We
have only to say, seeing how cold and how fierce
Christian theology has been thus far in history,
Heaven save us from such theology as we should

have if all the teachers of it were to be forever strangers to the duties and sanctities of home ; if the doctrine of God the Father were to be perpetually intrusted to the interpretation of men who know nothing of parental yearnings, sacrifices, and joys ; if the hands of little children were never laid upon the grim features of a monkish creed !

More self-denial has been exhibited in the Protestant order of a married clergy than the Catholic system nourishes or admits. The military hardships and fidelity of the Jesuits in their missionary enterprises look more dramatic ; but the life-long, uncomplaining wrestle with poverty by the hearthstone, which is the general law with the Protestant ministry of our country now, and the bloom of the sternest virtues and the gentlest graces in such ungenial circumstances, are a more precious contribution to the glory of the Gospel than the average character of a drilled celibate priesthood can ever show. Had Hildebrand's idea been the law for all Christendom, the church would have lost from the army of her martyrs the wives of the poor modern Protestant clergy, who will largely swell the number of those who are made perfect through suffering, and go through much tribulation into the kingdom of heaven.

Turn the eye for a moment from the righteousness of Hildebrand's movement, and raise the question of its success. Look at the Catholic priesthood and hierarchy to-day. So far as the

strength of a church, such as he dreamed of, is
concerned, the policy of his terrible decree is interpreted at once, when we ask ourselves how
much weaker the Romish system and hierarchy
would be if their priesthood were not, as now, an
order in the world and yet not of it; if they were
bound by domestic and social ties with the life
and passions of the communities which they serve;
if the whole energies of their nature were not, as
by the present system they are compelled to be,
pledged to the power and glory of the church,
and trained along those subtle trellises that lead
from every hamlet and every city directly to St.
Peter's and the Vatican! It may be of interest
to many of those who are devoted to the cause of
women's rights to learn that two women, prin-
cesses of Italy, were invited, by a letter from
Hildebrand, to preside over the deliberations of
that council that did so much to dishonor womanhood by making the acceptance of the family bond
and order a sin in every official servant of Him
whose first miracle was wrought at a marriage
feast.

While Europe was in turmoil from the effects
of that decree, Hildebrand struck a blow, still
more startling, at simony in the church, and at
the temporal power over spiritual officers. He
not only denounced all who had paid money for
their places, and deposed them, but he astonished
the world with the edict that "if any person ac-
cepts any bishopric, or office of abbot, or any

N

lower spiritual rank, from the hands of a layman, he shall not be regarded as a bishop, or an abbot, or a clergyman ; while every individual of the laity, be he king or emperor, who bestows investiture in connection with such office, shall be excluded from church communion." Remember that the abbots and bishops in the Middle Ages were not only officers of the church, but were also temporal princes. They held lands, forests, castles, and serfs. They were prominent supporters of the civil and royal order of society. The claim of Gregory, therefore, that they should be nominated in every country only from Rome, and should receive their badges of power from the sovereign pontiff, was nothing less than a social revolution. It made every bishop and priest dependent at once upon the papacy. It struck from the monarchy of every country its wealthiest and most learned adherents. It put half the land, and more than half the wealth, of Europe at once in the control of the pope. Carry out this plan, and the sacerdotal power is instantly a kingdom within all other kingdoms, as distinct from the body politic as a cancer is distinct from the frame in which it runs, and perhaps as deadly, by its steady absorption, to the forces of the body's life.

Gregory put all his passion and firmness into this movement, as he did into the edicts against concubinage. And here again, if we wish to know the permanent influence of Hildebrand, we may ask the question, Who appoints Cardinal

Wiseman to England, nominates the head of the church in France, invests the Archbishop of New York, or designates the Metropolitan at Baltimore? The arm of that crooked monk of Cluny reaches down eight hundred years, affecting our society, and keeping alive an interest in his schemes in our politics. With that decree began a long and strenuous wrestle between the papacy and the temporal power, such as the world had not seen before, and has never witnessed since.

The Emperor of Germany, Henry the Fourth, was a very young man. He had been badly educated ; was passionate, wilful, and vacillating ; and was surrounded by intriguing bishops who slyly encouraged his vices, and by quarrelling nobles who fretted under his authority. Gregory, no doubt, wanted to test and to establish his own principles in Europe by a rupture with the stripling monarch. A better opportunity he could not hope for. He had outwitted the father, Henry the Third, a very able ruler, by his diplomacy ; and he felt, probably, that he could easily overbear the feebler son by the prestige of his office and the energy of his mind. The young emperor showed no zeal in carrying out the new papal decrees against marriage and simony ; and his life was dissolute. Hildebrand wrote to him admonishing him for his crimes, and then, after a while, summoned him to Rome to answer there, before his tribunal, for various and undefined offences. It was a bold step even for a bold pope.

Henry instantly replied by a still bolder one.
Hildebrand's policy was getting to be intolerable ;
it perilled the liberty of priests and prelates as
well as kings ; and bishops enough were suddenly
collected from Henry's dominions to depose Hildebrand, by vote of a council, as a licentious
priest, a false pope, a cruel tyrant, and a sorcerer.
Such was the answer the young ruler sent by a
messenger, who delivered it roughly to Gregory's
face, as he was presiding over a council, in the
year 1076.   Hildebrand, we may believe, rejoiced
at the insult and the insurrection.   It offered him
the most splendid temptation to stretch his claims
of power to the utmost, — to clothe one of the
most audacious of his assumptions in a decree.
In full council he excommunicated Henry the
Emperor, interdicted him from the government
of Germany and Italy, and pronounced him de-
throned.   " I absolve all Christians from the
oaths they have sworn or may swear to him ; and
forbid all obedience to him as king.   I bind him
in the bonds of thy anathema ; that all the nations
may know and acknowledge that thou art Peter,
that upon thy rock the Son of the living God has
built his church, and that the gates of hell shall
not prevail against it."   It was the first time in
the history of Christendom that such a sentence
had been uttered against a sovereign, — the first
time that a pope had presumed to strike beyond
the soul of a monarch at his temporal crown.
Some chroniclers hostile to Gregory relate, in the

very spirit of the literature of the Dark Ages, that when the pope took his seat after this awful decree, the chair of St. Peter cracked asunder, though the wood was new and strong, as a type of the social distractions that were to follow that curse.

On all the bishops, also, who had aided Henry, the terrible edict fell. The Vatican blazed with wrath like Vesuvius, and maledictions spouted in showers from its crater through the sulphurous air. Hildebrand had no soldiers to support his startling pretension. The monks were pledged to him. He was making the first trial of the new machinery of Rome, — traditions in place of truth ; priests inviolable ; the recently established doctrine of transubstantiation ; bishops and abbots proclaimed as independent of secular authority ; and through these the mystic sanctity and despotism of the Holy See. His party were in the minority even in the church itself ; but he wasted no thought upon the seeming inequality of the struggle. He trusted to the moral effect which a papal decree would carry with it, and to the vigor with which his arm had hurled the doom against the most powerful monarch of Europe.

Henry affected to despise the judgment of the Vatican ; but he soon found that Hildebrand's anathema was abroad in all the air of Germany, and was slowly corroding the sinews of his strength. It was read in churches ; it crept along from castle to castle, from village to village, from house to house, disturbing bishops, making barons uneasy, frightening priests, appalling the people with subtle superstitious dread. Henry might be ruler of the earth; but Gregory was "prince of the powers of the air." The overarching region of sentiment, the impalpable mental element, obeyed the electric pulses of his mitred genius. One of the prominent princely agents in that insult to the pope died suddenly and mysteriously. The cathedral in which the partisans of Henry had excommunicated the pope was struck by lightning. Slowly the combination that had promised to support the monarch crumbled. Provinces revolted; bishops stole away to Rome to make their peace with the terrible Hildebrand, and, on their return, would have no intercourse with the emperor. Henry began to feel like a leprous man in his own dominions. In a few months he was almost deserted.

Gregory had threatened that, unless he made his peace with the church within a year from his sentence, orders should be given to elect a new emperor. The year was fast rolling away. It would close in February of 1077. Midwinter came, and Henry found that there was no hope but in bending before the proud priest who had laid such a spell upon his realm. He must turn his steps towards Italy. He must cross the Alps through winter snows and storms. But even nature was against him, for so bitter a winter had

not been known for years. With his wife and
infant son and one attendant, he set out on his
journey, and attempted the pass of Mont Cenis.

Is there any other scene so impressive in the
secular history of the world? The Emperor of
Germany toiling up the white and slippery preci-
pices of Switzerland, clinging to the shoulders of
the guide, creeping down the sides of icy ravines
on his hands and knees, or rolling along the
steeper declivities at the peril of his life, and
seeing his queen and infant drawn up and let
down by the mountaineers in great bags made
of the skins of oxen, in order that, by personal
humiliation and penance, the deadly spell might
be revoked, which the words of a monk, sitting
in St. Peter's chair, had breathed upon his power,
his hopes, and his heart! Look steadily at that
figure of the emperor among the Alpine snows
toiling towards Lombardy, for it shows you in
one scene the climax of the papal power in the
Middle Ages. Rome has no such other monument in its annals as that chilled emperor on the
summit of Mont Cenis, drawn from his palace in
midwinter by the power of an idea! And yet
pause, one moment more, to admire something in
that scene more lasting and more noble than the
power of the Vatican, — the love, the patient,
forgetful, forgiving love of a woman and a wife!
Henry the Emperor had ill treated the princess
who was his companion in that winter journey;
he had neglected her, had been faithless to her,

and had striven to be divorced from her. But she was always gentle and faithful amid her wrongs ; and now she clings to him in spite of papal ban and general desertion, — yes, though his own mother had forsaken him, — and braves the savage Alps with her delicate frame, to show us that there are affections in our nature that will jet out in unselfish heroism, as sublime as any stimulated by ambition or provoked by spiritual fear.

Hildebrand was at the castle of a faithful friend in Canosa. The emperor arrived at its gate, supposing that he should be instantly admitted to the papal presence, — that his winter journey would be accepted as a sufficient penance and abasement. But the end was not yet ; Hildebrand refused to see him. "Let him submit his cause," he said, "to a council in Germany over which I will preside." Eager to make his peace with Gregory, the emperor clothed himself in a thin white linen dress, and, passing through the two outer gates of the castle, stood bareheaded in the snow, on a bleak morning in January, before the inner wall. A second day found him in the same position. The third day he was still there, cold and hungry ; for the inner gate, like Hildebrand's heart, was still closed against him. At last he was admitted to the pope, — a noble-looking youth, tall and commanding in form, wearing an imperial grace, representing well the kingly idea, before the bent, diminutive, implacable Hildebrand ! The terms of reconciliation were cautious and severe. The earthly power must be utterly broken before the majesty of the church. Henry yielded to all, in order that the terrible excommunication might be revoked; and then attended church with the pope, to have his humiliation complete. Having granted him absolution at the altar, Hildebrand took the consecrated wafer, lifted his hands in presence of the crowd, and called on God to strike him at once with his judgment, as he partook of the Lord's body, if he were guilty of the charges his enemies had made, — if his motives were not pure. He ate the wafer, and stood unharmed while the congregation burst forth in cheers. He then offered the same ordeal to the emperor, to test whether his motives had been as clear; but Henry trembled, and declined the awful test. Hildebrand's victory was thus complete, but he had overshot the mark. The young emperor left his presence outwardly humble, inwardly enraged.

Instead of peace, therefore, this dramatic triumph of Gregory conjured a storm that desolated his later years. Henry broke all the terms of his compact, one by one. The tyranny of Gregory, in that personal interview, was like the point of Ithuriel's spear; — a manly spirit leaped out from Henry's degraded breast which astonished his subjects. He organized, with more energy than he had ever shown before, an opposition to the man who had trodden upon him so ruthlessly;

10

and even went so far as to depose him once more, and elect another pope in Germany, whom he determined to place by his sword in St. Peter's chair in Rome. Hildebrand consecrated another emperor, who was chosen by a portion of the Germans, in Henry's place; and so, for several years, the powers of church and state grappled each other in the wrestle for supremacy.

But Hildebrand's pretensions and schemes were not at all affected by the temporary fortunes of this strife, and went far beyond all that a favorable issue in the contest with Henry could have secured to him. He styled the council that elected another pope "an assembly of Satan, whose lives are detestable, and whose ordination heretical." Our contempt for them, he says, is in proportion to their seeming elevation. He excommunicates them all. His passions, and the weapons of his adherents, were engaged with one emperor; his mind was busy with plans of authority over all countries and all ages. No volumes in literature are so remarkable as his letters, — so amazing in the contrast of their pretension to authority with the power to execute it. Time after time, and in the boldest terms, he made the claims that the church must not only be independent of the civil power, but dominant over it; that kingdoms were only districts of the papal possessions, and that monarchs were his vassals. Claims that it should seem could be put forth only by a hot-brained fanatic in feverish diction,

he uttered in cool, square sentences, fortified by
logic, and sometimes by historic evidence. He
gloated over his title-deeds to nations, and unrolled them now and then in the face of Europe.
The great empire of the West, he contended, it
was his to give with the imperial crown; and so
he would never date his letters, as former popes
had done, according to the years of the emperor's
reign, but by a chronology of his own. Saxony
in particular, he pretended, had been given to St.
Peter by Charlemagne, who conquered it. Denmark he claimed, in a letter to its king, and
offered, for a consideration, to give him a province
occupied by heretics, as an independent domain
for one of his children. Twice he made, in form,
a claim that Spain belonged to St. Peter before
the invasion of the Saracens; and expressed his
preference that it should remain under infidels,
rather than under Christian monarchs who would
not submit to his authority. He informed rulers
of Sardinia that St. Peter owned their country, and
threatened to give it away if they were not more
obedient, — especially if the archbishop and his
clergy did not shave their beards, according to
the general Western custom. He informed the
King of Hungary that that country belonged to
the Roman Church, because the first conqueror
of it had sent a lance and a crown to the body
of St. Peter. He made the same pretensions to
Dalmatia, in a formal letter, and even to Russia,
in a missive to King Demetrius. The monarch

of France, also, is treated to similar epistles, and Africa he claims as part of his domain. Without an acre of ground which he could govern by unquestioned personal authority, he looked upon the world as his chess-board, with kings, queens, bishops, and castles as the subordinate instruments of his play. The insane man who gave the word of command, " Attention the universe ! By kingdoms, wheel ! " is a feeble symbol of the claims soberly put into literature in the epistles of Gregory VII.

Even to William the Conqueror of England he held a tone equally high. When William was about to start on his invading expedition, Hildebrand, not then nominally pope, supported his cause in the college of cardinals, sent him a consecrated banner, and also a ring containing, as he pretended, one of the hairs of St. Peter set under a diamond of great price. He commissioned William to bring back that kingdom to obedience to the Holy See, and re-establish forever there the tax of Peter's pence. Only from William the Conqueror in England, however, did he find determined resistance to his pretensions, in language as resolute as any he used. " I will pay tribute to the church," says the Norman king ; " but I will never swear allegiance. And if any monk of my dominions dares to carry tales to Rome, I will hang him on the highest tree of the forest."

We cannot but stand in admiration before a scheme of society in which empires become coun-

ties of a vast spiritual monarchy; which shows us
a living chain of priests running in rising links
from every land till they touch and encircle St.
Peter's chair, — each of them wearing a sanctity
inviolable in every latitude by any ruler; which
abases kings as the lieutenants of the great spiritual Caliph; which promises to do away with war,
in providing that all disputes between countries
and rulers shall be settled by a word from the
man whose blessing is the only virtue of a crown.
Futile as such a dream must be, we cannot but
admire the proportions of its vision; we cannot
but revere the intellect that could feel it as its
inspiration; could pour the life of logic and imagination into it; could calmly collect its almost
superhuman energies to intrench it on the earth;
and, above all, that could retreat within the majestic symmetry of it as a solace in time of
trouble!

Hildebrand was serene amid his greatest difficulties; his calmness was unshaken; his hopes
never flickered; his confidence in his mission and
the majesty of his office never failed. When
Henry turned against him the second time, —
when civil war was waging around him, he says in
one of his prayers to Jesus, "if you had imposed
such burdens as mine upon Moses or Peter, I
believe they would have been overwhelmed."
But then he says again, "When the good Jesus
stretches out his hand towards me I am filled with
joy." His enemies said he was in constant inter-

course with demons, and that his power was from
them; but he supported himself, he affirmed, by
the help which the Virgin mother vouchsafed to
him, and by his confidence in the righteousness
and triumph of his cause.

As difficulties increased around him his spirit
mounted, and the rhetoric grows more intense in
which he vindicates his scheme. When affairs
went against his party in Germany, as they did at
last, and Henry passed the Alps, — not, as before,
a suppliant for his pardon, but with an army to
inaugurate another pope in his stead, — so far
from listening to any terms, he writes to the
bishops who deny his power to absolve subjects
from their duty to a monarch, " What are kings
and princes if they do not live as Christians?
They are slaves of demons. Every exorcist has
power over demons, and so over them. And if
exorcists have this power, how much more the
great bishops of the church ? Can a king baptize ?
Can a king make the body and blood of Christ
by a word? Does not a king on his death-bed
implore a priest to save him from the eternal
dungeon of hell ? Nay, kingship itself is only an
invasion of the natural equality of man, ordained
by Providence on account of human wickedness.
It has no inherent, eternal sanctity. Good Christians, of the lowest rank, deserve to be esteemed
as kings more than bad princes. The first are
members of Jesus Christ ; the second are limbs
of the Devil." Well may a church historian ask,

concerning these sentences, "Are we reading a journalist of Paris in 1791?"

Such was the spirit of all Gregory's answers to the suggestion of compromise with his foes. Even when Henry held part of Rome, and Gregory was shut up in the castle of Angelo, his only terms were, "Let the emperor yield, and acknowledge my authority as the lord of princes, and I will pardon him even now!" But he was forced to see from his castle a procession pass to the great church in the Eternal City, headed by Henry the Fourth, to inaugurate the antipope. Yes, another scene, alas! more terrible, was to pass before his eye. Some Norman troops came to his relief; drove the soldiers of Henry from the city; delivered the pope from his imprisonment; but pillaged, sacked, and burned the city. Thousands of the Romans were sold publicly as slaves. He calmly celebrated mass and performed miracles — as was said — in the Lateran church while the city was in flames, and the blood of the innocent population was flowing in brooks around him. Neither Goth nor Vandal, it has been said, neither Greek nor German, brought such desolation upon Rome as this capture by the Normans, who rescued the pope. Hildebrand began his career as a thinker in the quiet of the monastery of Cluny, looking out upon its peaceful and cultivated grounds; he closed his course by flying from the city which he thought to make the spiritual capital of the world, ravaged and stained with fire, as the witness of what those principles had done in his lifetime which he dreamed over in his early years.

From Rome he hastened to Salerno in Italy, to breathe a quiet air before he passed away. He published edicts forbidding laymen to touch consecrated vessels, ordering an unequal number of signs to be made to indicate the mystery of the Trinity, and wrote again to William the Conqueror, urging him to set his imprisoned brother at liberty, because he had respected priests, who, said Gregory in his missive, are "the pupil of the eye of Jesus Christ!" In 1085, when he was seventy-two years old, he sank to rest. On his death-bed he was asked if he wished to pardon any who were under his condemnation. He breathed his character in the reply: "I absolve and bless all those who believe that I have the power to do it, except Henry the emperor, the antipope, and their adherents." Against them his fearful excommunication must stand. His last words were: "I have loved justice and hated iniquity; therefore I die in exile." The Catholic writers tell of miracles that have frequently been wrought at his tomb. In 1577 his entire remains, with the pontifical ornaments, were found in Salerno; but it was not till 1609 that his name was entered as a saint, and allowed to be honored by a public office in the church he served.

The dying curse of Gregory upon Henry preserved its vitality more than twenty years. His death was a tragic one; for his son rebelled against him, — that son whom his wife had carried in her arms over the Alpine ice : and in the midst of civil war he died of a broken heart. But his body was refused honorable burial. Under the condemnation of the church in life, bishops refused to let him sleep in consecrated ground ; and it was only after five years of contention that he was laid away in the vaults of his ancestors.

Hildebrand belongs in the list of the world's great men. He had a mind competent to conceive a vast constructive scheme of society, the first movements to establish which must be revolutions ; and he had the courage to start the revolutions, not from any love of discord, but as believing that the world would gain by the higher order and peace that would be permanently instituted. His ambition seems to have had little personal appetite for power in it. He lived in his ideas ; and his ambition was for the sway of the principle of which he happened to be the supreme servant. Among all the great men that have pledged their thought and power to the polity of the Catholic Church, he is undoubtedly the imperial intellect ; he saw in largest outline and most sublime proportions the majesty of that invisible kingdom which, for centuries, the genius of Catholicism has toiled with uncomplaining, wily, and persistent energy to establish in the earth. He stands out the ablest man of the eleventh century, indeed of several successive centuries, without a

10 *   o

second to divide with him the claim for breadth of mind and mental courage.

He stands, also, above his age by his superiority to many of the superstitions and to the fanaticism of his period. He was widely accused of sorcery; and yet, in a letter to the King of Denmark, he urged him to put a stop to the abuse of persecuting innocent women as witches. He believed in the absolute power of the church over souls; and he protested against the abuse of pardoning a single sin for mere outward penance, or on any other conditions than heartfelt sorrow and reform. He was educated a monk; and he lamented bitterly over the unfaithfulness of Christendom, as seen in the crowds that sought the quiet life of the monasteries, contrasted with the few who were willing to take up the harder and nobler task of fidelity to truth in the duties of the world. He reproved the Abbot of Cluny for receiving a duke within its shades, who wished to lead a pious life, instead of urging him to continue at his post; "for thus," he says, "my brother, you have left a hundred thousand Christians without their natural protector, and have gained only a single monk." He believed in loyalty to the church; and yet he could write these words: "To aid the unfortunate and oppressed, from love of God, I consider more than fasting, prayer, vigils, and other good works, be they ever so many; for true love is more than the other virtues." There is reason to believe also that he was not wholly sound on the Catholic dogma of transubstantiation, — that his powerful intellect saw through the grossness of that superstition which had hardened in a barbarous age.

As to the success of his labors. We must remember that he played for the future, and for an institution. No great institution rises in history except out of a soul which is the acorn of it. No speculation ever germinates of itself into a fact. Plato's fancied republic has been fruitless and harmless. It is an idea incarnate in a man, heated by his passions, swelling in all the veins of his personality, that strikes root in history ; and that "corn is not quickened, except it die." Hildebrand was planted, and the Catholic polity rose out of his grave. His first victory over Henry was premature, and his subsequent defeat was not fatal. His mitre worked miracles, the legends say, after he died. He began to live after he died. The great contest raged after his eyes were closed. The marriage of the clergy was dishonored in the Catholic Church in all aftertime by his uncompromising denunciation ; and, in another generation, the emperor yielded the right of investing any churchman with the symbols of office, and granted freedom of election. A little more than a century later beheld Pope Innocent III. practically as supreme in Europe as Hildebrand's policy would have asked. He left the church in the gristle ; it hardened into bone.

As to the good this man accomplished, we must give a divided judgment. So far as he has helped to suppress liberty of thought, through the strength and skill of the pressure which the Catholic hierarchy lays upon it now, he has proved an enemy to his race. But so far as he helped to confirm, in the Middle Ages, the power of the papacy, and build up the unity of Latin Christendom, he did an immense service; for only thus were the bonds of order knit through a society that would otherwise have dissolved: only thus was learning preserved through the Latin tongue, that was kept alive as the language of religion; only thus was "a bridge thrown over the chaos between ancient and modern civilization."

The central error of Hildebrand's system and life was that of confounding Christianity with any visible institution of the earth. Men are insensibly seduced into methods as worldly as his, betrayed into passions as violent, and tempted to schemes as bloody, by starting with the idea that Christianity must wear a visible body on the earth, and be served with outward implements. If we lodge our hopes of the Gospel in the success of any one proud institution, we shall find all the impurities, all the vices, and essentially all the crimes, that belong to the earthly man, vitiating the stream that flows from it, just as we have found it in the Catholic Church; because an institution having rank, honors, and wealth at its disposal will be managed by the earthly side, the unregenerate forces, of human nature. The kingdom of God cometh not with observation.

There is such a thing possible as a universal church. It exists now upon the earth. It is the salt, it is the life-blood, of civilization. Its fibres run across the boundaries of kingdoms; it holds the Christian world in unity. It has its outward institutions, though they are not such as the monk of Cluny dreamed of; it has its laws and ministers, though there is no order, such as he prescribed, in their coming and their rank. It is not a Catholic polity, nor an Episcopal one, nor a Presbyterian one, no, nor all systems and hierarchies combined. Its buildings and trophies rise out of the silent pressures, through public sentiment and private hearts, of the spirit of the Gospel. Hospitals, asylums, and schools of reform are dots in the landscape of its power, — though no papal voice, or decree of council, called them into being. Every church built out of the desire of worship is a symbol of its sway. Every work of art, showing how religion has refined and inspired the taste for beauty, is a graceful proof of its dominion. Every school that springs from a conviction of the worth of man and his right to education is a witness of its vitality. Every law that ordains justice over the clamorous interests of a class is a confession of its majesty. The affections that elevate and sweeten and hallow home, and the charities that flow out of mellow hearts to the needy, are streams of its life and promises of its triumph. Try to organize Christianity within one line of agencies, under the patronage of earthly power, and you kill it, or corrupt it. Unharness it, — let it work free as an elemental force — the spirit that bloweth where it listeth, — and you have the leaven in the meal, with its prophecy of quickening for the whole lump. And when, at last, by its secret agency through invisible veins, and in impalpable ways, — when, far on in a century whose distance we cannot calculate as yet, the spirit of the Gospel shall have poured itself through the trunk and in all the boughs of humanity, sending justice as the organic fibre, and charity as the sweet juice, from the lowest root to the topmost leaf of society, then will the hope of the world be fulfilled ; then will the scheme over which Hildebrand of Cluny mused and prayed be realized in a form higher than he or his stormy age could have conceived ; for then shall the promise and prophecy of Hildebrand's Master, the true Lord of the church, be completed in history, and the mustard-seed appear in the developed tree, where the birds come to lodge and sing with joy.

VI.

MUSIC.

I HAVE thought, ladies and gentlemen, that I could not more fitly discharge the duty with which your committee have honored me, than by bringing to you a brief address upon music.

I must throw myself at once upon your indulgence as critics, by confessing that, in the great temple of harmony, my worship is offered in the court of the Gentiles. Yet it is not without the profoundest reverence towards the inner enclosures that guard the Holy of Holies, nor without the most burning desire to be a " Hebrew of the Hebrews," in order to gain the privilege of penetrating to the central recess, and bowing at the most sacred shrine.

If I should acknowledge to you in advance that I do not practically know a note of music, it will not be the first time, perhaps you will think, that a clergyman has ventured dogmatically upon topics which he has not mastered, though perhaps you may be inclined to give me credit for an honesty in confession that is somewhat rare.

A friend of mine is fond of telling the story of a

minister who preached a thrilling discourse under three heads, which he had thus arranged : " Under the first head, I shall speak of matters, brethren, with which we are all acquainted ; under the second head, of those parts of the subject of which I know something, and you are ignorant; under the third head, of matters about which we none of us know anything at all." And they say that he was most interesting and eloquent under the third head.

And yet it seems to me that there is room for a man, who comes under the third head so far as the science of harmony is concerned, to speak without arrogance and assumption, in a literary way, of music as a force, an advantage, a privilege, and a joy, — just as a man may describe his delight in landscape, and enlarge upon the pleasures of a refined and sensitive taste for natural beauty, who knows nothing of the science of the sun-ray, or the chemistry of grass, or the subtle magic by which the evening symphony of color is executed upon the hills.

There are two prominent channels of communication with the outward world, — the eye and the ear.	Their mysteries of structure, action, and office are about equally marvellous.

They are both made to respond to vibrations. The first catches and measures the pulses of that wondrous ether, immeasurably more delicate than our atmosphere, whose shaking it is that produces light.	The other detects and interprets the vibra-

tions that travel to the mind as sound. The foundation of all art lies in the fact that the two eyes are a
stereoscope. So far as the senses are concerned,
things are shown to us double and upside down ;
the mind sees them single and right side up. So
two waves of vibration break through our ears
upon the brain ; yet they fall in perfect time
and are reported as one sound to the spirit that
rides thus its double set of senses through the
marvels of the world.

One of the striking wonders connected with the
science of vision is the power which the eye has
of seeing several colors in the landscape or a picture and receiving one impression of symmetry and
beauty. Each hue is caused by a certain fixed
number of vibrations upon the eye, of inconceivable
swiftness. To get the sensation of redness the
retina must be affected a certain number of millions of times in a second. A violet ray, or a yellow one, affects the retina a different number of
millions of times in a second. And therefore to enjoy a glorious view in nature, or a triumph of art on
canvas, where blue and gold and purple are mingled, the eye must be played upon incessantly by
different sets of vibrations, and yet be quick
enough in its reports to hold the colors distinct
for the inspection and enjoyment of the mind.

A kindred marvel is connected with the ear.
Each object in nature is endowed with a peculiar
power of influencing the air by vibrations. The
ear is delicate enough in its sensibility to distin-

guish this whole gamut of the voices of things; and when fifty different instruments, or several stops in a leviathan organ, are pouring sheets of braided vibrations through its narrow tunnel upon its drum, it is not overpowered, but analyzes them, trembles to the most subtile pulsations that thrill through the surges of tone, detects whether the instruments or pipes are properly balanced and combined, and enables the mind to discern the grade of the sentiment and the degrees of genius that dispose and vitalize all. We are sometimes asked to admire the power of Cæsar, who could dictate to six scribes at once. In the cultured musical ear listening to a symphony, we have the phenomenon of some threescore reporters talking at once to an inward Cæsar, who yet rapidly combines their incessant speech into orderly information, and is free to respond also with his imagination and heart to the quality — inspiring, pathetic, or amusing — of the news they bring.

The eye is the channel of more direct introduction to the intellect; the ear is the broad highway to the heart of man. It is a suggestive fact in the pathology of afflictions, that total blindness tends rather to refine the character and make the life more spiritual. It sharpens the other senses, and makes them atone in some degree for the loss of light. Total deafness tends, on the contrary, to harden the nature, to make it suspicious, and rather to impair than increase the energy of the sister senses. This is the tendency, not always the result, for inward sweetness and nobleness will often counteract and conquer the drift of obstacles and infirmities.

But in this tendency do we not find a striking testimony to the value of music ? We can spare the eye better than the ear in education. Sound is closer to the soul as a stimulating influence than light and color. The eye is the gateway to the intellect ; the ear is the avenue to the sentiments that are the glory of our nature. There could be a heaven without light, but not without song, not without love and praise. The cherubim may have the keener eyes ; but the seraphim, no doubt, have the sweeter voices and the more delicate ear.

In an article contributed several years ago to an English review by a living essayist, Reason and Faith were represented in a charming allegory as two sisters who had each been visited with a sad affliction from birth. Reason was deaf, Faith was blind. So they joined hands for their perpetual journeyings over the globe, where day and night fall alternate. By day the eyes of Reason were the guide of Faith ; by night the ear of Faith was the guide of Reason.

The holiest influences from the eternal world are always figured to us as voices, not as visions. Whispers come, but spirits are not shown. When Paul speaks of having been caught up to the third heaven he does not allude to any sights, but to " unspeakable words " which he heard, that " it is not lawful for a man to utter." And in the

Scripture the Holy Spirit is figured as the wind, parent of music. What statement of music, either, of its mystery and spirituality, is more suggestive than the words of the New Testament, which were first applied half to the Divine Spirit, and half to the moving air which is its symbol: " Thou hearest the sound thereof, but canst not tell whence it cometh, nor whither it goeth " !

One of the richest chapters of natural religion, showing how the outward world has been created to be the servant of man and express his quality, might be drawn from the power of musical expression hidden in things and ready to be combined by genius. The alphabet of the musician is far richer than the alphabet of literature ; for the notes which he writes have different qualities and meanings, as they are struck from or uttered through the different substances which he impresses into his service to speak them. And the progress of musical science has been immensely aided by the enlargement of the vocabulary of things, — in finding out, as one has said, how " every known substance, wood, shell, horn, glass, copper, iron, steel, brass, silver, strings, skins, pasteboard, and even india-rubber, wait to be voices of feeling, and sing the passions of the human spirit."

You know how charmingly the Autocrat of the Breakfast-table has written about the ripening of a violin. " There are no less than fifty-eight different pieces in a violin. These pieces are strangers to each other, and it takes a century, more or less, to make them thoroughly acquainted. At last they learn to vibrate in harmony, and the instrument becomes an organic whole as if it were a great seed-capsule, that had grown from a garden bed in Cremona or elsewhere. The wood is juicy and full of sap for fifty years or so, but at the end of fifty or a hundred more gets tolerably dry and comparatively resonant." Now these fifty-eight pieces that thus combine to form the most princely instrument are types or suggestions of how all matter is toned and tempered to start vibrations with various qualities in order to enlarge the compass of expression for genius, and the resources of social instruction and joy.

And, still further, the delicacy with which matter is attuned to respond to and express the nicest touch or impulse of genius in the playing of music, deserves prominent place in any treatise of natural religion that would show how things have been created to express Infinite genius, and for the service and training of man. Sound travels eleven hundred and thirty feet a second; and the vibrations from any instrument a performer is playing will convey, not only the loudness or softness, the precision and swell of the tones, but also how much the inmost quality of the man as well as his fingers, or his breath, is involved in his work; whether his intellect is chiefly engaged, and how much he has and what is the grade of it; or whether his sentiments are uppermost, and what is their level fineness and intensity.

If we were to attempt an appraisal and allocation of music in the hierarchy of Arts, we must give it the credit of being the greatest in the line of pure creativeness. Other arts are in a large degree copies or selections.

A great landscape is a transcript from an actual picture by the Almighty, and a man here comes into direct competition with the Infinite genius. Noble sculptures are either reproduced, or culled from living symmetries. There have been faces in flesh and blood as noble as the Apollo, the Clytie, or the Venus of Milo. Grand historic paintings are drawn from described scenes. Some of the richest conceptions of architecture have been borrowed from the arching boughs of elms ; from snow scrolls ; from the interblended spring verdure of pine groves far up above their stately trunks ; from vine-embroideries, from rock-spires and cones, and buttresses of mountains, and from the oversweeping dome of the sky.

But music is a pure creation. It is not a thing, and it is not a copy. There are no hymns, no choruses, no symphonies in nature. What we call the music of nature is in the rough. It is not organized ; it is thrown out in masses. In the voluble melody of birds, in the voice of cataracts, in the sweep of storms, and the wrestle of winds with the leaves of a wilderness, there are only notes, or simple chords to suggest harmonies that are not realized. Mere imitative music is of a low rank, and always wears a charlatan character.

Perhaps there is a music of the spheres, but we can only imagine it, we know nothing of it. I have sometimes thought that if a blind spirit could be supported in space so as to hear, as this globe rolled by him, the notes that are borne on it, — the myriad-voiced melody of birds, the sweeping of winds over all the zones, and the sheets of sound, now sombre, now cheerful, — they waken from the forests which they stir, — the low, lisping penitence of the peaceful sea, and, through all, the thunderous mellow bass of the stirred ocean, beating on a thousand leagues of rock, — that spirit might imagine it was a mighty organ rolling by, touched on every key, alive in every stop, and aroused by every pedal to the praise of God.

But we can only conjecture what the blended voices of this planet may be when heard as a whole. In the music of nature, so far as we hear it in detail, no idea is worked into and struggles through even its vast vibrations. And it is only when a mighty thought or sentiment rolls through waves of sound, combining them so that they co-operate on our heart and mind, that pure sublimity begins. All else that we call sublimity is only a surprise of the senses.

Not a great many weeks ago I stood on the summit of the White Mountain ridge that over-looks New England, and heard the north-wind scream and roar. And I thought, what if this power could be made articulate,—what if it could be poured as a musical force through some colossal organ that a master genius might utter with it his sentiment of the night and mountain glory, and God the ruler of infinite space ! What if it could roll over New England thus, instead of its fierce monotone, an accompaniment, such as a religious master would conceive, to the seventy-seventh Psalm : " The voice of thy thunder is in the heaven: thy lightnings lightened the world ; the earth trembled and shook. Thy way is in the sea, and thy path in the great waters, and thy footsteps are not known ! "

Nature in her music seems to strive simply to set us the example of pure tone, smooth swell in volume, and delicate cadence and vanish. Listen to the elocution of the sea as it talks with the shore, and find how mellow, how utterly purged of all coarseness the serried thunder of its ground swell is, and how gentle the lisp of its last ripple that runs up a mile, perhaps, in length, like an army of little white mice nibbling the sand as they advance. No wonder that Demosthenes spent so much time by the sea-shore, " filling his mouth," as Mrs. Partington said, " with paving-stones, that he might learn to be an oratorio." He was trying possibly to catch the secret of volume and tenderness in sound. Hear the melancholy crescendo of a gust through a brotherhood of pines, and with what exquisite art of gradation it sighs away into calm ! Hark, in the summer to the sweet dactyls of the Peabody-bird, the Canada sweet-whistler in the mountain valleys, and admire the smoothness of that high soprano, and how it slides and tapers into silence like the polished sting of the bee, in which the microscope can find no raggedness or flaw!

The most valuable lessons in the management of sound we learn from Nature. And as to purity of tone, we must stand reverent, in the religious sense, before what she teaches us. For in this, as in the clearness of clouds and the transparency of air and the blaze of the sea-foam and the sparkle of moving rivers, she suggests to us the purity and holiness of God.

A great religious writer of our country, now living, has said, in a passage which I think stands on the higher level of American literature: " In the lofty passes of the Alps I heard a music overhead from God's cloudy orchestra, the giant peaks of rock and ice, curtained in by the driving mist, and only dimly visible, athwart the sky, through its folds, such as mocks all sounds our lower worlds of art can ever hope to raise. I stood (excuse the simplicity), calling to them in the loudest shouts I could raise, even till my power was spent, and listening in compulsory trance to their reply. I heard them roll it up through their cloudy worlds of snow, sifting out the harsh qualities that were tearing in it as demon screams of sin, holding on upon it as if it were a hymn they were singing to the ear of the great Creator, and sending it round

and round in long reduplications of sweetness,
minute after minute, till finally receding and rising, it trembled, as it were, among the quick grat-
ulations of angels, and fell into the silence of
the pure empyrean. I had never any conception
before of what is meant by quality in sound.
There was more power upon the soul in one of
those simple notes than I ever expect to feel from
anything called music below, or ever can feel till
I hear them again in the choirs of the angelic
world ! I had never such a sense of purity, or of
what a simple sound may tell of purity, by its own
pure quality. And I can truly affirm that the
experience of that hour has consciously made me
better able to think of God ever since, — better
able to worship."

When we say that music is a pure and uncopied
creation, we mean that in nature there is no combination of great sentiment and the developing
of an idea or emotion in sound. Man is the organ
through which the Infinite Spirit creates this addition to the treasury of beauty and the resources
of life.

And it seems to me that the method of a musical
composer of the first rank in producing his work
is the most subtile of all the processes of genius,
and nearest in kindred with the movements of the
Creative Intelligence. A sculptor slowly moulds
from his thoughts into clay that is not perfectly
ductile, and then translates from clay into more
stubborn stone. The painter finds it often impos-

sible to clothe in color the idea which his sketch recalls. The poet often finds that he cannot report in language the fire and melody that flash through his imagination. But with the musical artist, the thought and the arrest of it are instantaneous. The grandest inspirations of great composers are caught for all generations, without distortion or deflection from their first majesty and grace. The sign that entraps them, the bars that hold them, show them to us just as they swept into the atmosphere of their genius from the breath of God !

So far as dignity and subtlety of genius are concerned I should rather have been Mozart than Shakespeare. I know not how the conception of Hamlet, or Lear, or Othello dawned and swelled on the great dramatist's vision until it was wrought out in rhythmic and stately fact. But the process could hardly have been so mystical, so supernatural, so akin to the Divine calling of the world from nothing in a moment, as Mozart's creation, according to his own account, of a grand passage in a symphony or an opera. It did not come to him in a thin stream of melody, or in a theme which he expanded by a conscious mental effort, arranging it for various instruments and composing it in harmony ; but it burst full-voiced, as it were, from an ideal orchestra or a celestial chorus into his imagination, from which it was only copied into a mortal score. It was as if a whole act of "Hamlet" or "King John," with all its characters, interplay of passions, words and rhythm, should have streamed in one condensed flash into Shakespeare's mind, ready to be clothed in type, and to remain forever in the uppermost range of the creations of the human intellect.

It is only from instances like this, which the sphere of music furnishes more than any other region of art, that we can catch a hint of the movements of Infinite thoughts from which the whole order of nature has issued, and is sustained every moment as a starry anthem in space.

Whenever it is possible, I go to the Music Hall, in Boston, to enjoy the feasts of instrumental harmony, or the oratorios that ennoble many of our winter evenings.

On the platform, towering over the singers or musicians, is the bronze statue of Beethoven, a noble monument of the genius of Crawford, representing the master with his head bent, and a music sheet in one hand, upon which the other had just written the first notes of his choral hymn of joy. Sometimes I find myself led off from the harmony in thinking of the last appearance of that great man at a German festival in his honor, when the Ninth Symphony, closing with that sublime chorus, was performed. He was almost as deaf amid its grandeurs as his bronze statue in Boston is to the surges of sound that swell around it. He could not hear the tumultuous applause of the crowded theatre at its close.

A friend touched him as he stood on the stage

with his back to the audience, and made signs that
he should turn round and see the enthusiasm of
the thousands whom his music had thrilled. He
turned with a listless face, which at once struck
the multitude with a fresh consciousness of his
affliction. And then we are told that as the flood-
gates of pleasure, compassion, and sympathy were
opened, there followed a volcanic explosion of
applause, which seemed as if it would never end,
and which the master could not fail to hear as
well as see.

And recalling that scene the miracle of genius
seems the more fathomless. This man's most
original and wonderful creations were produced
when his earthly ear had been almost paralyzed,
and it was painful to hear him attempt to play
the piano. It was in this state that, out of pulsations borne to the ear of his soul, he wrought out
the architecture of harmony. And I can scarcely
ever look at that statue without recalling those
words which were first addressed to it when it
was received into that hall, — words that seem to
me most vividly to describe Beethoven's music : —

" What a vast, majestic structure thou hast builded out of sound,
    With its high peak piercing heaven, and its base deep under
        ground :
    Vague as air, yet firm and real to the spiritual eye,
    Seamed with fire its cloudy bastions far away uplifted lie,
    Like those sullen shapes of thunder we behold at close of day,
    Piled upon the far horizon where the jagged lightnings play.
    Awful voices, as from Hades, thrill us, growling from its heart ;
    Sudden splendors blaze from out it, cleaving its black walls
        apart ;

White-winged birds dart forth and vanish, singing as they pass
    from sight,
Till at last it lifts, and 'neath it shows a field of amber light,
Where some single star is shining, throbbing like a new-born thing,
And the earth, all drenched in splendor, lets its happy voices
    sing."

And reflecting thus upon the endowment which
Beethoven's genius has left to civilization, and the
sad privations of his own nature here, I love to
think that the scene in that German theatre is a
feeble symbol of the thrill which his spirit feels
in surveying the vast and purifying joy that sweeps
through tens of thousands of souls on this planet
every year in response to those creations which,
I believe, give the heart that appreciates them a
fore-feeling of the intellectual rapture of heaven.

The greatest privilege of a city life seems to me
to be its musical opportunities. In the cultivated
or mountainous country a banquet is provided for
the eye. And there, too, we can have intellectual
pleasures, — communion through books with the
best minds, thoughts, and experiences of our own
age and of history. The city alone can give us
a chorus, a sublime organ, and an orchestra. In
these some of the rich and manifest advances of
modern over ancient civilization are summed up.

If an old Greek should return to us, we could
show him no statuary equal to that with which
Athens and Corinth were crowded. We could
point out to him no architecture of a grade up to
the average of the temples that crowned the hills,
or shadowed the squares in which Sophocles or

Plato once walked. But take him into an opera-house or into a great concert-hall to hear the work of a modern master, and we could introduce him into an advance over everything that the age of Plato or of Augustus knew as music, no less remarkable than the progress of our practical science beyond the attainments of the classic times.

The name of Handel carries us on to another state. The highest music is religious. And in speaking of orchestra, organ, and chorus as supplying the supreme civilized privilege of the city, let me go further and express my belief that the greatest fortune which can befall a person in the line of art is — more than seeing Rubens's picture of the Descent from the Cross, or Titian's Assumption, or Da Vinci's Last Supper, or Raffaelle's Transfiguration, or the Dresden Madonna — to hear Handel's Messiah, when it is given with a competent combination of power and gifts.

We have the profoundest and most laden eloquence of the Bible trembling of itself with the most solemn emotions which God's law and grace can arouse. We have the feeling which these words, and the immeasurable facts they stand for, wakened in a great soul who entered by sympathy into the deepest evangelical sentiment of Christendom, and was competent to enshrine it in music. We have the instruments — organ and orchestra, the endowment of an advanced civilization — to give the body and shading of the master's idea.

We have the accomplished singers to render air or trio or quartette, and the fourfold volume of the chorus to give the ground-swell, swing, and majesty to the gathering hallelujahs.

I always wonder when I hear that oratorio that in every city a grand cathedral service is not made out of it, or out of selections from it, once a month, — certainly every Christmas, — that the promise of Christ, and the blessedness of his grace, and the beneficence of his reign, and the glory of his triumph may have fit interpretation in words and in ways that oversweep the petty divisions of catechisms and creeds.

. . . . .

It might, perhaps, be profitable and pleasant, if we had time for it, to speak of music as a method of expression, and of the manifest differences of style among the great masters. It may be questioned whether a very critical ear, sensitive to the slightest faults of execution, is a blessing. I have one or two friends who suffer so much exquisite misery in the course of a year from this cause, that I have sometimes been tempted to adopt the philosophy of the friends of Job, and believe that they are great sinners in their hearts, and are visited in this way by the whip of the Almighty, — a jangling cat-o'-nine-tail of sound. It would be, perhaps, better, so far as happiness is concerned, instead of suffering from this gout of the auditory nerve, to take the ear of the man who was asked if he was a judge of music, and confessed that he

knew two tunes from all others, Yankee Doodle
and Old Hundred, but could never be entirely
sure which was which. There is no art in which
there is such a range of capacity of appreciation
among intelligent persons. A Chinaman of considerable culture delights in a gong. A Turkish
plenipotentiary, invited to an instrumental concert
in Europe, where noble music was played, being
asked which piece he preferred, said that he
thought the first one was by far the most interesting. It happened that what he referred to was
the introductory tuning and scraping of the instruments.

The sensitive ear for mere niceties of execution
in detail may not be worth desiring, but there is
no worthier exercise of mind and culture of taste
than the study of the general style, flavor, atmosphere, and level of genius in a prominent composer and master. The pleasure of feeling the
central effluence from the soul of a great musical
genius streaming out of a work as a whole — of
being borne by it, as it were, into the climate
of his spirit — is granted to, or may be gained by
those who are strangers to the technicalities and
the science of music itself.

The difference in effect between a perfect poem
by Tennyson and a faultless passage from Wordsworth is not the difference merely of the sentiments which the lines may interpret, or the pictures they may draw. Their rhythms are different ;
their melodies are unlike ; the landscapes of their

natures are as diverse as the Bay of Naples and a Scottish frith. A mind sensitive to the radiation of genius feels that there is scarcely a verse in a volume by one, which the other could have written. It is so when we turn from Carlyle to Emerson. No writers are so frequently compared with each other, as though one had borrowed from the other. Yet there is hardly a sprig or bunch of words in any production of one which could have grown on the mental stock of the other any more than a pine cone on an ash. They are as unlike as the scenery and breath of a clear winter night, and a thunderous, savage summer noon.

There is the same difference, as decisively and more delicately revealed, among musical masters, in the aroma and color, the breadth, dignity, and elevation, of their works. It is rare to hear a passage from Mendelssohn that seems to have stayed long enough on the tree and in the sun. It seems to have been plucked a little hard, and scarcely ripe ; while every creative movement of Mozart's mind shook off melodies, juicy, mellow, sweet, and blooming as peaches, fit for the palate of an angel. And one of the richest pleasures flowing from an educated taste and continuous interest in music comes from the feeling of the predominant quality of each master through every work. We learn how substantial music is, though its kingdom is that of the air, when we find the innermost quality of the man permeating every chord and cadence which he does not steal ; the sense of sublimity before the simple forces of nature and the holiness of God veined with a tenderness as if the Book of Ruth were set in the substance of the Pentateuch that belonged to Handel ; the wild waywardness of Beethoven's genius, sea-like and stormy, heaving up from troughs of sullen shadow crests of melody to flash in the fitful sun ; and we see a distinct quality imparted to every air, duet, and chorus by the honeyed Bellini, the weird Weber, the rhetorical, florid Donizetti, the sparkling, superficial Auber, the luscious Rossini, the sunny and joyous Haydn, or the half-spectral, wholly delightful genius of Schubert, whose soul seems to have been compacted of the most poetic, warm, and genial moonlight that ever turned an earthly landscape into a fairy scene.*

But, ladies and gentlemen, it is time to relieve your overstrained and failing patience. Such associations as yours, diffusing, feeding, instituting

* The time fails us to speak of patriotic music. The singers of our great struggle as yet are the poets. No new and commanding melody or chorus has been created to enshrine the faith of the loyal States and the beneficence to humanity of our immense war. When victory and peace come, perhaps the fitting ode, with the fit wings of music, will burst from the genius of the nation. Perhaps it is well that, when the emblem of our nationality shall be uplifted above the cities and countries of rebellion, there shall be no new strains to salute the ears of the recovered aliens, but the old rhythm of Yankee Doodle, and the Star-Spangled Banner, and Hail Columbia, with one tune a little strange, perhaps, of which, when they ask the name as it shall be played by Union bands in Charleston and Savannah, they shall be told it is the John Brown Chorus over the downfall of slavery, — " Glory, Hallelujah ! " (1861.)

the taste for music in the community, organizing singers by acquaintance, sympathy, common practice, emulation, and charity, " which is the bond of perfectness," enrich our civilization, and supply one of the crying needs in the character of our country.

" Topmost crown of ancient Athens towered the Phidian Parthenon,
  Upon freedom's youthful forehead, Art the starry jewel shone.
  Never is a nation finished while it wants the grace of Art, —
  Use must borrow robes from beauty, life must rise above the mart,
  Faith and love are all ideal, speaking with a music tone,
  And without their touch of magic, labor is the devil's own."

There are two universal languages that spread civilization and ennoble society. The first is mathematics, the sign-speech of the intellect. There is no Celt or Saxon, no Jew or Greek, in that tongue. Whoever makes a statement or clinches a discovery in it helps the race. His page can be read by the mathematician in Arabia and Russia, though it was written in Paris or Cincinnati. Yes, the laws of form and light and motion are the same through all space, and Newton's demonstration of the law of gravity, and Laplace's " Mécanique Céleste," and Young's " Treatise on Light " could no doubt be understood by an intellect in Sirius or the outer edge of the Milky Way. Music is the universal language of the innermost spiritual nature. It can be understood in its signs and its voices, by races and by grades of spirits that cannot understand each other's speech, and that are alienated in all other ways.

" Underneath its world-wide Banyan, friends the gathering nations
    sit,
   Red Sioux and dreamy German dance and feast and fight to it."

Yes, and all that we cultivate of its highest
spirit in its great religious expressions here will
go with us as preparation for eternity. We shall
not talk German probably in the future world ;
but I do not know why the Andante of the Fifth
Symphony of Beethoven may not be played in
heaven. The angelic masters must be inspired
beyond our present capacity of appreciation if
they can produce anything that will make that
seem meagre. We shall slough off, probably, our
English vocabulary and tongue in the grave ; but
even in the final gathering of the redeemed out
of every nation, tongue, and clime one strophe of
the consummate Anthem to the Lamb and through
him to the Infinite who shall put all things under
his feet, may be the Hallelujah Chorus of the
Messiah, contributed from this earth to form part
of the everlasting language of the skies.

1858.

VII.

I SHALL have the privilege of addressing you on the subject of Existence and Life.

The great object which the Creator seeks to produce and sustain by the economy of nature is conscious life. The globe is the bulb of which life is to be the flower. The calendar of the globe is not dotted by years nor by ages, but by advancing steps of life. The great strata, whose formation we study with a bewildering sense of duration, are simply the dull dial-plate on which the celestial time is marked by the creative energy moving from worm to mollusk, from mollusk to fish, and thence to reptile, and on to mammal, and at last to man. God does not publish himself by ages, but by creations. When a new tendril is produced, or a new sense appears, or a higher type is introduced, or the skeleton flowers out from a wing into a forearm, or from a paw into a hand, so that wider control is gained of nature, then a new minute is noted on the chronometer that keeps the time of the Divine plan. It is evident that the world is provided as the basis for human life ; and man is broadly related to nature by his faculties, — is put to pasture, we may say, in the universe, that its harvests may pass up and be transmuted into his experience.

Have you ever thought how the human frame represents all nature ? It is a singular fact that even the proportions of sea and land on the surface of the globe are repeated in the human body, of which three fourths are liquid and one fourth dry. The bones of the human body represent the rocky skeleton of the globe ; the flesh and skin, the soil ; the teeth, the minerals ; the arteries and veins, the river systems ; the hair, the vegetation ; the nervous life, the galvanic and magnetic currents ; while the food, which is drawn from all nature — air, ocean, land, forest, and lake, tropic heats and polar cold, — for the support of the civilized constitution, pictures the fact that civilized life should be a reproduction into thought and feeling of all the elements organized into nature.

It is, therefore, life considered in its sources, the breadth and variety of the supplies of it, — life on the side of reception, leaving out of view the expression and expenditure of it in action, that I purpose to treat and that I invite you to survey.

We must begin by thoroughly comprehending the distinction between existence and life. It is a great mistake to suppose that people live to the same extent, or that they are equally alive, be-

cause they equally exist. The idea of more or
less of dignity or meanness, breadth and power,
cannot be connected with the word " existence."
Physical animation, the feeling that one is a conscious fact in the universe, determines that. Life
is a higher matter. Life consists in the putting
forth of faculties that are sheathed in our existence. We live by communion with the substances
of the universe, and the fulness of any life is
determined by the number of objects from which
a person draws nutriment.

For instance, you may hold in your hand a
dozen seeds, and you must say of them that they
equally exist. But you cannot decide, as you
look at them, even though they may be of the
same size, the amount of life of which they are
capable. They are tiny possibilities. Drop them
in the ground and their life begins. Each pellet
then shoots out the latent forces of its bosom.
Its delicate threads fasten on the clods for foothold, and it pushes its way upwards, climbs to
feed on the sun, the sky, and the clouds. But if
one of those seeds is that of a fragile herb, and
the other of an elm, the amount of life they will
gain will be immensely unequal, because one has
vastly more capacity than the other to draw in
from the treasuries of nature and reorganize it
into itself.

So any hundred infants are human germs of
which the word " existence " is equally applicable ;
but the life they are to experience and exhibit

will depend on the number and vigor of the faculties that will strike down, reach wide, and tower up into the universe to import nourishment from the stores of things.

Our physical life, which is the basis and type of all other vitality, consists in incorporating the physical elements. The amount of physical life is simply the amount of power we imbibe from air, electric force, food. Each man is a divinely chartered corporation to trade in the elements and products of the universe, and transform them incessantly into bone, blood, muscle, and strength. When this process of commerce with the riches of nature, of suction from its substance, ceases, — when the ability to gain or renew power stops, the body ceases to live. It may maintain its existence a while longer till its old fund is used up ; but it has begun to die.

The relation of the body, thus endowed by all space, to the real life of a human being, is that of the flower-pot to the plant ; it is to give the spirit room and shelter in the physical universe, that it may branch into the finer world to bud and bloom. To live for the body, instead of by and through it, is therefore to abdicate the privilege of our colonization in the material world at the start.

Is it not, therefore, a dreadful satire on the highest form of civilization that it is continually generating from its deeps thousands of beings whose labor and wit must all be expended, not

in living, but in continuing to exist? Think of
the armies of men and women that must pledge
all their time, breath, and genius, if they have
any, in "keeping body and soul together," whom
it costs the whole play of their faculties simply
"to fetch breath," and then think how wealthy
and bountiful this universe is! The lungs of a
human being are fed for nothing. If there were
a thousand times as many on the earth they
could be supported as freely as they are now.
It costs nothing to store their nerves with electric
power. There is light enough for as many eyes
as can be crowded on the globe; splendor, truth,
and beauty enough for as many minds as can be
gathered here; mystery and inspiration enough for
as many souls as can find foothold on the planet.
God provides inexhaustible stores directly for
every faculty of man but the stomach. And the
earth is opulent enough to feed myriads more
than are supported on it now. But the arrangements for the digestive system are left to human
skill and organization; and is it any wonder that
schools of socialism are springing up among us,
when this is the only department of human sustenance that is so miserably mismanaged as to
fail; when human wisdom has proved unable to
distribute labor over the soil so as to tap sufficiently the exuberant bounty of the globe, or
even to organize the transfer of what the earth
produces to the mouths of men, so that food
shall be cheap enough to keep every human crea-

ture in existence easily; when we have books in our advance countries talking about an overstock of human beings ; and when the awful pyramid of poverty, broad-based with the pariahs of heathenism, shows in its sloping layers the beggars of Italy, the half-blind miners of England and her starving operatives, the rag-pickers and outcasts of republican America, coming to its apex in the miseries of needlewomen and the " Song of the Shirt " ?

Schemes of socialism are started by the pressure on the intellect of this problem, whether the land does not belong to the race, just as the atmosphere belongs to the race, — whether man does not own it, and not men ; and whether any system of property for the soil which prevents a large mass of the world from getting a living, or which forces them to pawn all the noble possibilities of their existence for a mere living, is not as transparently wrong as pre-emption-rights and squatter-sovereignty in the air would be, — were it possible, — so that it should be let out to the majority at so much per cubic foot, or as the getting rich in acres of sunshine would be, which a man should hold in his own right and suffer to leak out here and there upon a house or field, at a fixed price per quart ! It is well to penetrate to the intellectual roots of startling theories. If it is an open, debatable question whether the land is not an element like atmosphere, light, and heat, the title to which is vested in the human stomach, we must expect to see project after project of social organization, till some one is found that will distribute labor by perfect science, and so multiply the products of the globe that food will be insured to every descendant of Adam, and life, as something higher than existence, be offered to the lowest member of the race.

When we think that the impeachment of society has been moved by the modern intellect because it forces crowds of minds, hearts, and souls to be mere satellites of the stomach, it is interesting to turn for a moment, in passing, to the Epicureans who prefer that scheme of existence, and who deliberately live to eat, instead of eating to live. If a human creature, lifted above all compulsion to do so, chooses to live for the sake of sensations and physical delights, it is an interesting question whether he would experience any conscious irreparable loss if he were turned into a plant that should have the capacity of feeling diffused through it, — that could taste the earth by its roots, and drink mountain-dew every night with its leaves! What vacancy would the striking out of brain and of sensibilities to the exquisite world produce in natures of that class? Their life is really an underground one, like that of potatoes, turnips, and beets, — where the upper faculties are simply the appendage to the lower, and valuable for the juices they carry down ; not like the tree, where what is underneath is important for what it sends up to faculties that revel in the light.

Think of laying open the sources of a human being's life and finding that he is built up — the interests and delights of his mind as well as his body — out of venison and turtle, so that his epochs are Burgundy and salads, French pastry and Moselle ! The Psyche in him, that should burst into the butterfly, confined wholly to the grub ! What should we say of an engine which, if the power of taste could be imparted to it, should spend its existence in munching wood, becoming very critical in the flavors of birch, hackmatack, maple, and pine, filling its boilers with alcohol, feeling the fire as a subtle pleasure over its steely nerves, and puffing away the steam without doing any work, or running its wheels for any purpose but to generate an appetite for the coming meal ! Such a machine, as a curiosity, would rebuild Mr. Barnum's fortunes ; yet a little insight shows us human types of such, plentifully scattered over society as the marvellous results of civilization !

The distinctively human life begins when we rise into higher spheres than the physical, and appropriate into our own substance material which they offer. And so the first thing to do in order to understand the comprehensiveness of life, compared with mere existence, is to widen our conception of the realities in this universe from which it is fed. The mind has a digestive system for truth, and appropriates it, assimilates it, just as the body assimilates meal. The law of cohesion is a thing for the mind, just as much as a brick that is ruled by it is for the hand. The law of attraction is a thing for the intellect just as much as a piece of steel and a loadstone. And a man who perceives them, and enriches his reason with them, broadens his life vastly beyond that of the man who deals in houses and estates as matters of property alone. He gets vitally into communion with wide substances of nature, while the other man uses them only mechanically to extend the scale of his existence.

A man, also, who understands bread-making. why yeast makes it rise, and how it nourishes the body, deals with the realities just as much as the man who mixes and kneads the dough, and derives substance from it as truly as by eating the loaf. Or, further, the man who discerns the relations of gold to geology, in what age it was cast up, how it was washed into stream-beds or mixed with the quartz, and how it is purified and coined, owns money as an intellectual being, whether he has physical control over it or not, because his life receives nutriment from the truth which invests it, and by which it is stamped ideally as a precious metal by the wisdom of the Creator.

Thus every sense is an avenue or duct for transmitting material of life to the mind as well as to the body. Strike the eye from the human race, and human life would thenceforth be palsied to the whole extent of the truth that knocks for entrance into the spirit at the optic nerve. Destroy the ear, and life is robbed of the nutrition offered by the truth that rides towards us on waves of sound, in conversation, debate, eloquence, music. We live just to the extent of our reception into the deeper nature from the rational vesture and effluence of things.

And beauty is as real a thing as a flower. The exquisiteness of a landscape is as substantial as the land. Where a man's spirit is stimulated and refreshed by such aspects of nature, his life is increased as really as it is sustained by the products of the soil.

How many artists are fed by the White Mountains! The corn and parsnips which the Saco meadows bear find their way to the cellars of New England, every winter, as provision for the body; but these men carry the slopes, ridges, rocky tendons and imperial dome of Mt. Washington itself with them. They unravel the lines of its beauty and strength, and turn them into instincts for the creation of beauty. They wind their powers around it like an anaconda around a goat, and crush it into pulp, — breathe in its mists, lap its sunshine, drink the aerial wine of its morning and evening hues, and feel it dissolve into their being, like the juices which the bee absorbs from a flower, to exude upon canvas in the spiritual honey of art.

Again, going up still higher, we find that the

meaning of things is no less substantial than
things themselves. The man who finds the existence, laws, and wisdom of the Infinite hinted
to him continually in the colors of the earth and
the mystic order of the firmament deals with realities as much as the man who sees the science
of the earth and the systems of the sky ; and
both of them are in contact with the substances
of things as really as the man who owns land and
eats the products of it.

When you look at a great picture, what do you
call the essential fact before you ? — the canvas
which the fingers can feel, the pigments which
possibly can be scraped off in a murky paste and
weighed, or the proportions of a human form
which glow on the cloth, and back of this, the
saintly expression that steals through the hues, as
though the soul of an angel had condescended
to be imprisoned perpetually there in color? So
the nature that has only material relations to the
universe, and acts as though physical things are
the chief fountains of life, simply crumbles in its
gross fingers the web on which divine splendors
and mysteries are outlined and tinted for the culture of the intellect, the charm of taste, and the
feeding of the life of the soul!

The great question, therefore, concerning a
man's life is, What tendrils has he out? from how
many grades of divine substance is he drawing
sustenance and power? We are put here to secrete something everlasting out of nature. The

opportunities are rich, but it is the capacity, the fibre, that determines whether we shall do it ; for nature contributes to our life, not primarily according to its bounty, but according to the filaments in us that will solicit and incorporate its bounty. One man absorbs mathematical truth out of the heavens, while side by side with him a mortal exists that organizes nothing grand or stately into his constitution, — just as the mushroom can do no more than hoist its pleated parasol out of the same ground and in the same sunlight from which the oak-seed imbibed slowly its tremendous strength. Another man draws to himself the wisdom printed in the granite leaves beneath us, which earthquakes have turned for our benefit, and shows that he has ennobled his life by it, and represents it wherever he moves. A third wins the divine thought hinted in the old bones which the globe entombs ; while a fourth fastens on history, and compels the laws of it to filter through facts and ooze into his reason.

Isaac Newton shoots out mental fibres that twine around every planet of the solar system. He not only expends his energies on the algebraic problems they offer, but absorbs the secret of their harmony, and builds up the sinewy symmetry of his intellect out of the juices of the divine thought they hold. He squeezed the moon and wrung the nectar of universal law out of it, as a school-boy sucks an orange dry.

Goethe has told us how much each of his

12

paragraphs and *bon-mots* cost him in gold. But really his education and the healthy vigor of matured genius cost all history and all art. It cost Italy and the East. It cost the calm laws that thread and sway the fever of modern civilization. For these were the sources out of which that serene, cold scholarship and wisdom were slowly secreted by the branching faculties that seemed to let no sphere lie ungrasped by their tough ligaments.

Think what it cost to cultivate and perfect the genius of Turner, the English painter! Search for the treasuries of his life, and you find him twisted in vitally with the Alps and the sea, — with the grace suffused in trees that makes their limbs bend in Gothic arches, that flushes the west with sunset-pomp, and flings the unsubstantial gold of evening over the meadow-grass!

Lieutenant Maury drags the sea, yes, distils out of it the complex and subtile forces that penetrate its deeps, hem and hurry its currents, and rein in its bounding strength at the pleasure of Him who said, " Thus far shalt thou go and no farther." He carries the essence of the ocean with him, as a power, a trophy, and a resource of his intellectual life.

See how Carlyle feeds his shaggy intellect out of the French Revolution, the storms of the Middle Ages, and the commotions in England, — rioting in the bitter wisdom which he crushes out of the laws of retribution that run through all history, and, Scandinavian Titan that he is, drinking the aqua-fortis of the Divine justice from the skulls of empires, like savory wine.

Think how Dickens, instead of being accidentally related, like most of us, to the men and women of our neighborhoods, — shaking hands with them, and entertaining a few by outward hospitality, stretches the antennæ of his sensibilities, sympathy, and imagination far and wide into our modern civilization, and is capable of draining the moral substance of London, — striking some tap-root of his intellect, affection, or humor into every alley, parlor, and counting-house of it, to refresh and enlarge his genius.

Or look up from the poor surface-existence of the senses, in which we are so apt to suppose that life consists, — from the pride and silly pleasures of a man who thinks it a great thing to be distinguished by his house and his money, — to the intellect of Humboldt which no house can cover ; broad-based as a mountain in the physical truth of things, its sides clad with the tilted strata of the earth, lifting its summit above storms and vapors, and catching some wisdom from each brilliant point of the heavens, as every star of the night flings a sparkle on the frosty cone of Chimborazo!

We often talk about a " live man." It is very seldom that we see one of our fellows who is half alive. Indeed, a great many of us, as to our humanity, are not born yet. The faculties that

inspire life have not opened their eyes.   A really
live man would be one, every bump of whose
brain should be a hopper into which material
would be streaming from all quarters of the universe to be ground up into internal riches and
strength.

Somebody once asked an eccentric friend of
mine, who is quite a vegetarian, what he found
fit to live upon ; and a day or two afterwards
the old gentleman showed his questioner a little
poem he had written in reply, saying, that he
breakfasted on Socrates, lunched on Pythagoras,
dined often on Moses or Paul, kept Plato as his
rare Johannisberg, and used Charles Lamb as
dessert, Tennyson and Shelley as cream puffs,
with Sydney Smith for Worcestershire sauce.
There was a meat diet for you, a wholesome
cannibalism of the soul !   And so we were made
to live on stars, and strata, and the philosophy of
Bacon.

Thus, as Emerson says, "we sit by the fire and
take hold on the poles of the earth."   The skies
are the market, and the globe itself the cellar,
and history the larder, from which the manna and
wine of truth are to be gathered freely by the
human nature, which the body clothes to support
and ennoble its life.   We merely exist among
things, if we do not penetrate by some pungent
faculty into the essence of some district of nature,
and feel it transmuted into our own being.   "A
man is a centre for nature, running out threads

of relation through everything, fluid and solid, material and elemental."

We must see, therefore, that space has very little to do with our real life. By casting latitude and longitude you can tell only where a man exists : where he lives depends on where his deepest interest is.

One man exists in the world of business ; but there are a score of chinks and crannies between the stones of his warehouse, his bales, crates, and ledgers, through which his interior nature sends out aspirations and appetites into the world of substance. Another man exists in the world of business, and lives there, too, in a mean and perilous sense. Old Paracelsus used to say that every man carries a demon in his stomach, who conducts digestion by processes of alchemy ; and you now and then see a man enclosing a goblin to preside over liver, spleen, and pylorus, cunning enough to pulverize money and turn it into a heart and sympathies so hard that you might break the paving-stones of Wall Street against them. Another man exists in the world of business, and desires to live by nobler faculties outside of it, but has not force enough to push any intellectual and delicate filaments through the casings of counting-room and store. He is an appendage to his occupation. The things he owns cannot be called his possessions ; for they possess *him*. He is their secretary, to keep the moth and rust from them, see to their insurance, cast their interest, and attend to the law-business they involve. It is not seldom that an estate or a warehouse jumps, in this way, upon a soul and rides it lean, like the Old Man of the Sea on Sindbad's back.

Yet let us not forget to say that the great merchant's life is no more confined to the limits of his visible sphere, or to the material objects with which he deals than a great poet's, or a great artist's life is. " Might you penetrate the inner counting-room of some mercantile establishment, — the merchant's brain, — you would find at work there an imagination whose sweep circumnavigates the globe, penetrates the policies of distant cabinets, and anticipates the prospects of remote kingdoms; studies the play of social caprices, predicts the yield of fields he never saw, and the fertility of seasons yet to roll; weighs in his letter-scale the chances of peace and war; with a prophetic vision beholds and secures, in regions now waste and unvalued, the spots that population is presently to seek; picks out the single gifted projector, the solitary, sagacious project, among the thousand visionaries and the ten thousand visions that wear an equal promise in ordinary eyes, and doubles and redoubles his fortune on a capital in which sagacity, forecast, meditation, and faith are the largest figures." Such men are among the noblest trophies of modern society. They live half a poet's life. Their schemes, benefiting the world, enlarge our conception of the breadth of living, and show us how cargoes of hides and ship-loads of cotton and restless bills of exchange are the busy shuttles of a unity of life which national prejudices, animosities, and hostilities of faith could never weave.

Where a man's deepest interest is, — not in the space he occupies, — there is his life. The learned blacksmith, Elihu Burritt, blows his bellows and hammers his iron in Worcester, Mass. ; but if you could look at his mind you would see fifty languages shooting out their feathery wings on it : look at his spirit and it is flying from land to land, like a dove, emblem of the genius of our religion, with the olive-leaves of peace. If one had hunted for the Apostle Paul in Ephesus, he would have been found, perhaps, working on sail-cloth in a tent-maker's shop ; but this tent of time was tattered over his head while he was at his toil, and there were mystic breathings and melodies in the air about him, which no observer could have heard, and a subtler light than that of the sun played about his needle as he stitched the Cilician canvas faithfully, — "a light that never was on sea or land."

"A man may dwell in Paradise and dream of a cabbage-garden, or he may dwell in a cabbage-garden and dream of Paradise." The dwelling shows where he exists ; the dream determines where he lives. So some men exist in Boston, but live abroad : the social problems, the art, or the scenery of Europe supplying the atmosphere

of their taste and intellect. Another man exists
to-day, but lives yesterday. The past is the
mould in which his mind thrives. He is vitally
related with Pompeii and ancient society and
Greek poetry, more than with Washington and
Kansas and Dr. Kane. Now and then you see
a man who lives so far in the past that he may
be said to be not so much behind the age as
behind all ages.

A man who does not believe with his whole mind
and heart in freedom, who will ever suffer himself
to sneer at it, or to carp at the eloquent vigor
of its western Magna Charta, the Declaration of
Independence, and who will allow any catch-
word or technicality to detain his sympathies
from the side where the spirit of liberty struggles
against fraud and force for new foothold, cannot
be said to live in America. He is spiritually an
Austrian, warmed by a western sun, fed by
American wheat, using the Anglo-Saxon speech,
protected and enfolded by a history with which
he has no vital sympathy, and which he feels no
sacred passion to continue. Is it difficult to tell
on which side his affinities would have fastened
eighty years ago?

Your next-door neighbor, who bows to you
courteously and shakes hands with you every day,
may live more intimately with Cicero or Mozart
or Napoleon than with any dwellers in the block
he inhabits. Taste and learning dissipate at
once the bonds of space and time, and open the

world of wisdom or of artistic luxury for man's abode.

I have often thought of the magical changes that would be wrought, if the pressures and dead-weights of the body could be annihilated, and the myriads of beings about us, like balloons cut from their fastenings, should range themselves at once into a society according to the affinities and specific gravity of their real natures. Fifth Avenues and Beacon Streets would then be gained and held by actual culture and inmost refinement; and all who had not these intrinsic titles to such regions would fall to the alleys and byways of the permanent universe, by sogginess of spirit. The real President — representative in his nature of the whole diameter of American history, from the faith that gnawed its way into Plymouth Rock to the fortitude that rebuilds the hotel in distant Lawrence — would rise to the true White House. And instead of the seeming huddled anarchy of our visible society, the latent order, which only the prophet sees, would become the conspicuous and palpable order : tiers of spirits would sink to the deeps of dissipation, misery, or remorse ; others would float on the strata of envy, pride, and self-love ; some would find the brilliant district of the sphere of truth through their controlling intellectual hunger ; others the rosy realm of beauty ; the selectest bands would be seen in the serene, warm light of charity : and so society would show the order of Dante's great poem,

12 *   R

banding itself in circles of life that narrow downwards to the base of the pit, and sweep up and yet up to the joys of Paradise ! *

* This lecture Mr. King left unfinished. From his hasty notes it would seem that he intended to show that the Bible was emphatically the "Book of Life." "How life is packed into it," he writes; "not an abstract chapter, — life of all the faculties of man." Again, "If we could see men pictorially, with the constituents of their life around them, we should see bees swarming around one, birds glittering around Audubon, fishes swimming around Agassiz, Swammerdam enveloped in infusoria, and Herschel with a star on his forehead." Another item is to this effect: "A rolling stone gathers no moss: a whizzing soul gathers no wisdom."

VIII.

THE EARTH AND THE MECHANIC ARTS.

I ONCE had the privilege, in the Observatory at Cambridge, of looking through a powerful telescope at the planet Jupiter. It seemed to be a ball about as large as the moon at the full, not white or silvery, but tinted with straw color, except at the poles, where it was deadened into gray, and showing leaden streaks across the centre which at a low power of the instrument appeared like one unbroken equatorial belt. It is a magnificent world, that planet Jupiter, — the leviathan of our solar sea. It is fourteen hundred times as large as our own globe, and seventy thousand times the volume of the moon, — whose size it resembles through the telescope, — and there it hangs; its weight, its mass, its interests, its mysteries, all reduced to a striped and tinted film moving, swimming in the blue firmament.

So our earth appears to a distant observer within our system. To some of the inhabitants of the side of the moon which we see (if there be intelligence there), it is a glorious globe, fixed perpetually in their zenith, fourteen times as huge as the full moon looks to us, delicately colored,

like Jupiter, and marked by belts, not perpetual
but changing.   What a poetic spectacle it must
be !   What verses must be written in celebration
of it by the Tennysons and Wordsworths among
our lunar friends !

We may well wonder what they think such a
vast orb was thus bathed in beauty for.   It must
look to them, as they study it with powerful
glasses, like a floating Arcadia, not made for
work but for dreamy joy.   And if one could be
brought gradually nearer to it, till at last we
could see the line of the morning or of sunset
travel over it, bringing out the rose and gold on
its mountains, flooding its turning and white-
edged seas with purple, bathing its hundreds of
miles of forests, and sweeping broad leagues
of prairie-green, the splendor would be so over-
powering that no thought of toil could be associated with such an abode.   Or if any work was
connected with it in the mind of such an observer, it would be that of artists only, students
and executors of beauty.   Perhaps, if seen as the
shadows settle on it, and it turns its vast disk
into the gloom through which only starlight
gleams, it might seem to be a sanctuary-orb,
fitted up for cloister-spirits to meditate in and
send up the worship of reverent and quiet aspiration.

But this is the distant view and estimate of the
earth.   As we come nearer to it its roughnesses
start out, its poetic hues grow fainter.   It stares

at us as a rugged reality. It is no Eden, in the close acquaintance. It is a sphere for hard and bitter toil,—a world to be subdued and tamed. It was not made for artists chiefly, or for pietistic dreamers, but for men with working clothes, and vigorous muscles, and the conquering implements of mechanical skill.

I am to speak to-night on the nobleness of the mechanic arts, — the true and permanent ground of our reverence for them, and the respect due to those who represent them. And this is the first thought which must arrest and hold us : the world itself was made by the Creator as a field chiefly for the display and advance of the mechanic arts, and for the education of man through the exercise and improvement of them.

In saying this I do not mean to say that literature of the highest order is not better, as an expression of human nature, than machinery ; nor that painting, music, grand architecture, all exquisite things, are not of loftier grade, as human products, than ploughs, furnaces, and lathes. I do not mean to say or imply that noble character, that sincere worship, is not the highest attainment, the consummate flower of the globe and society. And I am very far from suggesting or believing that the doom of the majority of the race is to be coarse and unintelligent toil.

Men were made to attain ideas and to exhibit and illustrate intellectual power on the earth.

But the chief proportion of the ideas gained and of the mental power developed by the residents of this globe is to be shown, not through the finer arts, but through the arts that transmute matter and conquer nature. When a seed is planted the intention is that air and soil and light and rain shall be worked over into a vital and organized product. Now the human intellect is placed on the globe to work as a transmuting and organizing power on the matter of the planet, to subdue it to intelligent, useful, and moral purposes, and to set its forces in new and noble combinations for beneficent ends.

The mastery of the earth is the chief command and trust which the Almighty has committed to mortals here. It is this command which ennobles labor, and places the mechanic arts, through which alone the mastery of the earth is gained, in their central position as expressions of human power and symbols of human duty.

Some of the most striking and brilliant chapters of natural religion are opened by a study of the relation of man to the earth as the elaborator of matter. I recall with great interest and satisfaction the instruction I received, five or six years ago, from a little book published in New York, from the pen of Thomas Ewbank, entitled "The World a Workshop." Such a book does immense service by connecting large ideas with the branches of skilful labor, and I remember how deeply I was impressed by it as a new and rich contribution to natural religion. Every mechanic ought to own it, and read it and re-read it. I do not know that it is on sale in this city, or is in the libraries here. Possibly it is out of print now, although I hope not.

As soon as we grasp the conception that man was made to be an artificer of matter, to gain control of the planet, and build up civilization, and enlarge his own intellect and nature by that work, we detect distinct and charming revelations of Divine thought and plan in the connection between man and nature.

See the relation between the muscular power of man and the force of gravitation. That is the basis power on which, by which, and with which we are to work. If a man with his present muscular force were placed on the sun, he could not move. His frame would be crushed at once by the tremendous pull of the sun's mass upon him. Place him on Jupiter, and he would not be half so strong as now. He would stagger along as if he had not too much but too little spirit, or as if, like one of the German turners in the formation of the living pyramid, he had two men and a boy standing on his shoulders. Place him on the first of the satellites of Jupiter, and he would have ten thousand times the physical power he has here, and could easily jump ten or fifteen miles. We can easily conceive the relation between the strength of the frame and the force of gravitation to have been such that men would not be half so free, and that the mechanical powers could not have been half so efficient. Mechanic arts and triumphs are provided for in the primary fact of the proportion between our muscles and the globe's dead pull.

I will not speak at any length of the structure of the hand in relation to the arts by which matter is subdued. You are all familiar with what may be said on that point. Man alone is endowed with a hand; and in the combination it reveals of strength with variety of motion, in the nice adjustment of firmness to delicacy of perception, in the balance between the softness of the flesh and the sensibility of the nerves and the toughness of the muscles, in the forms and relations of the fingers and thumb, in the provisions wrought into its structure for holding, striking, pulling, feeling, weaving, spinning, and the numberless methods of service which the useful and the fine arts require, are seen some of the most recondite proofs of Divine skill and far-reaching adaptation that have enriched the science of natural theology. The strength of the elephant and the instinct of the bee would be poor compensation for the paralysis of a nerve, or the subtraction of a muscle from its composition. When God formed the hand of Adam, the mastery of the whole planet by the human race was prophesied and provided for.

Consider, too, the structure and composition of the earth's crust in connection with the call of man to be a great artificer. If the strata of the globe had been laid even, and in the order of their heaviness, and if the metals had been made by Providence in pure masses unmixed with ore, as coal is, or granite, the possibility of almost all the arts would have been annulled. But the comparative lawlessness of the distribution of the strata, the intermixing of material by convulsions and earthquakes, the creation of metals in the ore state so that they can be broken, handled, and artificially fused into masses compact and pure, place the globe at man's disposal, instead of making him its slave. The study of iron, coal, and granite, as related to civilization, and to their places in the earth's crust, opens one of the deepest, richest, and most mystic volumes that embody the beneficence of Providence. No man can help standing with uncovered soul before the organization and interests of labor, who becomes acquainted with the provisions, ages on ages before the advent of man, for the supply to the future workshops on the globe of coal and iron. The old forests of buried geological epochs, which grew when no human being could have breathed the planet's air, the play and fury of the central fires that seem in a narrow view only disastrous, and the lawlessness of the strata of the globe, which might be easily conceived the freak of chance, turn out eloquent witnesses of the presidency over all ages of a plan which contemplated man as the master-workman of the future, the large-brained and noble mechanic, for whom the most ample and various supply of material must be provided, that his cunning and his genius might be at once stimulated and equipped.

It is wrong to touch points like these, which require particular illustrations to vivify them, and to leave them in general statement. But the field of particulars is so rich that a lecture would be monopolized by any one department of them, and I must only sound the keynote, hint the music to which it points, and pass on to consider in another aspect the nobleness of the arts that are engaged in dignifying and transmuting matter.

For thousands of years society has been struggling against a prejudice that labor upon matter, except in the most refined and artistic ways, is degrading. According to the highest aristocratic prejudice, even the sculptor's and the professional architect's employment is demeaning, in comparison with the ineffable honor of plenty of inherited money, having nothing to do, and doing it. But all lower methods of handling matter, working it into useful forms, and putting ideas into it, are accounted incompatible with pretension to position, — utterly under ban. To be a soldier, an orator, a poet, — to be able to express skill and genius in destruction, or thought, fervor, and sentiment in breath and words, is consistent with some claim to social standing high and secure ; but to express conceptions in machinery that create wealth and happiness, to utter talent and genius through new combinations of matter and force, puts the ungenteel stamp upon the brow of the body and the spirit.

The literature of republican principle has been wrestling with this estimate for centuries. How to throw back this scorn of creative toil, how to prove, in behalf of labor, that direct dealing with matter is not degrading, and that the mechanical departments of work and service are of worthy rank, and are not to be abased before haughty insolence, and are not to be called on to defend themselves either, — how to do this, and make the protective argument felt as an impeachment of those who arraign toil, has been the eager aim of those whose sympathy with the race is widest and most penetrating.

It is well to point to the necessity of skilful and creative labor, and to show that what is necessary to the existence of civilization cannot but be honorable. It is well to call attention to the utility of such labor, and to make the vast array of services which the elaborating arts have rendered to modern centuries speak for the workers whose busy fidelity they express. It is well to wing and speed the arrows of satire at those who believe that dainty uselessness is the height of nobility, — that the pond, and not the river, is the type of excellence, — that the lotus, and not the oak wreath, is the true rewarding crown.

But the sovereign answer in behalf of labor is this : God is the great artificer. The Saviour

said, " My Father worketh hitherto, and I work."
The Infinite intellect is perpetually dealing with
matter. There is not a particle of it that is not
vitalized, moved, and moulded by him. You
think it low to be a carver of wood, do you,
my dilettante friend? Show me a square inch
of wood on this orb that the Creator has not
fashioned! Ship-building, or the construction
of timber-bending machinery, is not in accordance with the tests of the best society, is it?
Show me a natural oak-knee which the Creator of forests has not bent! Working iron into
innumerable uses by the aid of implements that
enable the hands to wield it, and to deal with it
when heated, imparts or suggests some social
contamination, does it? What do we say of the
Creator, who has beaten and heated and alloyed
every atom of the rough iron of nature? Opening mines and dealing in coal soils the conven-
tional position, by the world's ordinance. What
judgment have we for the Lord of all things, who
has carbonized and blackened and packed away
in the cellar of the planet every flake of the
countless myriads of tons of that subterranean
Ethiopia which is now yielding its crystallized
fervor to the needs of civilization?

The old mythologies depicted a separate Deity
for each district of nature. Jupiter presided over
the air and the lightning, Vulcan over the mechanical processes ; Neptune swayed the sea,
Pluto the central depths of gloom and fire. But

modern religion has brushed away these fancies. God is the vitality of all nature. He is the fountain of all force, and the giver of all law. He is in direct contact, not by arms and fingers, but by his spirit, with every atom of the globe and of all worlds. He is the artificer, and works in matter by bringing his spirit in relations to it far more intimate than we can by our muscular handlings of it, — more intimate than the dealing of our spirits with our bones and blood.

We speak of God as the artist of nature, — its painter and ornamenter. But he is also the infinite manufacturer and mechanician. Beneath all the polish of beauty is the roughness and strength of the Vulcanic labor. Talk of a plated iron warvessel that can float and yet resist a broadside ! Think of our globe as a granite-sheathed steamer floating on air, — her plates of mail compacted, bolted, and clinched by the Almighty himself, and the flame of Mauna Loa and the smoke of Cotopaxi hinting the deeps and terrors of her furnaces. Talk of a clipper that cuts the latitudes indifferent to frosts or fervid seas, and rounds Cape Horn with glee. Yes ! we may well be proud of her. Those that build her may well sing, —

> " Up ! up ! in nobler toil than ours
>   No craftsmen bear a part,
> We make of Nature's giant powers
>   The slaves of human art.
> Lay rib to rib and beam to beam,
> And drive the treenails free ;
> Nor faithless joint nor yawning seam
>   Shall tempt the searching sea."

Yet of the stanchest clipper we must say, —

> " Her oaken ribs the vulture beak
> Of northern ice may peel ;
> The sunken rock and coral peak
> May grate along her keel ;
> And know we well the painted shell
> We give to wind and wave
> Must float, the sailor's citadel,
> Or sink, the sailor's grave ! "

But think of a comet like our last visitor, that is built with fleecy sails to cross every latitude of the planetary world, to sweep far out beyond the Cape Horn of the system into boundless cold and night, and then to bend, to point her misty prow towards the invisible sun, to obey a helm that keeps her true through the bleak star-watched ether to move on till he becomes visible again, to hasten then as by a pressing breeze, to cross once more the track of the sluggish orbs, to fly nearer and nearer, seeing him swell as she approaches, and at last spreading more canvas, skysails, studding-sails, as she rushes into splendor, sweeping around him again, true to the predicted hour in a course of a thousand years, no soil, no barnacles, no tattered tackle upon her, and shaking out, as she passes the hot goal, a broad pennant of light that streams fifty millions of miles !

Or shall we raise the question of steam-engine building and a railway-track, and of its worthiness as a business in a social point of view? When we are about to settle it, suppose that we think of the sun and the solar system as an engine and train of cars, and ask who built them, and with what expenditure of time and thought and interest. For, besides the circular motion of the planets around the sun, the sun himself, with all his train of globes and satellites, is plunging on in space, four hundred thousand miles a day, towards a determined point among the fixed stars.

God is the artificer of matter. Not an ounce of it within the bounds of space that he is not upholding, penetrating, changing, moulding, every day. He deals with nothing else that we can see. He utters no audible word. He prints with no type. He puts his lessons to us, all his wisdom, all his warnings, all his eloquence, all his love that outward nature holds, into matter as he himself wields and shapes it. The world is a laboratory, a mill, a forge, a factory, as well as an expression of beauty; every particle of matter at some time passes through these stages to be subject to the hammers and the acids and the implements of the Infinite himself; — and we have not settled yet in our high places if labor is honorable, if we do not rise in worth and the scale of humanity as we get farther and farther away from any useful contact with forces and things!

We may be told, however, that all labor is honorable in the degree that it embodies and sets forth ideas, and therefore that literature must always take precedence of the arts of invention, because it deals directly with ideas, and reaches the intellectual nature as an educating force immediately.   I acknowledge the principle that the grades of nobleness in labor are determined by the amount of intellect involved in them, or uttered through them.   And I maintain that the mechanic arts of the last fifty years are not humbled at all before the printed or spoken literature of the last fifty years, as expressions of thought, imagination, the toil of the highest intellectual faculties.   Can there be any question where the greatest amount of original thought has been shown during the last generation, — in the records of Patent-Offices, or in the catalogues of publications by the chief booksellers in Christendom ?

When we talk of sentiment, tenderness, aspiration, pathos, love, the moral qualities that breathe through books, or the musical creations of great artists, and the sweetness of rhythm and the delicacy of form in poetry, we talk of things which cannot be measured with any of the triumphs of inventive art.

But as to pure force of intellect, I believe that far more has been expended upon the world, in the last two or three generations, through the channels in which labor flows, than through the avenues that are esteemed especially intellectual.

What speech has been made in seventy years, which displays such original triumphs of reason and imagination, which holds in solution the results of so many weeks and months of severe thinking, as the steam-engine, even as Watt left it ? I doubt if there is such a thing in all literature.

What volume of essays is so new among the products of thought, is so original as a piece of thinking in things, as the carpet-loom, or the carding machine, that seems alive with pure intellect, or the sewing-machine, — I will not say which one for fear of bombardment, — or the last and bust lathe, which will turn you out, as you please, the model for a Chinaman's boot or a marble facsimile of Daniel Webster?   Where will you find a stroke of statesmanship to rival the conception that spans the St. Lawrence with welded iron tubes, in spans of a thousand feet, and bolted so that the heaviest laden trains shoot through them as on granite?   What theory, on any large problem of church, state, law, or civilization, has been so thoroughly worked out and harmonized with facts, in the last century, that it can compare as an expression of sinewy and comprehensive thought with a model iron steamer, which mechanicians can now build so that it may be suspended by stem and stern, with all its machinery on board, or poised in the middle, leaving the extremities unsupported, without breaking·?

Or let me invite you, in part through the glowing language of another, to visit an immense foundry, and witness " the costly preparations for some great casting of iron, — the bed-plate of a vast marine engine, for instance.   The sooty workmen, at mine and furnace, have been long at work digging the ore and blasting the iron.   There it lies corded in yonder piles of ugly crudeness and

13   s

grim strength! Here, beneath this lofty roof, full of rough and shapeless materials, of vast cranes, and monstrous tackles and chains from which the world might hang, with the dying light of day struggling in from windows in the roof, and the flaming light of furnaces flashing up from its floor, the preparations have been and are still going on! For months the skilful workmen, in the moulding-sand that forms the floor, have been busy, with firm and cunning fingers, forming the mould, with every mortise, bolt-hole, groove, stay, inclination, anxiously adjusted and arranged; and there it lies buried in the ground. Near by, the furnaces, heated seven times hot, hold the obdurate metal seething and boiling in their hellish jaws. From minute to minute the doors are opened, and out flows — amid flames and sparks that threaten the destruction of the building, and amid which the workmen stand as unharmed and unterrified as the three men that walked in the prophet's furnace — buckets of molten iron, that are borne with staggering steps and emptied into the vast caldron, from which the mould is finally to be filled. The long-expected and anxiously prepared-for moment at length approaches, nay, it is precipitated; for the door of the reservoir leaks with the immense weight of its raging contents. At a word the channels for the molten iron are cleared; the foreman stands at the bursting gate; the workmen, with bars and tools suited each to its end, take their posts; while the master, standing over the mould, and looking calmly but earnestly round, finally gives the signal! Up flies the gate, forth leaps the furious current, the channels blaze with fire, the mould trembles and smokes with the rushing contents, the loosened gates explode from their tubes; but silence and suspense hold the assembly yet. The master stands intently watching the shrews for signs of any superfluity of metal. Perhaps there has been miscalculation and not enough! Perhaps the mighty weight has crushed the mould, and the metal is sinking into the ground! Perhaps the casting is a failure, and the labor of months is to be repeated! A moment must settle the results of a whole quarter's toil; the profits of years of industry are at stake; the pride of the engineer, the suspense of the workmen, all feelings of sympathy are concentrated in this anxious minute. But lo! just here bubbles feebly up the tardy metal, rises a few inches above the surface, and stops, — not a gallon of metal to spare, not a hundred pounds over, in a casting of forty tons! Success— proud, happy, glorious success — has crowned the arduous work!" *

Think of that adjustment of means to ends, that careful, thoughtful insurance of harmony, symmetry, and strength, in the immense product! How many novels have been written in the English tongue, since foundries like this first saw the light,—how many plays have been wrought upon

---

* Bellows's "Restatements of Christian Doctrines," p. 298.

paper! And what number of novels, do you suppose, have shown a plan so broad, a mould so
strong, a relation of parts so cunning and exact,
a proportion of power so admirable, that they can
as intellectual achievements compare with such
a casting of a bed-plate? There is hardly a novel
written in English now, whose work does not look
flawed, distorted, pinched, or "sloppy" in the
contrast.

Turn from the department of pure literature to
the government of the world, and you shall see
new testimony to the amount of intellect that has
been poured through the mechanic arts in the
last fifty or sixty years. Great mechanics have
done far more in that time than great politicians,
great statesmen, or great generals to affect permanently the fortune of nations.

Men in the places of civil power think that
they chiefly mould or modify public interests, by
their direct dealing through votes, speeches, and
schemes with a nation's laws and life. But however much they do, it is the movement of the
great social forces below political ones — the
drift of things — that determines good or evil for
a people. And these social forces are guided,
intensified, or changed very much by the control
gained and established over the powers of nature.
Think what wonders the mechanic arts of locomo-
tion have wrought on colonization the last forty
years, — the moving of myriads from one country
and clime to another without serious social jar!

Think how the mechanical aids of industry, increasing many fold the wealth of the world, have raised labor into power in the state, and stealthily modified constitutions to meet and fit the new conditions! It would be impossible, hereafter, for France to sink to such a social condition as she was in during the two generations that preceded, caused, and justified the French Revolution of 1789. It was not the eloquence of Grey and Brougham, but the declamation of the steam-engine, that produced the passage of the Reform Bill a generation ago in England ; and the machinery of the island is now pulling, straining, altering her social charter, her whole system of church and state, with a leverage and a piston and pulley power which are resistless, in favor of larger representation of the people who crowd the factories and feed the furnaces and looms.

Even in morals the effect of improvements wrought by mechanical skill is often wonderful, and puts to shame the intentional consecrated labor of moralists themselves. In the countries where fires are necessary for a large part of the year, think what beneficent influence on family life, on temper, on the spiritual as well as real atmosphere of home, the invention must have been that utterly prevents smoky chimneys! And I have no doubt that the cheap production of gas and the kindling of the gaslight in the streets of cities have directly prevented more crime, in the last twenty years, than half

the sheriffs and half the philanthropists have succeeded in doing.   In the Book of Job we read
of the morning light taking hold of the ends of
the earth and shaking the wicked out of it, —
majestic poetry clothing thus in imagery the
hostility of light and crime.   And now in the
streets of great cities the ruffian cannot say,
" Surely the darkness shall cover me," for, as by
the presence of God, " the night shall be light
about him," and a noontide safety is poured over
walks that border the lairs of iniquity.

Geologists tell us that in some districts of the
earth the whole land, mountains and all, from the
shore-line, is slowly rising, borne up by quiet
continental forces underneath.   We conceive the
inward energies of the planet as acting through
volcanic throes and earthquake fits of passion
solely, which are nothing to the noiseless power
that works below the earthquakes, and lifts the
rock-foundations of an empire.   So in the moral
raising of society, through the progress of mechanic art, ennobling labor, spreading comfort,
giving power to the people, befriending the good
causes and interests of civilization in a thousand
subtle ways, we notice the play of the continental moral forces working from beneath the explosive ones, and bearing up more and more of
society in light and better air.

In whatever point of view, from whichever side
we study it, the fact appears that the human race,
as a whole, were made to be workers in matter, to

change it into new forms, to get education in doing it, to express their education again in doing it, to advance civilization thus, and in such ways to rise into fellowship with the Omnipotent chemist, geometer, and mechanician of the world.

Every man who is fixed for life in an occupation ought to have the habit of regarding it at times from the highest point of view, and especially of rising into a feeling of kindred with the illustrious masters of it. If a man is a preacher, let him consecrate some hours by the thought of the men — Mason and Chalmers and Channing, Fénelon and Bourdaloue, Luther and Knox, Bernard, Chrysostom, and mighty Paul — who have worn the same robe on souls electric with the Holy Ghost. And let the thought that he is of that lineage inspire him, whatever be the proportions of his gifts, and keep him true.

If he is a teacher, let him feel what his profession, as a whole, is doing for the world to-day, and, remembering that Agassiz is daily employed in it, and heroes like Dr. Howe, and that the name of Thomas Arnold glows on its roll, let a consecrated pride in its worth and its names animate his will and encourage his heart.

If he is a merchant, let him not fail to feel, now and then, that his warehouse or office is one tile in the vast edifice of credit, interblended interest, and confidence, whose arches span from London to Canton, which, more than any other influence, knits the nations into unity ; and let him vow that his character by its looseness or its knavery, shall not be an element of danger or decay in that noble pile.

And if he is a mechanic, let him think how the globe was wrought out on the creative wheel through patient and expectant ages when man was not, but was foreseen in the creative thought. Let him think of constructive toil as

> " A blessing now, — a curse no more ;
> Since He whose name we breathe with awe
>   The coarse mechanic vesture wore, —
>   A poor man toiling with the poor ;
> In labor, as in prayer, fulfilling the same law."

And let him study the biographies of the great mortal masters of the mechanic powers, the stalwart thinkers in God's dialect of force, — Watt and Franklin, Arkwright and Cartwright, Whitney, Fulton, Whittemore, Stephenson, and Brunel. Literary men read the stories of their struggles, their wrestle with the great secrets of nature, like Jacob with the Spirit, refusing to let go till the blessing was yielded, their single-eyed devotedness to their track and their truth, with admiration and with touched hearts. How should they who are of the same calling follow the record of their careers and triumphs ! There should be niches in every mechanic's memory, where, through faithful and repeated readings of their lives, these spirits should stand as noble monitors and friends.

The papers tell us that, next week, commissioners will be chosen to represent the Pacific Coast at the World's Fair at London next May.

If we were to choose from the whole planet a
score of men to represent us on some other globe
or in some other system in a great human fair of
the universe, it would not be kings, dukes, prime-
ministers, the richest men, we should appoint as
ambassadors to show what our race is, and what
it is doing here, but the great thinkers, artists,
and workers, the thinkers in ink, the thinkers in
stone and color, the thinkers in force and homely
matter, the men who are bringing the globe up
towards the Creator's imagination and purpose ;
and on this mission the leaders of mechanic art
would go side by side with Shakespeare and Milton, Angelo and Wren, Newton and Cuvier.

In England, now, they are preparing statues of
Brunel the engineer, and the Stephensons, father
and son, to be finished and erected about the
same time with those of Macaulay and Havelock.
The nation is beginning to bow to the occupations and the genius that have added to her
power ten thousand fold, — is beginning to bow
to labor, noble, glorious, sacred labor, which, in
partnership with the thoughts of genius, is changing the face of the planet as by a wand of miracle,
preparing in no slight degree the advent of His
kingdom, and fulfilling His deep purposes, who
labored on the planet myriads of years before
Adam was moulded, a breathing statue from the
dust, and who now calls man to partnership in
his plans.

And how can we honor labor and the arts that
raise it, most successfully ? By right thoughts of

it ; by ennobling ourselves, if any form of it is our calling ; by erecting statues of its great representatives in our hearts ; and by the fervor, the duties, and the sacrifices of patriotism now.

For our national struggle is not only for a capital city, for the old geography, for the Mississippi and Missouri, for the hallowed parchment of the Constitution, it is also for the dignity of labor. The daggers of conspiracy strike at that. Through the rent Constitution, through the holes of the Declaration of Independence, which they scorn, the traitors seek to stab the doctrine of the humanity and rights of the classes everywhere that toil. They proclaim, at the mouths of their artillery, that the state is built right when votes are restricted, and when lords stand high and insolent on the trampled muscles of those that toil. Their three-barred flag, emblem of infamy in every thread, is symbol also of this apostasy. Let us accept the challenge. Let us see in the stripes and colors of the dear old national banner the streaming representative of the rights and worth of labor ; and let every bared arm and swelling muscle swear fealty to it now, with the deeper passion. Let it be ready, if need comes, to throw down the hammer for it and take the sword. And let the crime against it be avenged, as it only can be, by the smiting down of every tattered rag of the rebellion, before the spirit and valor of men who will suffer no empire to be founded in America on perjury, treason, and insult to toil !

1861.

IX.

DANIEL WEBSTER.

ON one of the mountains of New Hampshire, in the Franconia Pass, hangs a great stone face, which tens of thousands of tourists from all parts of the country have looked up to with awe. Many, doubtless, who now hear me have seen it, and remember how they felt when first

> "The giant image broke on them,
> Full human profile, nose and chin distinct,
> .   .   .   .   .
> And fed at evening with the blood of suns."

So, for many years, for the full space of a generation, the brow and features of one man seemed to stand out high and majestic from the solid ridges of New England character and intellect, — a prominent part of its natural scenery. The very name of the man suggests the texture and strength of granite by the combination of its syllables, — Daniel Webster.

I shall never forget the first time I saw him. It was on Bunker Hill, the 10th of September, 1840, at the great Whig gathering there of twenty thousand, in the Harrison campaign. Half a dozen stands were erected on different parts of the field for speakers ; but, a boy of fifteen, I was indifferent to all speaking, and was in search of the figure of the great Senator. I was eager to see the fountain-head of the eloquence we had been declaiming at school. At last I descried on one of the far-off platforms a mass of dingy grandeur which was unmistakable, and struck what is called a "bee-line" for it through the crowd. I pressed up very near to the platform, and caught the flash from under the thunderous brows, and saw a genial glow upon the face. He was introducing a tall Virginian to the living mass around him. These were the first words I heard : "What shall I say of you, my friend? This, gentlemen, is Benjamin Watkins Leigh of Virginia, a Whig true to the backbone." Then he slapped him on the shoulder with a force which proved that Mr. Leigh, without question, belonged to the class of vertebrata among politicians.

When a shower suddenly scattered the thousands, I managed to keep close to Mr. Webster as he left the field, seizing every opportunity with the utmost impudence to see the play of his features. And at any time after that day I would have gone farther to look upon his face than to see the Notch of the White Hills or Niagara. It was my fortune to listen to his great speech in 1842 in Fanueil Hall, after the Ashburton Treaty, when he flung back the taunts of his party because he had remained in the Cabinet of Mr. Tyler.

His oration on Bunker Hill at the completion
of the monument in 1843 I listened to. I saw
him in Fanueil Hall in November, 1844, on the
evening of the day that brought the news of Mr.
Clay's defeat. The vast room, dimly lighted,
was packed with men in a quite sombre mood.
And when the swarthy statesman stepped upon
the stage, and suppressed the cheers that hailed
him with the opening words, proudly declaimed,

> " What though the field be lost !
> All is not lost ; the unconquerable will,
> And study of revenge, immortal hate,
> And courage never to submit or yield,
> And what is else not to be overcome !
> That glory never shall his wrath or might
> Extort from me,"

the scene was a grander representation than any
picture by Martin of the council which Milton
paints, when the defeated spirits gathered to hear
their dread commander, who,

> " Above the rest
> In shape and gesture proudly eminent,
> Stood like a tower."

Afterwards in 1849 I heard him deliver a historical address on the Constitution ; then in 1850
the speech in Boston when he said that Massachusetts must conquer her prejudices ; after that
his final speech in Fanueil Hall.

Vividly do I recall the last time I saw him.
It was a warm day of the spring of 1852. Mr.
Webster was walking very feebly along Washington
Street, Boston. His hat was pulled low over his

brow, and he seemed anxious to escape the notice of the crowd that gathered to follow him. He wore an olive-green frock-coat, and around his neck and shoulders hung a massive gold chain. Possibly you will like to hear the inscriptions on its clasp. On one side was engraved, "To Daniel Webster, the Defender of the Constitution, and the Advocate of the Union." On the other side, "Manufactured by Woodruff and Addison, San Francisco, California, September 29, 1849." In reply to the letter which presented it he wrote thus about California : "At last we have seen our country stretch from sea to sea, and a new highway opened across the continent from us to our fellow-citizens on the shore of the Pacific. Far as they have gone, they are yet within the protection of the Union, and ready, I doubt not, to join us all in its defence and support. [Yes, we are ready still !] They are pursuing a new and absorbing interest. While their Eastern brethren continue to be engaged in agriculture, manufactures, commerce, navigation, and the fisheries, they are exploring a region whose wealth surpasses fiction. They are gathering up treasure in a manner and in a degree hitherto unknown, at the feet of inaccessible mountains and along those streams

'Whose foam is amber and their gravel gold.'

Over them and over us stands the broad arch of the Union, and long may it stand, as firm as

the arches of heaven, and as beautiful as the bow
which is set in the clouds ! "

The old man, ten years before, had saved his
country by the Ashburton Treaty from the desolation of war on the easternmost frontier.   It was
fit that, as he walked in the streets of the oldest
city of the Union, a few months before his death,
he should wear a decoration to associate his
genius with this youngest city of the extreme
West, the farthest limit of the empire which, so
long as it obeyed and revered the Constitution,
could not outrun the reach of his love.

Then came the solemn Sunday, October 24,
1852, and the tolling bells to tell us in Boston,
before church-time, of the death in Marshfield : —

> " What ails the morning, that the misty sun
> Looks wan and troubled in the autumn air,
> Dark over Marshfield ?   'T was the minute-gun :
> God ! has it come that we foreboded there ? "
>
> " This mighty spirit is eclipsed ; this power
> Hath passed from day to darkness ; to whose hour
> Of light no likeness is bequeathed."

And speedily was reported to us there, speedily to
the whole land, too, the final scene in the statesman's sick-chamber.   We speak of the death of a
great man in old age sometimes as the wreck of a
weather-stained bark on pitiless rocks, sometimes
as the furling of tired sails in quiet port.   Neither
of these images fits that death-scene.   Neither
of them is profoundly Christian.   The calm fulfilment of every duty, and the reining up of the
faculties to obey the mastery of the will; the

desire to know when the experience of dissolution was to commence; the solemn tones of prayer, laden with the riches of his language and humble with penitence; the farewell to family and friends, majestic and tender, as he felt that he was floating out beyond earthly reckonings and the outlines of human charts; and then, after the broken ejaculations of the psalm for the Divine rod and staff, the silent close ! — not a wreck on the desolate coasts of mortality, — it is we that are on the shore, — the fading rather of a noble ship into the mists that curtain the horizon, its sails all set, bearing one great and serene form beyond our gaze into the ineffable light, and into an experience where he could say more truly and intensely than on earth, " I still live ! "

We must now give some minutes more particularly to his biography.

Mr. Webster was born the 18th of January, 1782, in Salisbury, N. H. When his Puritan father built his log-cabin there, no pioneer hut sent up any smoke or prayers into the sky between this clearing near the head-waters of the Merrimack and Montreal. The young Daniel was born in midwinter, on the frosty verge of Pilgrim civilization, under the auspices and influence of the North Star.

The name is Scotch, and the large majority of the Webster stock were of the Scottish type, — of light complexion and hair, tall, slender, and bony. But Daniel's grandmother (Bachelder by name) was of the dark and bilious mould and temperament. Mr. Webster said in 1840 : " We are all indebted to my father's mother for a large portion of the little sense and character that belongs to us." The boy Daniel was of her type, not of the Scottish pattern, — youngest and darkest of ten children. General Stark told him once that his complexion was admirable for a soldier, because burnt gunpowder would not smutch it. He never obtained, however, even amateur military distinction. When fifty-four years old, he wrote from Washington to one of his sons who was disappointed in regard to a military appointment : " We are predestinated not to be great in the field of battle. I once tried to be captain, and failed ; and I canvassed a whole regiment to make your uncle an adjutant, and failed also. We are not the sons of Bellona's bridegroom. Our battles are forensic ; we draw no blood but the blood of our clients."

His father had served in the French war and in the Revolution, and on the little farm in Salisbury was engaged in a genuine Puritan hand-to-hand fight with nature and the wilderness, wringing subsistence for a wife and ten children out of a thin penurious soil, and a climate divided into three parts, — nine months winter, two months breaking up of winter, one month setting in of winter.

There were no luxuries in the farm-house, and

T

very few books. So much the better. There
was opportunity for the farmer-boy to learn the
Bible thoroughly, and know Watts's Hymns by
heart, and commit a cheap pamphlet-copy of
Pope's " Essay on Man " to memory, and get a vigorous appetite for knowledge from the annual visits
of the almanac, whose poetry and anecdotes were
devoured with an eagerness that left a smack
on the mental palate. If you want a boy to have
tough mental fibre in after life, keep him in childhood on a few strong books that he must chew.

When he was eight years old, he saw in a
country shop a cotton handkerchief with something printed on both sides of it. He gave his
whole stock of hoarded pennies to secure it, and
absorbed its contents that night with his keen
dark eyes, on his father's kitchen floor, by the
light of the roaring chimney-fire. What painter
will be first to make that scene perpetual in our
country's history and art? It was the Constitution of the United States, just then in the dawn
of its beneficent power under the lead of President Washington, that the New Hampshire boy
was then stamping on his brain. He told the
story himself in 1850, and archly said, " I have
known more or less of that document ever since."
If a Californian, without excess of reverence, had
heard him say that, he would have been apt to
break out in the Pacific vernacular, and exclaim,
" You bet ! " Forty years from that winter came
the great Hayne debate. But I would travel

farther to see a master's picture of the lad, reading the Constitution in the rude home on the
edge of the northern wilderness, than to see
Healy's great painting of the orator in the senatorial struggle against the theory and passions of
secession ; as I would go farther to see a picture of the springs of the Amazon, far up under
the cold white splinters of the Andes, than the
most adequate representation of the imperial
river's tropical tide.

The father had not been able to give any of his
children an education. But Daniel, the youngest,
was of too feeble constitution to work much on the
farm, and he was sent to an academy. The father
pinched himself sadly to bear the burden. The
New Hampshire hunters after moose buckled a
strap around the stomach in their journeys, and,
when provisions were very scant, drew the strap a
hole or two tighter to prevent or deaden the gnaw-
ing of hunger. That is what the old father did
morally, — he drew the strap tighter to give one
boy an education, and the older sons said that
" Dan was sent to school, that he might know as
much as the other boys."

He gained rapidly as a student, but could never
get courage to stand up and declaim before his
companion-scholars, — a difficulty which did not
seem to affect him seriously in the Senate in later
years. His father then determined to send him
to college. He tells us what a warm thrill went
through his frame when the old man, toiling up a

hill in the snow, broke the news to him, and how he leaned his head on the sturdy father's shoulder and wept. At fifteen he became a freshman in Dartmouth College ; at nineteen he was graduated, all the class feeling that he was destined to eminence.

But when half his college term expired he determined that Ezekiel, his brother next older, should be educated also. And so rapidly was the purpose carried out that, in the year in which he graduated, at nineteen, Ezekiel, twenty-one, entered college.

And then how he worked for him, to pay the expenses of Ezekiel's college life ! He went to Fryeburg, near the White Mountains, to teach school for thirty dollars a month. But he found that in the winter evenings he could earn twenty-five cents each by copying deeds, and that in a long evening he could copy two. By this extra toil he paid his board, and saved his monthly salary untouched, to gallop with to the tall, light-complexioned, serious Ezekiel, who in looks seems to have been a Scotch Apollo. Thirty years afterward Mr. Webster told a friend that the ache was n't out of his fingers from that Fryeburg copying. No, and the nobleness was not out of his soul !

In college he seems to have blended a very serious intellect with a great deal of humor ; and in the letters that have been preserved which he wrote to college friends after his graduation, from nineteen to twenty-three, there is a rich overflow of fun. He was given to rhymes. After his first

experience of the weed he versifies his profound
gratitude to its soothing quality : —

> " Come, thou, tobacco, new-found friend,
>   Come, and thy suppliant attend,
>   In each dull lonely hour ;
>   And though misfortunes lie around,
>   Thicker than hail-stones on the ground,
>   I 'll rest upon thy power.
>   Then, while the coxcomb pert and proud,
>   The politician learned and loud,
>   Keep one eternal clack,
>   I 'll tread where silent nature smiles,
>   Where solitude our woes beguiles,
>   And chew thee, dear tobac."
>   WEBSTER (*nineteen years*).

Young ladies in the country seem to have had
a tendency to fall in love with the large-browed,
sad-eyed, dark, and handsome youth. Comte,
the French atheist, considered the eye imperfect,
and thought the solar system could be improved.
In a letter to a friend the young Webster makes
this physiological proposition : " If there should
be a new edition of human nature, I think it would
be found expedient to give girls stronger ribs, and
a thicker covering for the heart. I say a plague
to the girls, if they can't keep their little beaters at
home." (Suppose that nature should refrain from
making pale, olive-skinned geniuses, with noble
features, and eyes large, sad, unworldly, incapable to be fathomed. Perhaps the ribs would be
strong enough then.)

There certainly were no pecuniary temptations
to great softness in the left side of the dam-

sels towards the young graduate, for he writes thanks to one of his classmates for his excellent receipt for greasing boots, but says, "mine need other doctoring, since they admit not only water, but peas and gravel-stones."

> " What nonsense lurked within the pate, oh !
> Of definition-making Plato,
> Who sang in philosophic metre,
> ' Man is a rational and biped creature ' !
> Many do think, and so do I,
> Old codger, that you told a lie ;
> And yet perhaps, you surly lout,
> There is a hole where you 'll creep out ;
> Males you call rational, but no man
> E'er heard you say the same of woman ! "
>
> WEBSTER (*twenty-two years*).

The richest records of those years of earliest manhood relate to his efforts to keep Ezekiel afloat in college. It was no easy task, after the Fryeburg school-keeping and deed-copying were over. Genius was maturing, but to a young law-student in New Hampshire dollars came hard. A farmer's dollar is not made as Mr. Emerson tells us the city dollar may be, by the skit of a pen; his bones ache with the work that earned it. Ezekiel writes from college : —

"Money, Daniel, money. As I was walking down to the office after a letter, I happened to find one cent, which is the only money I have had since the second day after I came on. It is a fact, Dan, that I was called on for a dollar, where I owed it, and borrowed it, and have borrowed it four times since, to pay those I borrowed of. Yours without money,

"EZEKIEL."

Daniel writes from Salisbury : —

"I have now by me two cents in lawful federal currency; next week I will send them, if they be all. They will buy a pipe ; with a pipe you can smoke : smoking inspires wisdom ; wisdom is allied to fortitude ; from fortitude it is but one step to stoicism; and stoicism never pants for this world's goods. So perhaps my two cents by this process may put you quite at ease about cash. We are at home in the old way ; boys digging potatoes with frozen fingers, and girls washing without wood. Write me ; tell me your necessities, and anything else you can think of to amuse me. Be a good child ; mind your books and strive to learn. "DANIEL."

So for two or three years the correspondence runs on, filled with records of poverty, affection, and fun. Daniel's spirits seem always to wax as money wanes. He says he has discovered what the fulcrum was which Archimedes needed to move the world, — cash. Once he borrowed eighty-five dollars to send to Ezekiel, and it was lost by the stage-driver. Here was a blow indeed. These are the young Daniel's reflections in a letter to his brother, — I am afraid you will not discover in them a senatorial stateliness or severity : —

"Fol de dol, dol de dol, di dol ;
I 'll never make money my idol;
For away our dollars will fly all.
With my friend and my pitcher,
I 'm twenty times richer
Than if I make money my idol;
Fol de dol, dol de dol, di dol ! "

Through all he had a presentiment of coming fortune. In another letter he writes: "Zeke, I don't believe but that Providence will do well for us yet. We shall live, and live comfortably."

He did see Ezekiel through his troubles. He helped him into position, fame, and competence. Ezekiel became one of the first lawyers of New Hampshire, and one of the noblest, as he was one of the most majestic men of New England. Mr. Webster always spoke of him as the most commanding and imposing person he had ever seen. Until Ezekiel was comfortably established, the two brothers had but one aim, one purse, one welfare, and one hope. Their love was as that of David and Jonathan, "passing the love of women."

In 1804 Mr. Webster went to Boston as a law-student, and was a poverty-stricken youth there, where fifteen years later his income was over fifteen thousand a year, — a sum equal to more than double that amount to-day.

In 1807 he opened an office in Portsmouth, N. H. I was a school-boy in Portsmouth thirty years ago; and people then told with affectionate pride of the young lawyer with the slender frame and splendid eyes; and how he used to improvise the most humorous stories for children, about people that passed by the window; and how superbly he read Shakespeare in evening circles; and what a powerful opponent the great Jeremiah Mason found him in the courts; and

how Mr. Mason used to say that never was such
an actor lost to the stage as he would have made
had he chosen to turn his talents for humor and
mimicry that way.

Six years he served at the New Hampshire bar,
and was then sent to Congress, at thirty-one years
of age, in 1813.

Clay, Calhoun, Lowndes, Pickering, Gaston,
Forsyth, were the commanding names there. Mr.
Webster had never before been a member of a
deliberative assembly. He had not studied the
ropes of that ship. He never was a member of
any State government, except for ten days in the
Massachusetts Legislature, and then he introduced
and carried a bill that no man should catch trout
in the State in any other way than by hook and
line. At one bound, when he first took the floor
in Congress, he put himself in the first rank of
American parliamentary speech and thought.
His address on the war-question was so weighty
with historical knowledge and temperate logic ; it
was so lofty and calm in tone, so free from rant
and " splurge," so fit to go into permanent literature as a piece of strong and decisive writing ; it
was arranged with so much tact and uttered with
such dignified force, that Chief Justice Marshall
made the prophecy that the new speaker would
become among the very first, if not the first
statesman of America. And Mr. Lowndes said,
" The North has not his equal, nor the South his
superior."

14

Two terms he served in the House, and then, in 1816, removed to Boston with his family and devoted himself to the profession of law. In 1818, when thirty-six, he argued in the Supreme Court of the United States the Dartmouth College case, and won a position as a great constitutional lawyer, not merely of the first rank, but of a new type. In 1820, at thirty-eight, he sounded a new note in American literature, by his Plymouth oration on the second centennial anniversary of the landing of the Pilgrims.

I once heard a Yankee farmer compare Mr. Clay and Mr. Webster thus: "I 've heerd 'em both: with Mr. Clay the hearing on 't is more than the reading on 't, but with Mr. Webster the reading on 't is enough sight more than the hearing on 't." In Plymouth the old citizens will tell you, to-day, how sublime the spectacle was, when Mr. Webster, towards the close of the address, uttered his denunciation of the slave-trade: "In the sight of our law the African slave-trader is a pirate and a felon; and in the sight of Heaven an offender far beyond the ordinary depth of human guilt. If there be, within the extent of our knowledge or influence, any participation in this traffic, let us pledge ourselves here upon the rock of Plymouth to extirpate and destroy it. It is not fit that the land of the Pilgrims should bear the shame longer. I hear the sound of the hammer, I see the smoke of the furnaces where manacles and fetters are still forged for human limbs. I see the visages of those who by stealth and at midnight labor in this work of hell, foul and dark, as may become the artificers of such instruments of misery and torture. Let that spot be purified, or let it cease to be of New England. Let it be purified, or let it be set aside from the Christian world ; let it be put out of the circle of human sympathies and human regards, and let civilized man henceforth have no communion with it." He stood in front of the high pulpit to utter his address. The pulpit was filled with clergymen. Soon he turned half round, extended his hands, and lifted his blazing eye to the preachers that were leaning over, and said in tones, such as Moses might have spoken, and with a look such as Moses might have worn, fresh from the awful holiness of Sinai : "I invoke the ministers of our religion, that they proclaim its denunciation of these crimes, and add its solemn sanctions to the authority of human laws. If the pulpit be silent, whenever or wherever there may be a sinner bloody with this guilt within the hearing of its voice, the pulpit is false to its trust."

Alas for the perishableness of eloquence! It is the only thing in the higher walks of human creativeness that passes away. The statue lives after the sculptor dies, as sublime as when his chisel left it. St. Peter's is a perpetual memorial and utterance of the great mind of Angelo. The Iliad is as fresh to-day as twenty-five centuries ago. The picture may grow richer with years.

But great oratory, the most delightful and marvellous of the expressions of mortal power, passes and dies with the occasion. It is

> " Like the snowfall on a river,
> A moment white, then gone forever. "

But the reading of this address was as " great " as the " hearing " of it. It seemed like the utterance of an incarnate century. Old John Adams, then more than fourscore, wrote to him : " Mr. Burke is no longer entitled to the praise, the most consummate orator of modern times. The address enters more perfectly into the spirit of New England than any production I ever read. It ought to be read at the end of every century, and indeed of every year forever and ever. It will be read five hundred years hence with as much rapture as it was heard."

The sentences may be printed, word matched with word and thought linked to thought in perfect sequence, caught by the nimble cunning of stenography ; even the punctuation, each semicolon and every stop, may be arrested and made perpetual. But the cadence and the tones, the swells and sweeps and subsidence of feeling, the terror and the pathos, the vivid poetry of gesture and attitude and eye, — the living lightning that poured through words from the deeps of the soul, from the mystic deeps of spirit, — all this is evanescent as the lightning. Even music may be immortal here. The symphony can be raised, generation after generation, from its dumb signs.

The cavatina and the chorus may be retranslated, by adequate voices, age after age. But the orator in his sovereign oration, — Demosthenes speaking for the crown, Cicero against Verres, Massillon over the body of Louis XIV., Sheridan denouncing Hastings, Webster pouring out appeals massive and gorgeous for the integrity of his country, — each of these is an organ shedding a music which can never be played again.

In 1822 Mr. Webster, then forty, was chosen Representative to Congress from the city of Boston. During the next six years he made his celebrated speeches on the Greek question and on the Panama mission ; his oration at the laying of the corner-stone of Bunker Hill Monument, in presence of Lafayette, and his eulogy on Adams and Jefferson ; his great speeches on the Tariff and the Judiciary in Congress, and among other important arguments in the Supreme Court of the United States, the splendid, novel, and triumphant argument in favor of a citizen of Georgia, by which he broke down a monopoly, in the State of New York, of certain rights within their waters, and maintained the ground that the commerce of the country, under the Constitution, was " a unit, " so that the rights of ship-owners of all sections were equal in all waters of the Union. New York was beaten and Georgia triumphant, although every court of the Empire State had decided in favor of its State rights. But New York did not call a convention, or threaten to secede.

These eight years, from 1820 to 1828, were Mr. Webster's happiest years. The range of his powers had been exhibited. He was on the way to a large fortune. He was in full health. He was happy in the affections of a devoted family. He had risen to the head of different professions which seem to require powers that one would think cannot be joined in one man.

It is not for me, to-night, to speak of Mr. Webster's party-position, or to give any opinion upon the questions of tariff, bank, or treasury upon which he was so widely at issue with other honest and eminent men. I am to speak now of his genius. The remarkable fact in his genius was that he was so eminent in different and rival spheres. In the fulness of his powers he was master of the best method of speaking to a jury, of the best method of speech to the Supreme Court of the nation, of the most fitting style of address to a great popular audience on a commanding anniversary, of the highest style of parliamentary debate, and of the eloquence most pertinent to the Senate of the United States.

His leading brethren at the bar have remarked this, that the lawyer did not hurt the statesman, nor the statesman the lawyer. What man of all the great names of dominant Englishmen in the last hundred years has been first in the House of Commons and first in the highest English courts? It has been felt there that supremacy in one department is unfitted for supremacy in the other.

He seemed to be like a monster cannon, — good for a jubilee when it is eloquent roar that is needed, good for the field when it is a sixty-four-pound shot that must be sent to plough through the battalions of the foe. Yet this was not due to a remarkable flexibility or versatility of genius and faculty in Mr. Webster.

If one could reach the pole, he would stand at the meeting-point of all the lines of longitude; he could turn at pleasure, and by a few steps enter Europe or America or Asia. Mr. Webster stood at the focus of many lines of intellectual power and utterance, at the meeting-point of popular, forensic, statesmanlike, senatorial oratory and influence.

Mr. Webster's eloquence was always founded on facts and the broadest view of facts. It was not a display of sensibility or imagination or speculative skill. Nothing is more dry than facts given by items, summed up by addition, when the mind is enslaved to them and stands below them. Nothing is more winning and fascinating than facts set in broad lights by a mind that masters a large field of them and stands above them. The country looks prosaic when you trudge slowly through it, rod by rod : see it from the mountain-side, and you have the gorgeous colors of poetry poured at once over the whole domain. The landscape is instantly eloquent and kindles all classes of mind into delight.

Mr. Webster's power before jury, senate, audience, and court was in this broad view which made facts sublime. A critical friend of mine at the East was fond of saying that Mr. Webster was inductive, Mr. Calhoun was deductive, Mr. Clay was seductive. This is as true as it is brilliant. Mr. Webster never attempted to seduce the judgment of his hearers by playing upon their impressibility; nor to drive them into a logical corral, by acute deductions of practical results from speculative assumptions, narrowing as he came down. He tried to induce conviction by throwing open the facts, and asking his hearers to rise with him where they could see the broad masses of light and shade. He was a great reasoner, not a reasoning machine.

His understanding embraced the whole extent of a subject, methodized its complicated details, discerned its general laws and their remote applications, and exhibited the whole to view with a clearness of arrangement which rendered it perceptible to the simplest apprehension. As a reasoner he had hardly an equal among his countrymen, either in the sharp, swift, close argumentation of vehement debate, or in the calm survey and powerful combination of facts and principles.

By this method he held a jury as he held Chief Justice Marshall or Judge Story; he commanded the Senate as he commanded Faneuil Hall, or an acre of Whigs at a mass meeting.

And his style was admirably wedded to such a method. How broad it is, and yet how clear; how rich, and yet how simple ; how energetic, and yet free from all coarseness and audacity ; how easy, and yet what dignity ; how rugged, and still not rough ; how impassioned often, yet never passionate ; how opulent in imaginative suggestions, and yet how severe in its rejection of ornament !

You will not find a dozen figures of speech, you will not find half a dozen elaborate similes, in all the published productions of his pen. In this how different from Burke ! The " Arabian Nights " is not so gorgeous as Burke. His later pages are like the sunset : Mr. Webster's great pages are like the noon. He hated adjectives. He did not, like Mr. Choate, " drive a substantive and six." He loathed all " splurge." Sinew and simplicity, nouns and facts, he clung to, and made eloquence result from the breadth of the field of fact on which his intellect cast light.

I recall here his criticism of a line of Watts about an angel moving " with most amazing speed." This, he said, was bad. What meaning is there in the phrase " most amazing speed " ? It conveys no sense. " It would amaze us," he said, " to see an oyster moving a mile a day ; it would not amaze us to see a greyhound run a mile a minute." He loved statement, comprehensive and decisive, positive utterance, downward inflections, — not the fervor that stirs, so

14*

much as the emphasis that settles feeling. If he could make a thing seem great, he would leave out the adjective " great."

Byron said that he had heard Curran talk more poetry in a speech than he ever put into verse. Mr. Webster's sensibility was always under control ; his imagination and his passions worked through his reason, never overriding it ; no rhetoric or fancy or sentiment escaped him raw, in mere gushes from an excited temperament, but his most fervid or gorgeous passages were weighty with thought. Generally he kept close to the earth, or if he mounted it was by climbing, ridge above ridge, steep beyond steep. But when he soared, it was no movement of flimsy fancy ; it was the solid condor's body that was borne aloft on the mighty wings of feeling, high over the Cordillera spires of his understanding.

And his personal presence was part of his genius. What he said seemed to be truer and grander at the moment for his saying it. When Thorwaldsen, the Danish sculptor, saw the cast of his head in Powers's studio in Rome, he said, " Ah, a design for a Jupiter, I see ! " He would not believe the artist, when assured that it was an actual cast from a living American. The coalheavers in England, Mr. Emerson says, followed him with awe, as a representative of one of the elemental forces of nature. Sydney Smith remarked that he was a steam-engine in trousers, and complained of him as a living lie, since

nobody on earth could possibly be as great as he
looked.

When he rose to address a great audience on a
theme that possessed him, he was the full incarnation, to the eye, of a philosophic statesman.
Then the words of the Old Testament rose into
new meaning : " This Daniel was preferred above
the presidents and princes, because an excellent
spirit was in him." Then the highest office
seemed to be nothing but the proper pedestal to
set the proportions of his greatness in appropriate position and relief. Every one felt that there
was an ample mind fitly embodied, — itself a
spiritual state-house or capitol, rich with the annals of constitutional history, filled with the lore
of national and civil war, studded with apartments
that were crowded with records of diplomatic wisdom, freighted with the principles and statistics
of public economy. Every one felt that his eye
was constructed to see the truth and proprieties
of national relations ; that he knew the coasts,
shoals, and soundings of national experience ;
that his arm had vigor to grasp and guide the
helm of state.

And when he spoke, even in his simplest passages, the power of a great personality was manifest. His common-sense was ponderous and
even sublime by the momentum which his arm
and inflection gave it, and the dignity which his
diction imparted to it. No triumph that he ever
won seemed to require the whole of his resources,

or to drain the hiding-places of his strength. The movement of his mind was like the sluggish might of the sea. Though his genius has thrown up into literature the most brilliant spray of rhetoric and imagination, its natural movement and suggestion was the ground-swell of a resistless and unfathomable power. And hence his eloquence had always the serious and self-assured strength that made it competent to the utterance of a nation's thought and purpose. He would have been more fit, by language and manner, than any other man reared on this continent, to represent the American republic in a world's congress of prime ministers and kings.

Some three or four years ago there was a literary party in London at the house of the venerable poet, Samuel Rogers, then ninety years old. He had known Burke and Pitt and Fox and Sheridan personally. And late in life he became acquainted with Mr. Webster in England, and corresponded with him. At the party, on the mention of our dead statesman's name, Mr. Rogers said, " I knew him ; I received letters from him. Edmund," he continued, turning to a servant, "bring to me Mr. Webster's letters. Daniel Webster," said he, when he took the letters in his hand, "was not only the greatest man of his age, — he was the greatest man of any age."

The years from 1820 to 1828, as we said, when every step of his complicated genius had been sounded, were his prosperous and happy years. His resource from care was fishing. Trout and blue-fish acknowledged his genius as well as courts and senators. They flocked to his hook. In bait and debate he was equally persuasive. Feeding cattle, or wading for trout, or hauling blue-fish through the surf, when they pulled like horses, he would say to his companions, "This is better than wasting time in the Senate, gentlemen!" It was while fishing for trout in Marshfield that he composed the celebrated passage on the surviving veterans of the battle for his first Bunker Hill address. He would pull out a lusty specimen, shouting, "Venerable men, you have come down to us from a former generation. Heaven has bounteously lengthened out your lives that you might behold this joyous day." He would unhook them into his basket, declaiming, "You are gathered to your fathers, and live only to your country in her grateful remembrance and your own bright example."

In his boat, fishing for cod, a day or two before the address was delivered, he composed or rehearsed the passage in it on Lafayette, when he hooked a very large cod, and, as he pulled his nose above water, exclaimed, "Welcome! all hail! and thrice welcome, citizen of two hemispheres!"

For many years an Indian was the servant-companion of his fishing recreation. Mr. Webster was very generous with him, and the Indian was a strongly attached and faithful dependant. But once or twice he became sadly intoxicated (the Indian, of course), and was forgiven on serious vows of abstinence. The third time he was found "half-seas over" when he ought to have been on land fit to follow the streams. As soon as he recovered, Mr. Webster, who had found the whiskey-bottle still half full, lectured the penitent Indian on his ingratitude. He stood near a cart, looked poor John, who crouched before him, in the eye, and proceeded to enumerate and enlarge upon his offences, raising the whiskey-bottle over the cart-wheel. The Indian kept two ears open to the rebuke, and two eyes open to the danger of the precious bottle being broken on the wheel. He sobbed and cried ; but, just as the bottle was coming down with a mighty gesture, he jumped and begged, "O, please don't, Mr. Webster ! anything but that !" Again the orator set out, poured a deeper flood of indignation over John's fall, set his sin in more appalling colors, raising his arm and brandishing the bottle with the mounting fervor. But when the falling inflection was due, the Indian sprang again, "O, please not, Mr. Webster ! don't break him !" The third time the statesman started on his flight for the climax and the swoop. The Indian trembled with awe and shame, but the third time he leaped up and caught the descending arm, beseeching that he might be flogged, if the bottle could be saved.

Mr. Webster used to tell the story as the great defeat of his life. He could change the currents of constitutional law by an argument in the Supreme Court room, but he was not master of eloquence enough to make a wretched Indian, who trembled before him, forget half a bottle of rum !

In 1828 and early in 1829 Mr. Webster met great sorrows. His wife died, and his noble brother Ezekiel in his fiftieth year, in the prime of great powers, of majestic beauty, and a solid usefulness, fell dead in a court-room while arguing a jury-cause. The blows were very heavy on Mr. Webster's heart. He felt the fatigue of wide labors. He took less interest in causes. He announced his intention of retiring from political life. Man proposes ; God disposes. It was then that he was turned to the work which was the honor and crown of his life.

At this time he became convinced that the plan of a Southern confederacy had been received with favor by a great many of the political men of the South, especially of South Carolina. The four censuses of 1790, 1800, 1810, 1820, had shown that the North was growing in population and power disproportionately to the South ; and it was believed that the protective policy to which the Middle States were ardently committed was responsible for a large degree of the increasing disparity. Mr. Calhoun had supported the policy of incidental protection in 1816, and had denounced disunion then as " a word which comprehended the sum of our political dangers." His tariff sentiments of that year were framed and hung up with Washington's Farewell Address in the parlors, hotels, and bar-rooms of Pennsylvania.

Mr. Webster, who had opposed the protective policy in its origin, became a partial supporter of it when it had become established ; and in 1828 he and Mr. Calhoun, who were on opposite sides in 1816, had *chassé* across on the national floor, and were still facing each other as antagonists. But with a remarkable difference. Mr. Webster's position was this : Union tariff, or no tariff. Mr. Calhoun's was : no tariff, or no Union. Mr. Webster's feeling was that of a patriot ; Mr. Calhoun's that of a partisan.

Mr. Calhoun, by urging and keeping the election of General Jackson in 1828, hoped to break the protective policy of the country. If that hope should fail, or if General Jackson should prove false, he intended to put in force a new theory of the Constitution, namely, that a State had the right first to nullify a law of Congress, and then secede.

Mr. Webster foresaw the trouble looming. The cloud no bigger than a man's hand — the hand of Mr. Calhoun — he saw might become a tempest, a sectional typhoon, and he determined to be ready to meet it. His labors in the Supreme Court had led him to a profound study of the Constitution ; and now he bent himself to a thorough investigation of the relations of the States to the central government, and of the powers and duties of the Federal centre towards every possible movement of treason. He made himself master of the whole subject. He told some of his friends, in after years, that there was no imaginable form of conflict between State and Federal authority which he did not consider, and feel prepared to debate and to meet, acccording to what he believed to be the true theory of the Constitution.

General Jackson was elected, and was inaugurated March 4, 1829. Mr. Calhoun was chosen Vice-President. Friends of his were in the Cabinet, and his influence was weighty, if not controlling, in the White House.

The first Congress under that administration assembled in December, 1829. Mr. Clay was not in the Senate. No very prominent Whig or representative of New England ideas and the protective policy was there but Mr. Webster. The talent was largely preponderant on the Democratic side.

Very soon protection, New England, and Mr. Webster were made the subject of a combined, powerful, vehement, and imbittered attack. Mr. Calhoun, who presided over the Senate, but could not speak in it, knew Mr. Webster's power, and knew that it was necessary for his own purposes that his probable influence in the country should be crushed.

About a month after Congress assembled, in January, 1830, Mr. Webster, who had been engaged in a cause in the Supreme Court room, stepped into the Senate on his way home, with a bag of law-papers under his arm. Mr. Hayne, a young, accomplished Senator from South Carolina, a gallant, chivalric, and fiery debater, a friend and confidant of Vice-President Calhoun, was delivering a speech in which New England was severely handled. Mr. Webster, preoccupied as he was with a cause in the Supreme Court, at once replied, and in a speech which is one of the models of vigorous debate in Saxon literature.

Mr. Hayne now took up the warfare in hot earnest. Mr. Benton built and kindled the fiery furnace, and Mr. Hayne, in a second speech of two days, made the flame seven times fiercer, to punish the great Daniel and his friends. A speech so intense and so sectional had never then been heard in the Senate of the country. It was uttered with great declamatory skill and energy; it bristled with facts that had an irritating look and sound, — all the more provoking because they seemed undeniable, — and it put forth cautiously the new doctrine of the right of nullification, — setting up an image of the Union, like that of Nebuchadnezzar's dream, standing on the right of secession, — standing on brittle feet of clay.

The speech made an immense and intense impression. Hundreds said that Mr. Webster was annihilated. A Senator from North Carolina, Mr. Iredell, observed to one of these jubilant friends of Mr. Hayne: " He has started the lion, but wait till we hear his roar or feel his claws."

The roar and the stroke came the next day. I am not going to describe that reply of January 26, 1830. Slim, agile, impetuous, fierce, in his intellectual assault, Mr. Hayne's attack was that of a leopard upon a good-natured, sluggish, sleepy lion in his prime. The eyes opened; the mane bristled; the muscles swelled; he uttered his voice; he sprang; he struck.

Every noble element of power in debate is represented in those seventy large octavo pages of the second reply to Mr. Hayne in 1830. But there is no mean, malignant, taunting, or sarcastic passage in it. It is as generous as it is terrible. A distinguished scholar who heard it said that nothing so completely realized his conception of what Demosthenes was when he delivered his "Oration on the Crown." But the great speech of Demosthenes is veined with the fiercest invective. He played with Æschines and then poured vitriol on him. Mr. Webster demolished his antagonist's speech, and yet spared him and South Carolina. It was not only crushing, but Christian.

The marvel is that the speech, six hours long, running the whole gamut of senatorial eloquence, fit to be stereotyped at once with the noblest orations of literature, equally fascinating in the market-place and the college, was extempore. The language of not a page of it was committed to memory. The brief consisted of half a sheet of letter-paper. Mr. Hayne finished in the afternoon of January 25; Mr. Webster replied the next morning. Mr. Everett spent the evening with him, and found him entirely at ease, sportive, and full of anecdote. "He was as unconcerned," Mr. Everett says, "and as free of spirit, ... as when floating in his fishing-boat along a hazy shore, gently rocking on the tranquil tide, dropping his line here and there with the varying fortune of the sport. The next morning he was like some mighty admiral, dark and terrible, casting the long shadow of his frowning tiers far over the sea that seemed to sink beneath him, his broad pendant streaming at the main, the stars and stripes at the fore, the mizzen, and the peak ; and bearing down like a tempest upon his antagonist, with all his canvas strained to the wind and all his thunders roaring from his broadsides."

His brother Ezekiel had died a year before. When, after the Hayne speech, his own praise was sounded over the length and breadth of America, he said, when some one was extolling his merits, "How I wish my poor brother had lived till after this speech, that I might know if he would have been gratified ! "

A friend of mine, who was a very intimate friend of Mr. Webster, received from him once a statement of his feeling when he rose to address the crowded Senate, which is very striking and which has never appeared in print. "Not until I took the floor, and saw the concourse, and felt the hush," said Mr. Webster, "did I feel the slightest trepidation. Then it rushed upon me, the re-

sponsibility of my position. It very nearly un-
manned me. A strange sensation came. My feet
felt light ; they seemed not to touch the floor. It
was as though I began to rise and float. Instantly
I thought how my brother Ezekiel died, a year
before, falling while making a speech, and dead
before his head touched the floor. By a strong
effort I subdued the trepidation and the fear.
Soon my feet felt the floor again. Then they
grew heavy. Then they seemed rooted like rocks.
My brain was free. All that I had ever read or
thought or acted in literature, in history, in law,
in politics, seemed to unroll before me in glowing
panorama, and then it was easy, if I wanted a
thunderbolt, to reach out and take it as it went
smoking by."

The fiery furnace built by the Jackson and
Calhoun men for Mr. Webster did not singe
him. It served other uses. In the reply to
Hayne Mr. Webster drew out and stated more
clearly the latent doctrine of nullification and
secession which his antagonist had dallied with,
and exposed it to an elaborate and merciless examination. This part of his speech was entirely
extempore, not a note for it had been prepared on
his brief ; and it was the first time that the Constitution, in relation to State rights and State wrongs,
had been treated on the floor of Congress. He
showed that a government over twenty-four States,
where any one of them has the right to checkmate
Congress, the executive, and the Supreme Court,

was a parody on government. A thing, he said, with such a principle, or rather such a destitution of all principle in it, should not be called a constitution. "No, sir. It should be called, rather, a collection of topics for everlasting controversy, heads of debate for a disputatious people."

The chord he struck sounded rich and deep all over the land. It roused a new tone of patriotism. It called out a letter from the aged Madison, who indorsed his doctrine as the doctrine of the framers of the Constitution, and who said "it crushes nullification, and must hasten the abandonment of secession."

But it did the most efficient work in the Senate. It compelled the Democratic statesmen to consider the question in the egg, and take sides. Mr. Calhoun presided over debates in which his theory found less and less favor, and which seemed to show that the administration would not be committed to his ulterior plans.

Yet he did not despair. A few weeks later the birthday of Mr. Jefferson was celebrated in Washington. The nullifiers, Mr. Madison said, attempted "to make the name of Mr. Jefferson the pedestal of their colossal heresy." Mr. Calhoun and the new President were at the table. The regular toasts were ambiguous and shaky. Mr. Calhoun's ran thus : "The Union : next to our liberty the most dear ; may we all remember that it can only be preserved by respecting the rights of the States, and distributing equally the benefit and burden of the Union." This is conditional, roundabout, metaphysical. Andrew Jackson was at the table. Mr. Calhoun, the Vice-President, was his intimate confidential friend. But Old Hickory had done a large deal of thinking, with a pipe in his mouth, over Mr. Webster's reply to Hayne. He had a sentiment to offer. It did not take many words. "Our Federal Union: it must be preserved." The electricity bristled on the hero's hair, and gave a healthy shock, at the right moment, to the great Democratic party of the land. Mr. Webster's speech had become a wedge between Calhoun and Jackson. Mr. Calhoun might indoctrinate South Carolina as a State; but Mr. Webster's speech rose like Fort Sumter, which is built on courses of New Hampshire granite, frowning over his path with solemn muzzles, and bearing aloft, full high advanced, the gorgeous ensign of the republic, " its arms and trophies streaming in their original lustre, not a stripe erased or polluted, not a single star obscured, and bearing for its motto, in characters of living light, blazing on all its ample folds, the sentiment, dear to every true American heart, — Liberty and Union, now and forever, one and inseparable ! "

But more trying times were at hand, — times not only for debate, but for action. The Tariff Bill of 1832 was passed, which was felt — and perhaps justly — by South Carolina to be oppressive and tyrannical. And the State which had, sixteen years before, dropped the seeds of the protective policy, prepared for nullification and secession. The feeling in parts of the South towards large portions of the North, and especially New England, was very bitter, scarcely less so than to-day. But it was redeemed often by a wit which is not common now. Here, for instance, is a chemical analysis by Satan of a Yankee soul, which was circulated among our Southern brethren : " Cunning, $12\frac{1}{2}$ per cent; hypocrisy, $12\frac{1}{2}$ per cent; avarice and falsehood, each $12\frac{1}{2}$ per cent; sneakingness, $12\frac{1}{2}$ per cent ; nameless and numberless small vices, 14 per cent; the remaining $23\frac{1}{2}$ per cent being divided between New England rum, essence of onions, codfish, molasses, and beans." (This ought to satisfy some of my German relations, who were anxious a few weeks ago to hear me state of what the blood of a Yankee professor is compounded.)

Here, too, is a picture of a Yankee, Virgil Haskins, hauled up in the next world before Rhadamanthus, to answer for deeds done in the body. Rhadamanthus says : "I find you charged, sir, with selling, in one peddling expedition, 400,000 wooden nutmegs, 280,000 Spanish cigars made of oak leaves, and 647 wooden clocks. What do you say to that charge?" The Yankee ghost replies, "Wal, that was counted in our place about the greatest peddling-trip that ever was made over the Potomac." The judge continues : "To stealing an old grindstone, smearing it over with butter, and then selling it as a cheese." The ghost: "Jimminy! surely ye would n't punish a man for that, would ye?" Rhadamanthus again : "To making a counterfeit dollar of pewter, when you were six years old, and cheating your own father with it." The ghost, with glee : "Daddy was mighty glad when he found it eout. He said it showed I had a genius." The Yankee was condemned by Rhadamanthus to be thrown into a lake of hot molasses with a grindstone around his neck.

This was one way in which the effect of Webster's reply to Hayne was nullified.

The Tariff Act of 1832, which a Democratic President had signed, was dealt with thus : A convention was called in South Carolina and the act was annulled. Duties enjoined by it were forbidden to be paid in the State. No appeal to the Supreme Court to attest the validity of nullification was to be allowed. If the government attempted to enforce the tariff laws, South Carolina would secede. Mr. Hayne was now governor, and he resolved to carry out the programme. The State was almost unanimous. The military were ready. Blue cockades with a palmetto button in the centre were the rage. Even medals were struck, with these words: "John C. Calhoun, first President of the Southern Confederacy."

The President replied in a proclamation which indorsed the constitutional doctrines of Mr. Webster, and was made up in part of his language. He poured intense scorn on the new doctrine that a State had the right to secede under the Constitution. "Was our devotion paid to the wretched, inefficient, clumsy contrivance which this new doctrine would make the Constitution? Did we pledge ourselves to the support of an airy nothing, a bubble that must be blown away by the first breath of disaffection?" He outlined the prosperity and happiness of the nation of which South Carolina was a part, and of which her blood had been the cement, and he said: "Say, now, if you can, without horror and remorse, This happy Union we will dissolve, this picture of peace and prosperity we will deface, this free intercourse we will interrupt, these fertile fields we will deluge with blood, the protection of that glorious flag we renounce, the very name of Americans we discard. And for what, mistaken men! for what do you throw away these inestimable blessings? for what would you exchange your share in the advantages and honor of the Union? For the dream of a separate independence, a dream interrupted by bloody conflicts with your neighbors and a vile dependence on a foreign power."

Such is the rhetoric that befits the White House when the cockatrice egg of treason is hatched and the young serpents, whose look is venomous when they have grown, begin to hiss.

Mr. Hayne in response to this proclamation

declared that South Carolina would resist the general government to the extremity.

General Jackson told one of his friends once that he never had a tremor of the hands in his life. "My nerves are like steel bars." An old military friend called on him in the midst of the secession storm. He was smoking a favorite pipe. "Sam," he said, "they are trying me here, you will witness it; but by the God of heaven, I will uphold the laws." His friend hoped that things would yet go right. "They shall go right, sir," said Old Hickory, on fire, — and he shivered his pipe on the table. He did not save his pipe and shiver his country, and puff his duty off in smoke. They say that the General never was able to believe the earth was round. One thing he believed, — that his country was a whole, and he did not mean to see it torn into shreds while he had power to strike the wretched treason.

Mr. Calhoun was still in South Carolina, and still Vice-President. He resigned that office, was elected Senator of South Carolina, and hurried on to Washington to defend the attitude of his State and the right of secession in the midst of the storm. Jackson could deal with the treason ; but who could meet the intellectual leader of it, and vanquish him before the public sentiment? One man only, Daniel Webster, who was at fatal issue with Jackson on all the other measures of his administration. He had taken slight part in the debate ; but now he struck hands with the hero of New Orleans, — the stateliest intellect and the firmest will in the land compacted by patriotism against arrogant treason.

The Constitution was threatened ; the country was in danger ; the foundations of American liberty were marked for approach by sappers of treason. Mr. Webster saw that it was no time for party lines and feuds and titles. He threw away the name "Whig"; he forgot that Andrew Jackson was a Democrat. He remembered only that he was an American, and that General Jackson was a patriot, and he pledged to him all his strength of brain and arm, just as to-day Mr. Dickinson and Mr. Douglas and Mr. Dix and General Butler, strong opponents of President Lincoln's party platform, refuse to know anything about platforms when the Constitution is struck at with daggers and the flag betrayed !

The debate of February, 1833, on the bill empowering the President to collect the revenue in South Carolina, was a very different one from the Hayne debate of three years before. This was discussion with hands upon swords. Mr. Calhoun was the Hector of this Iliad, not unlike Homer's Hector either,

> " Prepared
> And ardent for the task ; nor less he raged
> Than Mars while fighting, or than flames that seize
> Some forest on the mountain-tops ; the foam
> Hung at his lips ; beneath his awful front
> His keen eyes glistened, and his helmet marked
> The agitation wild with which he fought."

Mr. Webster was the Achilles of the contest, —
Achilles, whom Homer calls the "godlike."

> " His ponderous helm
> He lifted to his brows ; star-like it shone,
> And shook its curling crest of bushy gold.
>
> .   .   .   .   .
>
> He drew his father's spear forth from his case,
> Heavy and huge and long.   That spear, of all
> Achaia's sons, none else had power to wield.
>
> .   .   .   .   .
>
> " Then his corselet bright
> Braced to his bosom, his huge sword of brass
> Athwart his shoulder slung, and his broad shield
> Uplifted last, luminous as the moon."

Yes, it was his country's shield, rinsed with the
ocean, as that of Achilles was.   And the fate of
the secession theory in that mental combat was
the fate of Hector.   It was dragged at the conqueror's wheel.

Mr. Calhoun's speech of two days in February,
1833, to prove the constitutional right of nullification and secession, was a splendid intellectual effort.
But it was acute, artificial, and metaphysical.   It
puzzles you while you read it ; it melts away from
you when you lay it down.   It is a consummate
piece of logic, but it does not stand to reason.
And, like a Prince Rupert's drop, break it anywhere, and it flies to pieces.

Mr. Calhoun was fond of subtile speculations.
He would rather take a machine to pieces and
spoil it, to find out the method of its action, than
to see it run.

When he was a student in Yale College, he

one day delivered a disquisition on a very strange and apparently absurd proposition, which he defended with great acuteness. The president of the college said to him, when he had finished, "Calhoun, that is a brilliant piece of logic, and if I wanted anybody to prove that shad grow on apple-trees, I would appoint you."

To argue the right of secession as granted in the Constitution was to attempt to prove that a very scaly shad grows on an apple-tree.

While he was delivering it in the Senate before an enormous crowd, a man in the gallery shrieked out, "Mr. President, something must be done, or I shall be squeezed to death!" That is the way we feel in reading it. It is an immensely able, but speculative and artificial process of logic for making any one State superior, in an emergency, to the United States, and for squeezing a large-limbed patriotism to death. Mr. Calhoun's theory of nullification was a theory concocted to meet a fact and justify a passion.

The drapery in the old United States Senate-room was looped up and fastened by supports in the shape of stars. When Mr. Calhoun had fairly commenced his nullification speech, one of these stars fell to the floor of the chamber with a startling noise. No wonder!

Mr. Webster replied to him at once in a speech of five hours, which met every turn and twist of the secession hypothesis, unfolding the Constitution as a power sovereign forever, for certain purposes, over all the States and all the individuals in them, and to be interpreted by Congress and the Supreme Court. Mr. Calhoun contended for the constitutional right of nullification. His conception of the government was like an engine with a sieve for a cylinder. Mr. Webster demonstrated that no such right was revealed or hidden or hinted in the Constitution, that it was an absurdity, and that it was treason.

His argument was a noble piece of reason contrasted with logic. It stands square on the facts of the Constitution and the early administration of it. It is self-consistent and self-luminous.

In closing, Mr. Webster said that if the friends of nullification succeed, "they will prove themselves the most skilful 'architects of ruin,' the greatest blasters of human hopes, that any age has ever produced. They would stand up to proclaim in tones which would pierce the ears of half the human race, that the last great experiment of representative government had failed. The doctrine of the divine right of kings would feel, even in its grave, a returning sensation of vitality. Millions of eyes of those who now feed their inherent love of liberty on the success of the American example would turn away from our dismemberment, and find no place on earth to rest their gratified sight. Amidst the incantations and orgies of nullification, secession, disunion and revolution would be celebrated the funeral rites of constitutional and republican liberty."

Mr. Webster rode in General Jackson's carriage to the Senate-chamber when he made the speech. This was General Jackson's summing up of the Websterian principles : "If this nullification goes on, our country will be like a bag of meal with both ends open. Pick it up in the middle or endwise, and it will run out. I must tie the bag and save the country."

Mr. Webster tied the bag in theory ; General Jackson tied it in fact, and saved all the meal, even the South Carolina portion. He was ready to arrest Mr. Calhoun, and have him tried and executed under martial law in the District of Columbia for treason. The great Senator was visited one night, and his danger revealed to him in bed. But his neck was saved by the compromise tariff measure, which was forced through Congress by Mr. Clay about the time that the Revenue-Force Bill was passed. Mr. Calhoun was coerced into voting for it, and South Carolina stripped off her military robes and avoided the open conflict with Jackson's unyielding will.

General Jackson declared in his last sickness, that in reviewing his life his chief regret was that he had not executed Mr. Calhoun for treason. "My country," said he, "would have sustained me in the act, and his fate would have been a warning to traitors in all time to come."

As a display of varied and sweeping eloquence,

the speech cannot be compared with the reply to Hayne, three years before. It is of another character. It is an exhaustive discussion of the one great question, " Is the Constitution a sovereign power of government within its limits, directly reaching the people of the States, or is it a league or treaty which any State may construe, and from which any State may withdraw when it suits her interests or pleases her passion ? "

Mr. Calhoun maintained that there is no such thing as the people of the United States as one body. There are separate communities only, each owing supreme loyalty to the State constitution ; and whenever a State convention votes the United States Constitution of no authority within its borders, no man within that State owes a particle of allegiance to the central government. In Mr. Calhoun's conception the general government is like a large sheet of postage-stamps, all ready to be detached in a moment, and each having no connection with the others that can be injured vitally by being torn off.

Mr. Webster regarded the State divisions as the lines and squares rather on a chess-board, over which the great power of the government moved freely according to prescribed rules, and so related that no one square and no seven squares could be separated from the rest without breaking up the whole board and destroying the possibility of the game.

He followed up every winding and artifice and
15 *

sophism of the secession hypothesis, and exposed it. His ponderous intellect never played with more vigor, never showed its weight of metal and the fatal force of its blows more superbly, than through the five hours of this demolition of Mr. Calhoun's heresy.

His strokes fell like a trip-hammer. The doctrine of secession was pounded down by it, beat after beat, not into gold-leaf, — for there is not any gold in it, it is only a slug of pewter, — but into pewter thinner than tissue paper. Mr. Webster hammered it down by the plain language of the Constitution, by general reasoning on the powers that belong to all government, by fair interpretation of its delegated authority, by the history of its formation and adoption, and by showing, through logical satire, dignified but merciless, what an absurdity, in every possible respect, a government would be, composed of a score or two of states, any one of which could annul its action at any moment by a decision of its local courts and legislature.

Mr. Webster disapproved the tariff compromise. His position was, "No ground can be granted, not an inch, to menace and bluster. No measure ever passed Congress," he said, "during my connection with that body, that caused me so much grief and mortification. The principle was bad, the measure was bad, the consequences were bad." He believed, with Mr. Benton, that "a compromise made with a state in arms is a capit-

ulation to that state." He wanted the strength
of the government tried, to determine the point,
once for all, if we have a government worth
cherishing and worth taxing ourselves to support.
General Jackson would have carried the country
through without the compromise; Mr. Calhoun
saved his head by it; and yet just enough was
yielded in it to give him the excuse for saying
that the government receded before his State in
arms.

The debate between Mr. Webster and Mr. Calhoun was free from all personal heat, from all
bitterness, from every tinge of ungentlemanly
allusion. In 1847 Mr. Webster toasted the
memory of Hayne at a public dinner in Charleston. In 1850 he spoke weighty, respectful, and
noble words over Mr. Calhoun in the United
States Senate. And on his death-bed Mr. Calhoun spoke most respectfully and kindly of his
great antagonist, saying, "Mr. Webster has as high
a standard of truth as any statesman whom I
have met in debate."

They rest from their labors and their works do
follow them. Error is not innocent. Mr. Calhoun
was a pure, lofty, narrow man. His thought has
done more than any other single force to disinte-
grate the republic. It has been the slow corrosion
of acid and frost. Mr. Webster's thought was a
compacting, confederating, organizing energy. Mr.
Calhoun was the chieftain of a clan; Mr. Webster
the representative of a continent.

Mr. Calhoun would have written or branded on the soul of a man the word " Kentucky," or " South Carolina," or " Ohio," or " Maine." Mr. Webster would have these written only in small letters, for a small area, — but in large capitals, fit to be read in Europe, and everywhere on this round globe, under every sky where a seventy-four with the stars and stripes may penetrate, the word " American."

After his great debates of 1830 and 1833 he wore the title " Defender of the Constitution." He was in the general regard less a politician than the epic poet of 1787. The work of the great convention that framed our government seemed nobler to the people when reflected in his capacious understanding, and as its ideal rods and beams and valves worked without friction in the bright medium of his imagination. He did not grow tired through years of pleading for devotion to the Constitution and Union. The rhythm of his speech had peculiar majesty, a tone of Hebrew grandeur, on this topic, recurrent and ever fresh.

It may be a sign of the secondary grave of his genius that the idea of right, in its abstract sublimity, did not burn as his beacon. No abstract principle or sentiment withdrew him from a careful measure of the good which an actual system would secure to men in the long run. The cotton handkerchief which he bought in boyhood was absorbed into his brain and blood. His eye always seemed to take in the moral and civil scenery of the country, — its thousands of happy homes, its schools and churches, its factories and workshops, the vast fleets of its commerce, and the widening line of civilization before which the wilderness was falling, — and when he spoke the word " Constitution" or " Union," in senate, in caucus, in festive hall, in journeys north or south, he made it embody and exhale all the gladness and the grandeur which so much prosperity and plenty, so much order and happiness, awakened in his breast.   For this reason he called on his countrymen to cherish the sentiments that should make that word sacred.   For this reason he continually used the awful imagery of the breaking up of constellations, and of anarchy in the firmament, to state the terrors and woes that would attend an explosion of the forces which bind the States together.   His intellect seemed to feel that their combination was not of man, but was an organic miracle, and to be constantly conscious of the delicacy of their poise.

In 1850, when California knocked for admission into the Union, and he was ready, as he was not in 1833, to meet clamor with compromise, — and there were so many who loved him that could not go with him, — he did not act from base motives. He was not indifferent to the evils which are covered and partially maintained by our national bond, but he would not look at the evils exclusively or minutely.   He saw an immense overbalance of good, — benefits more various, more

substantial, and more precious than any polity on
earth had ever secured to men.

And the great future of America (if explosive
passions could then be kept down) charmed his
imagination. He comprehended what the country
would be centuries hence.   In swelling speech he
loved to bid future generations hail.   And he
seemed to see, I doubt not, the upturned faces of
the Saxon millions yet to come, beseeching him,
by their looks and by their prayers, to pledge all
the resources of his intellect and his influence to
preserve the unity and peace of a nation upon
which their fortunes and happiness were at issue.
He thought that a little concession then would
be final. He thought the North was bound by
oath and obligation to return the fugitives.   He
granted the concession. He put his lips to the
trumpet and called on the North to obey the Constitution.

But no word from his fervid speeches and
countless letters of those last years is in the re-
motest degree kindred with the logic and the
passions of secessionists to-day or of their abettors,
or of the lukewarm supporters of the Constitution,
which are the most despicable tribe. (A man
may well be perplexed to know what course of
action is wisest in the head of the nation, but if
he is lukewarm in feeling towards treachery and
towards his country's Constitution and flag and
Congress and President, the nation says, in the
voice of the Apocalypse, " So then, because thou

art lukewarm, and neither cold nor hot, I will spew thee out of my mouth.")

Mr. Webster did not propose to alter the Constitution to appease rebellion. He proposed to make it obeyed in the North ; and every man ought to say now, that the Constitution must be obeyed in the South, — arms grounded, forts yielded, stolen money returned, the flag run up and saluted, and Abraham Lincoln acknowledged as rightful President of thirty-four States, before the convention shall be called that is to consider an alteration of the Constitution of the land.

A year after Mr. Webster's 7th of March speech, in his oration, 4th of July, in Washington, in laying the foundation of the new wing of the Capitol, he denounced the spirit of secession then smouldering in South Carolina and Mississippi in language at once ponderous and impassioned. He said that the trouble there was excessive prosperity under the Constitution, and for that the advice of the secession doctors, he doubted not, would be a sovereign remedy.

Call up his swarthy ghost to help secession ? It is Saul calling up Samuel, to hear denunciation and the prophecy of doom !

The spirits that come at the call of patriotism perplexed — Washington and Hamilton, Jefferson and Adams, Marshall and Story, Jackson and Webster, Benton and Clay, representing the suffering and victory of the Revolution, the early joy on the adoption of the Constitution, the peaceful

civil struggles under it, and every form of the
prosperity it has poured upon East and South and
North — preach, in common tone, to all sections,
obedience to the central law till all the people
shall legally dissolve the bond ; they frown upon
disruption ; they counsel common devotion to the
common and just ends of government; they plead
for the return of fraternal sentiments ; and they
appeal to the rising life of the land in the words
of Webster shortly before he passed into immortality : " The young men of this generation, and
of the succeeding generations : may they live forever, but may the Constitution and the Union
outlive them all ! " *

MARCH 19, 1861.

* After the rebellion broke out, Mr. King added the following
passage to this lecture : " Mr. Webster and Mr. Calhoun, we say,
are dead. No ; they 'still live.' On the floor of the Senate they
were for twenty years the able, fit, and courteous representatives
of hostile principles. They might be respectful and kindly towards
each other, and shake hands as friends, but their principles were as
irreconcilable as two railroad trains approaching on the same track
under full steam. Mr. Clay, in 1833, switched them off just in time
to save a collision. But now the crash is about to come. There
is no switch-man now ; and nobody wants any. Those two men
are ruling America at this hour by the hostile array of their ideas
for a final collision.

" Mr. Calhoun's thought has taken form in the conventions that
have voted down the Constitution, and yet have not submitted their
treason to the votes of the people ; in the three or four millions of
white men that refuse the name 'American' and say that the
fathers of the republic were mistaken in their doctrines of freedom ; in the booming cannon that fired at the national flag over
Sumter ; in the arming of privateers against American commerce ;
in the appeal of the confederate traitors for fifty millions to be
spent in striking at the national flag still more passionately ; in the

doctrine dramatized in disaster and war, that the minority ought to be allowed to rule.

" Mr. Webster's thought breaks out afresh in the proclamation of the President that America is one and cannot be broken ; it bursts forth in the banners thick as the gorgeous leaves of the October forests that have blossomed all over eighteen or twenty States ; it shows itself in the passion of the noble Union men of the South who will not bow to Baal ; it floats on every frigate that rides the sea to protect our shipping ; it leaps forth and brightens in the sacred steel which patriots by the hundred thousand are dedicating, not to ravage, not to murder, not to hatred of any portion of the southern section of the confederacy, but to the support of the impartial Constitution, to the common flag, to the majestic and beneficent law which offers to encircle and bless the whole republic ; it utters itself in the thunder-voice of twenty millions of white citizens of the land, that in America the majority under the Constitution must rule, and the public law must be obeyed.

" And when the work of the government shall be accomplished,— when the stolen money of the nation shall be refunded ; when hostile artillery shall be withdrawn from the lower banks of the Mississippi ; when the flag of thirteen stripes and thirty-four stars shall float again over Sumter, over New Orleans, over every arsenal that has seen it insulted, over Mount Vernon and the American dust of Washington, over every State capitol, and along the whole coast and border line of Texas ; when every man within the present limits of the immense republic shall have restored to him the right of pride in the American navy, and of representation on common terms in the national Capitol, and of citizenship on the whole continent ; when leading traitors shall have been punished, and the Constitution vindicated in its unsectional beneficence, and the doctrine of secession be stabbed with two hundred thousand bayonet wounds, and trampled to rise no more, — then the debate between Mr. Calhoun and Mr. Webster will be completed, the swarthy spirit of the great defender of the Constitution will triumph, and a restored, peaceful, majestic, irresistible America will dignify and consecrate his name forever."

X.

BOOKS AND READING.*

I CANNOT imagine how a speaker can more profitably use the hour in which you honor him with a listening ear than by an address on Books and Reading.

The supreme privilege and advantage which modern society enjoys over society five hundred years ago is printed literature. There are scores of blessings connected organically with civilization that raise the plane of our life ; but over all secular boons this one is sovereign, — the printing-press, which arrests and cheapens, which accumulates and scatters, the victories of genius and the stores of intellectual toil.

Our education is conducted by the first masters in each department through the help of books and their cheapness. We go to a college, possibly, where only third-rate professors preside and teach, or we may be too poor to attend any college or academy ; but for a dollar or two we

* This lecture, written in San Francisco, had an extraordinary popularity in every city and town in California where it was de· livered.

may be in Faraday's class in chemistry, force
Buttmann to teach us Greek, listen to Owen on
anatomy, make Schlegel interpret the masterpieces of literature, and detain Macaulay or
Guizot at will, to unfold their knowledge of the
laws and the heroes of the last eighteen hundred
years.

Books are our university. Spirits are our
schoolmasters. The quintessence of truth, for
which a man has spent years and genius and
thousands sterling, too, is compacted into a pack-
age that does not waste by multiplying, and, for
a few shillings, is a force of education to crowds
by the Mississippi, near the Yuba, and "in the
continuous woods where rolls the Oregon."

All other helps to culture are feeble in importance contrasted with books. To hundreds of
thousands the whole sky is less than an ordinary
treatise on astronomy, and, if they should live
under it through twenty generations, could never
suggest a thousandth part so much. A tolerably
cultivated man might thread all the passes of the
Alps, and travel along the table-land of the
Andes with eyes wide open, and know less of
mountains, and be stirred with a feebler sense
of sublimity, than by reading the fourth volume of
Ruskin's "Modern Painters." The Wandering Jew
might gossip to you the details of Europe during
the last ten centuries, and leave with you immeas-
urably less of history than a compend by Vico,
Montesquieu, or Hegel would impart. The first

would show you a pageant; the second would disclose the laws on which centuries are strung. And the careful study, during the evenings of a week, of the "Essay on Classification," about two hundred pages long, which introduces Agassiz's great work on the Natural History of our Country, would disclose vastly more of the creation to a man of average brain, than if he could see all the living creatures of the globe march by him, two and two, as the animals went into the ark, and could then be conducted through a museum crowded with fossil exhibitions of every species entombed in the planet's crust. The sight of all the facts would be like looking upon a shapeless heap of types. The study of the essay by the great naturalist would show you something of the thought of the Creator expressed in the animal world, from the birth of the first creature with sensation, hundreds of thousands of years ago, to the turtle that lies now on his back in Clay Street, awaiting promotion to soup and humanity.

To the mass of the world, who have not the leisure or the ability to wrest truth at first hand from its hiding-places, contact with books is of more account than immediate contact with all of the Divine wisdom that is directly poured into the universe.

There is no danger, therefore, that, with all our stilted apostrophes to the printing-press, we shall overrate the privilege of libraries and literature. There is far more danger that, because of this din of turgidness, we shall lose the sense of our boon, or fail to take its measure.

Plato, in one of the most charming of his Dialogues, disparages books as a means of instruction, in comparison with conversation. "Written truth," he says, "resembles painting. Its productions stand out as if they were alive; but if you ask them any question they observe a solemn silence. And so it is with written discourses; you would think that they spoke as though they possessed some wisdom; but if you ask them about anything they say, from a desire to understand it, they give only one and the self-same answer. And when it is once written, every discourse is tossed about everywhere, equally among those who understand it, and among those whom it in no wise concerns, and it knows not to whom it ought to speak and to whom not. And when it is ill-treated and unjustly reviled it always needs its father to help it; for, of itself, it can neither defend nor help itself."

Now it is by the grace of the printing-press that we are able to know this criticism of the great Plato, and to make Plato repeat his best sayings at our pleasure. By books we, in fact, go into the society of the best men of all ages, and hear them say their best things. I know that a man is greater than his noblest book, and that to know him thoroughly and have intimate communion for years with his genius in its private and flexible play, is better than to know all his

editions by heart.   But no talk with Milton could
give " Paradise Lost " or " Comus " or even " Il Pen-
seroso."   If one could have made a call on Newton in his library, or at his office in the mint, he
might have been in a peevish mood, you might
hear him fret over his quarrel with Flamsteed, or
he would possibly talk a little about the philosopher's stone.   You would not get a chapter of
queries as to optics out of him, or a demonstration of the speed of the moon's fall towards the
earth every second.   You certainly would not
get the whole " Principia."   Suppose you could
have dropped in to see Shakespeare in his com-
fortable country home.   He would have treated
you to as much sack, no doubt, as you could
" stagger under," you might have gone away " happy " as Cassio, but do you think that in your interview you could have been carried up into the
region of his genius where Imogen and Hamlet
started into life, or down into the depths of his
feeling whence the richest sonnets issued?   Call
on Thackeray, in London, and there is danger
that he will engage the time with his grievances
against his fellow-member of a literary club, who
photographed his broken nose too vividly in a
letter : he would not sketch Mrs. Henry Esmond
for you.   Nor would Dickens, seek him with the
warmest letter of introduction, unveil to you that
tropic region of his sea-like heart from which the
Agnes of " David Copperfield " rose as Aphrodite
from the foam near Cyprus.   He might be too

busy with details of domestic trouble. I have
seen letters lately from friends in Florence which
describe most temptingly the vigor and passion
of old Walter Savage Landor's dinner-table conversation. But you can take a volume of his
" Imaginary Conversations " and overhear what he
would say at a dozen dinner-parties, if he could
have the winnowed genius of two thousand years
for guests. Perhaps the report which a genial
and appreciative gentleman once gave me of a
long interview with Thomas De Quincey, who
lately died in Scotland, came as near affecting me
with envy as any literary tidings of that kind I
ever heard. Yet for six " bits " I can buy De Quincey's " Suspiria de Profundis," the sequel to his
" Opium-Eater," and, whenever I please, can sink
into the music of that prose which, I believe, is
the most rich and masterly since Hooker's.

No doubt there are a great many persons who
think thus with themselves when they desire a
firmer or clearer Christian faith : What a privilege it was to live in the time of Jesus ! to see
him pass through the village of Capernaum or
Sychar, or resting in Bethany ! to hear the sentences of the Sermon on the Mount fall from his
lips ! to see him take little children in his arms
and bless them ! to be present when he unsealed
the sight of Bartimeus, and know thus that he
was from heaven ! or, greater privilege still, to
have been with him a witness of the transfiguration ! The first disciples, some are apt to say,

had unspeakably richer opportunities than we can have to know the truths and to live out the spirit of the Christian religion.

Yet, have we ever thought of the fact that, by means of a book that would not make more than two hundred duodecimo pages, we know more about Jesus than any inhabitant of Nazareth, any citizen of Cana, any dweller in Sychar, could have known ? They knew only a fragment or two of his experience. They heard only a parable, or saw only one wonderful act performed as he went through their streets on his way to Jerusalem. Which has had the ampler earthly opportunity to get into communion with the mind and spirit of the Saviour, the woman of Samaria, who listened to his talk with her by the well, and misunderstood the most of it, or you, who are present, whenever you please, though the printed biographies, at that interview, and are within "earshot" also of his dialogue with Nicodemus, his parable of the Good Samaritan, his conversation with the young Pharisee, his various calls to consecration, his interpretation of God's character in the picture of the prodigal's father, — you who have the whole outline of Christ's career, and scores of avenues, by his acts and his instructions and his prayers, to reach the inmost riches of his soul ?

Books are our crowning privilege in modern civilization. With a taste for books and music, let every person thank God, night and morning, that he was not born earlier in history. "Books and music," did I say? Books are music. What was it to know Beethoven personally in comparison with knowing and hearing the andante of the Fifth Symphony, the scherzo of the Seventh, the adagio of the Ninth? Books contain the hidden harmonies, the ecstatic melodies of the spirits that are touched to fine issues. If an organ was conscious and could play itself, what would its broken phrases, its irregular fantasies, its musical chatter, however rich in separate tones, or occasional chords, be to the overhearing it some vesper-time, or at midnight, pour out the full capacity of its tenderness and passion through a fugue or mass or Hallelujah Chorus? It is the chatter of genius that we get in the ordinary play of the personality of Shakespeare and Wordsworth, Scott and Carlyle. Sit down alone with "Macbeth" or "The Excursion," with "The Cenci" or "Wallenstein," with "Pilgrim's Progress" or "Guy Mannering" or "Sartor Resartus," and you begin to hear the organ swells and symphonies.

If books cost in proportion to their grade or value, or if the higher levels of composition and creation were, of necessity, so written that they could be understood only by severe application, like that of learning a foreign language, or the higher mathematics, how would society be affected with a fresh and worthy sense of the privilege of books and reading! If only the aristocracy of wealth could buy Dante and the Waverley Novels, and the literature of the age of Elizabeth,

16

or could read of Copernicus, the law of gravitation, and Herschel's astronomy, or could own the Prophets and the four Gospels!

No, — we do not say the empire of letters, the kingdom of letters, the aristocracy or oligarchy of letters, but the republic of letters. Knowledge of the alphabet is your card of invitation and your unquestioned ticket of entrance to its sessions and feasts. A friend of mine said once at a public dinner in New York that it was no wonder the age was bearing on all nations and institutions to greater freedom; "for," said he, "the steam-engine is a snorting democrat." It does have a short-jacket, grimy, shoulder-striking look. Every steam-engine seems to me as though it would like to say, "Take a good stare at me, — I am one of the boys." Only it is not a disunion democrat. It wants free range up and down the country, east and west and criss-cross; and pants for the time when it can scare a herd of buffaloes on the central plains, and make Brigham Young stop his ears, as it screeches through Utah, on an excursion westward with the great United States mail behind, and the old flag flashing through its smoke with no star less than it bears to-day.

So is the steam-press a democrat. Men may hoard money and hide it; but the cylinder-press screams to the people: "If there is any truth uttered in any part of the world, and you want it, let me know and you shall have it cheap." A great man may reserve his personal conversation for a favored few, but the large talk of his soul is poured out through literature to whatever crowds will gather around his page, and even his private correspondence, after one generation, is rummaged for the entertainment of everybody. A man of genius, if he have affluence, may be mean and niggardly with it. He may build a palace for selfish enjoyment, and may wall himself out from sympathy with his kind, while he devotes his means and time to the acquisition of knowledge as a private luxury. But the palace of truth which he rears thus over his spirit, — its foundations of visible fact, its pillars of law, its dome solemn with the glimmer of mysteries, — from this he cannot exclude the race ; our little ticket of the alphabet admits you and me; he cannot fence off his ground or patent his key ; it is open forever to all pilgrims, and "no man can shut the door" ; it is free to you if you have fellowship with his thought, and can be kindled by it, as St. Peter's is to the poorest believer in Rome.*

> * "But we, brought forth and reared in hours
> Of change, alarm, surprise, —
> What shelter to grow ripe is ours?
> What leisure to grow wise?
> Too fast we live, too much are tried,
> Too harassed, to attain
> Wordsworth's sweet calm, or Goethe's wide
> And luminous view to gain."
>
> ARNOLD'S *Obermann.*

When we begin to talk more practically about the privilege of books and reading, of course we must lay heavy stress on the word "selection."

The largest collection of books in the world, the Imperial Library of Paris, contains more than 800,000 volumes and about 100,000 manuscripts. Now we often talk about an omnivorous reader and a very widely read man. But "art is long and time is fleeting." At the rate of a volume a day, stopping on Sundays to rest the eyes (and go to church), it would require almost 3,000 years to finish the job. A man who should have begun it in the reign of King David would be just about checking the last book on the catalogue to-night.

If single copies of every book that has been published since the invention of printing could be placed lengthwise in this State, the line would stretch from the vineyards of Los Angeles to the snowy beard of Mount Shasta. And all the paper that has been printed to be bound into books would doubtless cover every State and Territory, lake, river-bed, and mountain-range of the United States. Yet no man lives, — no threadbare book-worm, no German professor whose blood is a decoction of tobacco-smoke and beer, — that has read through probably half as many volumes as the Mercantile Library in this city contains. So important to the greediest reader does Nature — which does not build our lives on the scale of Methusaleh — make selection.

A hundred volumes, I believe, could be selected, the mastery of which, by attentive reading, would make a man better furnished with instruction, and better able to comprehend and enjoy the advances of knowledge, under the lead of the explorers of this generation, than any scholar or literary man we have in our country to-day. So important is wisdom in selection for its practical benefits!

Of course, I am talking now of reading for the sake of enjoyable knowledge, not for the sake of a profession, or for practical application to any branch of labor, or for the purpose of exhaustive acquaintance with any science or any department of literature. Each of these demands hard study in narrow and exclusive lines. A great German grammarian in Latin, reviewing his career, said that if he could begin his life over again, he should devote himself entirely to the dative case. (Perhaps he is at it now, in the next world.) If a man is ambitious of eminence as a leader or master now in any branch of science or art, he must pour his power thus concentrated in a very restricted groove. But to become an appreciative reader, and to know in pretty full outline the results of the best thinking, discovery, and literary productiveness of this globe, with a general acquaintance, too, with history, I repeat my belief that a hundred volumes, well selected and read carefully and repeatedly, can make a man of average intelligence in this city who can command five hours of leisure out of the twenty-four, better informed than any except the few supereminent literary men of the land.

The prominent classes into which the products of the press may be distributed are three. Books of fact, books of life, and books of art. The first class, or books of fact, include all scientific treatises or manuals in which the discoveries in nature, up to the line of humanity, are registered and interpreted. Books of life include all histories and biographies, and all speculations and inquiries concerning society, morals, and faith. In these two classes the substance of truth is the all-important thing, without regard to elegance of form or attractiveness of arrangement. The third class, books of art, comprehend all the works in verse and prose in which not abstract truth, but exalted pleasure is the object, in which form is as necessary as the matter itself, in which truth appears robed in beauty, for purposes of inspiration. In this division, all poems and dramas, the whole mass of fictitious literature, and every work that asks admission into the department of belles-lettres, must be placed.

Now if a person reads for information, not for practical skill or exhaustive attainment in any line, a very few volumes wisely selected from the first class, the books of fact, will start a man rightly on the road of knowledge, and be an undrainable resource besides. All education, it seems to me, should be based on the revelations of science concerning the scale of space and time. It is a sad shame that so little is known by the general mind — known "for certain," known so as to set our life and our interests in the fit contrasts of glory and gloom, magnificence and mystery — of the results of astronomy and geology. The results may be understood and appreciated by everybody; the processes by which the results are reached of course can be followed and comprehended only by the elect intelligence among men.

Geology opens to us the cellar department, and astronomy the dome, of our home in nature. Mrs. Somerville's "Connection of the Physical Sciences," Lyell's "Elements and Principles of Geology," Nicoll's fascinating work on the Planetary System, or Mitchell's eloquent "Lectures on the Phenomena of the Heavens," or the treatise by Buckland, and the masterly one by Whewell in the Bridgewater Treatises, or parts of the lucid and cheap series by Dr. Lardner, in the course of one winter, if faithfully read, would stretch a man's mind so that he could not go to his business in the morning, or see the evening star steal out from the prison of daylight, without feeling the preparation that has been made for his existence here, and the laws that bind the order of the universe.

No man has a right to go on living in a world whose upholstery is so gorgeous and foundations so sublime, without knowing something of both.

Napoleon, speaking once of courage, said that the highest order was " the two-o'clock-in-the-morning kind," — the courage a man would show in a pressing disaster reported to him when just aroused from sleep.   Now there are some things which a man should know with a two-o'clock-in-the-morning knowledge.   Wake him from deep slumber, and he ought to be able to tell you his birthday, his age, how many feet front his house-lot is, what neighbors live in the same block with him, and what notes he is to meet on steamer-day.   And he ought to be able to tell you as clearly at once the number of full-grown planets in the solar system (of course no one can keep the run of that straggling litter of asteroids, — the pup-orbs of the family), the millions of miles which the earth beats in a year, the reach of the sun's gravitation, the number of States, Territories, and square miles in his country, the salient facts and dates of its history, the probable number of years that the Mississippi has been running, and the dead certainty that he is against secession so long as the Mississippi runs down the line of our climates into the Gulf of Mexico.   [There are some planets within the solar confederacy that do not come out into the visible order and beauty of the family.   One has lately been discovered within the orbit of Mercury, with a very swift, narrow, and fiery track, the Hotspur, the South Carolina, of the confederation ; it has never been seen except as a round dot of darkness hurrying across the great sun's disk (the planet I am talking of); but it would not do to let it go, or to let the sun swallow it. It would be bad for it, bad for the sun, and bad for us.]

A man ought to know all the facts I have alluded to with as decisive and intense a conviction as if he expected to be examined on them every year before the school-board of San Francisco. A late traveller in Liberia tells us that there are inhabitants there who can see the satellites of Jupiter with the unassisted eye. Every person that has had a common-school education ought to carry with him a sub-consciousness of the immensity of the zodiac and the splendors of the space in which his life is framed.

And half a dozen fascinating books will tell all this, and the distance of the nearest fixed star, and how near Lord Rosse's telescope has come to seeing houses on the moon. All it needs is that they be read, not as water is poured upon sand, but as water is poured upon the root of a tree, to be absorbed and incorporated into instinctive knowledge.

The books of fact include every department of science, organic and inorganic, — sciences of force and sciences of law ; and in every department the results have been popularized for parlors as fast as demonstrated, and can be understood and enjoyed by anybody who has mind enough to cast interest for months and days at one and a half per cent. The constitution, laws, and speed of light

16 *

can be investigated and proved by very few, but anybody who can peel a potato can enjoy the eloquent description of their mystic witchery. You need not drag the sea to appreciate Maury's entrancing book upon it. Physical geography is one of the most winning and simple of studies in such a work as Guyot's "Earth and Man," the compressed oil of ten thousand books of travel and the geological delving of countless explorers. Without a tithe of the toil which it would require to add by discovery or culture one to the three hundred and twenty thousand species of plants which botanists distinguish, you may learn their classes, the processes of botanic growth, and the laws of their distribution. And of the two millions of forms of organic life which the zoölogists have enumerated, though you never hear or read the names of a hundred of them, you may become acquainted with the thoughts of the Creator which they express, and the exact plans of structure on which all the myriads have been strung from this hour back to the morning of the fifth day of the creation. Very few of us could learn to build a grand piano. Not a soul in this land could write a melody of Mozart any more than he could make a nightingale's throat. Comparatively few can learn to play one, when properly imbedded in its harmony. But how many can appreciate and delight in one when played! In the chief sciences the instrument is built, the music is written, skilled performers are playing it to us ; the question is simply if we will unstop our ears and listen.

Books of life, I suppose, are naturally more attractive than books of fact, that detain us outside of humanity. History and biography are the prominent branches of this division ; and in both departments human genius and industry seem to have been exerted to the utmost strain, since this century began, to increase the resources of easy knowledge and delight for the average mind.

The most important events in the deciphered history of nations may be gained in one winter's reading. Of course, histories are an endless task : but history, its epochs, outline, and mountain-swells of controlling and determining facts, is within the grasp of six months' consecutive, interested reading in leisure hours.

Of course, the method would have to be a little different from that of the English country gentleman, who, to cultivate his mind and solace his lonesomeness, concluded to attack the "Vicar of Wakefield" in successive evenings. He placed the book-mark properly every night to note his progress, which was ten pages a sitting, and as regularly a roguish niece put the mark back, before the next sitting, about eight pages. His advance was almost as slow as that of the toad in the well who jumped up four feet and fell back six. After some months, however, the squire did jump out of his well, and the niece asked him how he liked the volume. " O, very well, but don't you think there's a little repetition in it ? "

If we do not put the book-mark back too often, we can learn the deepest facts and truths which thirty centuries hide, in a year, so as to have a track of twilight, at least, in our memory over its expanse. How much that one book about the fifteen decisive battles of the world, which costs about a dollar, clears up to a reader who knows the general divisions of history and relations of empires !

And what can be more refreshing and stimulating than Prescott's histories connected with Spain, and Macaulay's England ? They ought to be read always in connection and contrast, to learn something of the art of historic painting, and how various are the methods by which ability of equal range and level communicates itself and produces its effects.

The first thing to do, in reading either of those works, is to become acquainted with the truth which the authors have quarried for us and arranged. But the processes of arrangement are no less interesting in their way as studies. Go from a chapter of Macaulay to a chapter of Prescott, and you are affected with an unpleasant sense of thinness in the sentences, poverty in expression, commonplace in the reflections, and watery paleness in the color. Macaulay is so opulent in vivid detail, exuberant in rhetoric, affluent in discriminating logic, and the palette from which he enlivens his canvas is so rich with deep, strong Rubens-hues! You feel, in contrast, that it is a very limited dictionary from which Mr. Prescott draws ; it seems doubtful if he will be able to find words enough to get through a dozen pages more ; and half his space seems to be filled with crayon-outlines, because he had not pigments enough for his brush.

But read a volume of each and compare the results in your memory! How superior Prescott is in the ability to handle and dispose all the facts of a reign, or to open a vista through the entangled politics of a continent! He is consummate master of historical perspective. Macaulay's canvas is all foreground, packed with vivid characters the drawing of any one of which is a triumph. No man so competent to finish a portrait in an essay : but his history is a collection of essays and a succession of portraits ; and we miss at the close the higher art which subordinates parts, masses and reduces detail, graduates light, concentrates splendor, and gives the grateful impression of large space, unity, and repose. In these qualities of a great historian, — in the arrangement of background and distance, and the relation of events to prominent characters, and one policy, and final unity of impression, so that facts group themselves into the sternest unspoken moral, — Mr. Prescott is as superior to Macaulay as he seems to be inferior in the treasury of gifts which a historian, one would think, requires as an outfit.

I must not dwell on such points here, however,

for they belong properly under the last head of the lecture. I allude to it, in passing, to indicate the stores of enjoyment as well as instruction at the command of those who read histories with open eye. Each prominent name— Gibbon, Thirlwall, Thierry, Grote, Guizot, Merivale, Milman, Michelet, Carlyle, Bancroft, Motley — is a painter on a large scale ; can be compared with some master in the art of color ; and yields from his volumes the double joy, when wisely read, of immense information and peculiar art in the grouping and illumination of it.

But the richest region in the wide literature of life is the department of biography. We need science enough to give us the scale of our existence here, and history enough to show us in a general way how old we are, and who are our fathers, and what are the chief moral strata of the past ; but it is still true that "the proper study of mankind is man."

The readers may be few who can appreciate the kinds of genius displayed in the laying out and filling in of a great history, but every person of moderate attainments and leisure can appreciate and enjoy the masterpieces of biographical literature. If I were to begin life now, and to lay anew the foundations of a library, it should be controllingly a biographical one, — literary portraits, memoirs, and correspondence. There is no way in which history is taught so vividly, and by which we get so close to the springs of it.

There is no way in which so much anecdote, wit, vivid and sparkling truth, can be acquired. There is no way in which moral impressions so healthy and deep may be left on the conscience and heart.

And think of it, each week may introduce you to some man or woman of genius, — monarch, general, priest, statesman, philanthropist, scientist, traveller, inventor, discoverer, poet, artist. You may see his whole life — the dawn of his genius, his struggles and sorrows, his wrongs and triumphs — in the pomp of his intellectual strength, and in his dressing-gown and slippers. You may take a look through him at his century ; you may see how he treats his wife and children ; you may know what he had for dinner and the best things he and his guests gossiped about : you may rummage even his private letters. Eaves-dropping and keyhole listening are contemptible, unless we do it at the remove of a generation. Then it is biography. The queen is very strict with the reception-invitations and etiquette. St. James Street is wary and scrupulous as to cards to dinner and soirées. Wait a little while, and the walls are thrown down and the rabble look on. Histories are the large landscapes. Biographies are the stereoscopic interiors of the past.

The third department of literature I spoke of comprehends books of art, or books in which the

subjects are either fictitious and ideal or in
which the form and moulding are integral elements of their value.

All novels are included in this department.
This in all popular libraries is the most attractive
alcove. We can-see that our city library is no
exception ; for by the monthly statistics it continues true that about ten times more works of
fiction are sought from its store-house than from
any other line of literature.

It is useless to quarrel with this fact, if we
dislike its intimations ; for it is useless to quarrel with a primal passion of our being. And it
is folly for any intelligent man to cast a slight, or
utter any indiscriminate scorn against novels as
a class. There is no such thing as novels as a
class ; we might as well speak of human life as
a class or history as a class.

Fiction is a mighty branch of literature, including under it different orders, classes, genera, and
species of books. English fiction and German
fiction no more belong to the same species than
a leopard and a hippopotamus. Modern French
fiction has a vitality as different from the modern
Anglo-Saxon as the life in a healthy body differs
from "the worm that dieth not" in the carcass
due to Gehenna. Sans-Culotteism in 1789 broke
up into Paris from the pit of flame. The By-
ronic spirit in literature is often characterized as
the Satanic school. But as Milton's fiend could
never get to the bottom of his abyss, finding

beneath each deep "a lower deep still threaten-
ing to devour" him, we see in the latest schools
of French novels the presiding demon of all can-
cerous corruption in the human heart, rising, not
from Stygian gloom and flame, but with appropriate effluvium from what Swedenborg describes
to us as the excrementitious hells.

The Saxon intellect has hardly shown its richness and soundness more marvellously during the
last sixty years, in the progress of science and the
miracles of invention, than through its fertility in
noble fictions, from Scott and Miss Austen to
Thackeray, Dickens, Kingsley, and the painters of
Jane Eyre, John Halifax, and Adam Bede.   Such
creativeness has not been known since the age of
Shakespeare.

And after biography, no reading can be made
more profitable, if the substructure of education
has been attended to, than novels.   Of course,
they must be read for something beyond sensations, — as products of art and of thought.

A library of novels is like a gallery of pictures.
One man saunters through the gallery and sees
what the pictures are about, — one is a battle-
piece, one a sunset in Italy, one a love-scene, one
a Madonna, one a mountain-range, one a sea-
storm.   Another man goes through the gallery,
sits before the chief pictures, and sees what the
artists were about, — what is the range of the powers of each, the degrees of their technical skill,
and the directions in which they lie open to the

Infinite.   The first man sees the paint, all of it ;
the second man sees the paintings.   The first has
whiled away an hour, and had a sensation ; the
last has enjoyed himself intelligently and fed his
mind.   Novels — good ones — have all the range
and all the characteristics of the higher classes of
paintings, — color, tone, grouping, precision of
drawing, perspective, and the quality of the lesson,
or the elevation of spirit, that looks out through
all.   And when read with one eye to the story —
the left eye — and the other — the right — to the
art of the book, the pleasure is intellectually as
profitable as it is noble.

Suppose an intelligent reader of Walter Scott's
novels — one who has gone through them all two
or three times — should attempt to account to
himself for his reading, and force himself to give
a rational verdict which novel, or which triad of
them, shows the ripest power ; or suppose a
reading-circle should devote two or three evenings
to the point why "Guy Mannering" is a greater
book than "Ivanhoe," which has more glitter,
and "The Heart of Mid-Lothian" than "Quentin
Durward" or "Count Robert of Paris," the reflection and the discussion would bring out into distinct relief the real privileges of fiction-reading.
Nobody concerned could help, after that, perusing
a novel more carefully.

Or let us imagine a reading-circle attempting to
classify novels by these tests.   Which of them
deal most faithfully with the ultimate realities and

passions of human nature, and which are conven-
tional, drawing character within a very narrow circle of society and experience, or what recent
novelist deals most nobly with the passion of
love, and what one with the religious sentiment?
or what is the organic difference between the
methods of drawing a life-portrait by Dickens and
by Thackeray? Still further, let a reading-circle,
or any devourer of books, propose these queries
for outward or mental discussion : Why Mr.
Charles Reade, so brilliant in swift sketches and
dialogue, cannot unfold and develop a character
without degrading it ; why Copperfield stands
head and shoulders above the range of Mr. Dickens's stories ; why it is absurd and libellous (for
I believe it is both) to say that Mr. Thackeray's
writings are mere satires, and weaken faith in the
reality of virtue ; why the close of Bulwer's work,
" What will He do with it," — a work in which
incidents are handled, woven, and untangled with
such a masterly hand, — is such an unmitigated
piece of snobbery that one feels like pitching
book and author into a region where types are
nevermore set up; why " Charles Auchester "
must have been written with ink weakened by
milk-and-water; why Mrs. Stowe's " Dred," the
first volume of which is by far the grandest volume
she has written, runs down so swiftly into weakness and failure in the second ; why the drawing of Rochester, so melodramatic in attitudes and
color, is the feeblest portion, intellectually, of a

book which is more marvellous on the tenth reading than on the first, — Jane Eyre ; and wherein
consists the literary art by which Miss Brontë
could describe the furniture of a room and a
sleety day so that they are more vivid than light
and experience could make them ; why the au-
thoress of " Adam Bede" is the most eminent
of living feminine English novelists, and why the
largeness of handling, the freedom from all spasm,
the reserve, and the depth of moral space out of
which each character shines like a star from the
boundless blue, make it superior to the more narrow, more coarse, a little more bitter, though still
very able and vigorous, " Mill on the Floss."

These hap-hazard queries relate rather to the
artistic qualities of novels, and show by casual
suggestion how varied and deep they are. The
moral interests in all eminent and decent fiction
is no less. What is more dreary than moral
philosophy, or the abstract discussion of questions
of ethics bearing on the grades of sentiments and
conflicts of duties ? But no question was ever
raised, possibly, by the acutest casuist which has
not been set at work vitally and dramatically in
some modern novel. And if all novel-readers
were compelled, when they close a book, to write
out the main doctrine or proposition which is the
axis of the incidents and plot, it would be better
for their moral education than if they could listen
once a week to the best lecture on ethics that is
delivered by the foremost professor in civilization.

One of the most practical, impressive, and strong-headed preachers in this country is a constant student of novels. They are the staple of his reading. They furnish him with a museum of characters, and with revelations of the status and needs of modern society which no other reading could furnish. He sees the world, he tastes life, by means of them, as we all may, if we will approach them for something besides their pepper and salt, for what their condiments merely flavor. And I have often thought that the pulpit could not do better with one sermon in every quarter, than by preaching on the health or disease of the most prominent novel which all parishioners are reading, and showing wherein and how far its main characters illustrate or reject the spirit of life which glows through the incidents of the four Gospels from " the Word made flesh."

In other departments of books of art, in all the higher forms of prose and in poetry, the key to the richest enjoyment is a sensitive taste for style, for differences and peculiarities in richness, melody, and rhythm.

It is said that, with his eyes shut, a man could not tell the difference between beef and mutton, veal and rabbit, pork and elk. Let them be put in his mouth without seeing or smelling, and his tongue could not tell "which is which." It may be so, but it is no reason why a man cannot tell, and ought not to be able to tell, with his eyes open.

There are persons who seem to be utterly im-
pervious to the flavors of literature. One book
reads as much like another, to them, as one mul-
tiplication-table like another. But since the first
book was written which belongs in the artistic
region, no two styles are alike. They differ even
in prose, as faces, forms, gaits, differ. They differ
because souls differ. No two living books, to the
end of time, will have the same style. Often the
very best and most precious thing about a noble
book is its style. It is, as to its matter, what the
atmosphere is to a landscape in Southern Italy.
Banish its unctuous opaline lusciousness, and
hang a New Hampshire air over it, and see how
much is gone. Strip the style off and leave the
matter in Mr. De Quincey's essays, and you would
find that it is like taking the sound out of a grove
of pines.

This miracle of style has not been sounded
yet, — why, when one man writes a fact, it is cold
or commonplace, and when another man writes
it, in a little different, but equivalent phraseology,
it is a rifle-shot or a revelation. One can
understand a little how the wink or twinkle of
an eye, how an attitude, how a gesture, how a
cadence or impassioned sweep of voice, should
make a boundless distance between truths stated
or declaimed. But how words, locked up in
forms, still and stiff in sentences, contrive to tip
a wink, how a proposition will insinuate more
scepticism than it states, how a paragraph will

drip with the honey of love, how a phrase will trail an infinite suggestion, how a page can be so serene or so gusty, so gorgeous or so pallid, so sultry or so cool, as to lap you in one intellectual climate or its opposite, — who has fathomed yet this wonder?

"The style is the man." Education for enjoying and fathoming books of art consists in becoming sensitive to their air and music. There are elements in Hawthorne's romances, all of them, as repulsive to me as anything, not openly immoral, in literature. But his style, so sweet, natural, genial, perspicuous, easy in its most curious felicities, the purest and most artistic English, I believe, written by any pen in a living hand to-day, — English of a higher order even than Washington Irving's, though akin to Irving's in showing something of "that sleepy smile that lies so benignly on the sweet and serious diction of old Izaak Walton," — this makes me love his genius, and believe that it is destined for richer service yet in the universe, when the unhealthy spot shall be taken by the proper medicine or surgery out of his soul.

A man with leisure and a tendency to reading, who has no appreciation of the subtleties of grace and meaning in styles, is to be pitied as a man is to be commiserated to whom a banana and lemon taste alike, and who should eat the berries and fruits of summer — apricots and plums, Bartletts and early Crawfords — as a turkey gobbles oats and corn. How often I have heard people class Mr. Emerson and Carlyle together, and say that one borrowed from the other, — men whose philosophy of life bear as much resemblance as a tropic thunder-storm and an arctic night, and whose styles are as much alike as the light of a pitch-pine knot blazing and smoking in a wild mountain pass and an icicle hanging with still, clear, pitiless brilliance in a winter noon.

I cannot enlarge upon this point with illustrations to enforce it ; but can only say that it applies to poetry as manifestly, at least, as to prose.

One of the strangest things which a deep student of Shakespeare learns is the variety of his music and rhythm in the same ten-syllable blank-verse. No other writer of his age commanded such music ; and the movement and measure of his Macbeth and Romeo, Hamlet and Antony, Lear and Tempest, are as different as if different writers — on the Shakespeare level — had given each the training of a life to one of these plays. And in each case the movement or melody is a subtle accompaniment to the passion or the law that informs and ensouls the piece.

The reason why Goethe cannot be translated is that no equal Goethe stands on the English side of the line to link the equivalent words with equivalent music. The process of rendering Goethe or Beranger into another tongue is that which a German, not over-familiar with our phrases, uses to describe translation; he says such a German book has been "upset into English."

A reader with an ear for melody has a feast spread for him in Saxon poetry fit for Apollo. Many a person imagines that a poet's office is akin to that of wood-sawyers, — that it is their business to saw up language into measure, and pile it even and gracefully, rhymed at the end. But with the ear for rhythm, Milton and Wordsworth, Coleridge and Shelley, Keats and Tennyson, are richer than an organ in the house. It was Hood, I believe, who divided poetry into two kinds, "verse and worse." The verse is what has melody, that which has it not is worse. Charles Mackay's verses seem as though they were composed on an even, hard-trotting horse upon a macadamized road. Whittier writes as though a trumpet was continually sounding through his Quaker soul. What an advance in melody in Longfellow, from the "Voices of the Night," with its "sweet sixteen" poetry and sentiment, to some of the chapters of "Hiawatha" and his last lyric in the Atlantic Monthly, "Paul Revere's Ride"! What exquisite meditative imagination in the slow sinuous harmony of Bryant's "Thanatopsis"! Coleridge — and in this respect Edgar Poe was like him — seemed to write fragments only to show how superior is the suggestion of sound to the expression of sense in verse. Shelley's words,

17

in many of his songs, appear to stand there simply
to prevent the melody from melting into utter
spirit.   And Tennyson's "Idyls of the King," the
crowning work of his genius, needs the rarest
voices that have been attuned on the globe to
read it, and set free the melody healthy and delicate as the echoes which his own Bugle Song
describes : —

> " O hark, O hear, how thin and clear,
> And thinner, clearer, farther going,
> O sweet and far, from cliff and scar,
> The horns of Elfland faintly blowing."

So from souls on the western shore of the Atlantic,
and from the borders of the Pacific, too, the echoes
return of his genius.

And here we must pause.   The distance of a
star, the age of the planet, the flow of history, the
stores of biography, the vast and crowded spaces
of fiction, the richest music borne from infinite
deeps through the rarest pipes of genius, — such
knowledge, such society, such inspiration, or such
solace may be ours through a library of a hundred
books ; no more.   If you have taste, you may find
leisure to win something of the luxury of truth or art
in the busiest life for the uplifting of your spirit.

Mrs. Browning in one of her early poems, " A
Vision of Poets," describes a church she saw in a
dream, and the approach of the great masters of
verse and passion at midnight up its aisles to its
altar : —

> " Here Homer, with the broad suspense
> Of thunderous brows, and lips intense
> Of garrulous god-innocence.

" There Shakespeare, on whose forehead climb
 The crowns o' the world.   O eyes sublime,
 With tears and laughters for all time !

   .   .   .   .   .

" Electric Pindar, quick as fear,
 With race-dust on his cheeks, and clear,
 Slant, startled eyes that seem to hear
 The chariot rounding the last goal.

   .   .   .   .   .

"Lucretius, nobler than his mood;
 Who dropped his plummet down the broad
 Deep universe, and said, ' No God,'

" Finding no bottom : he denied
 Divinely the divine, and died
 Chief poet on the Tiber-side.

" And Ossian dimly seen or guessed ;
 Once counted greater than the rest,
 When mountain-winds blew out his vest.

   .   .   .   .   .

" And Goethe, with that reaching eye
 His soul looked out from, far and high,
 And fell from inner entity.

" And Schiller, with heroic front,
 Worthy of Plutarch's kiss upon 't,
 Too large for wreath of modern wont.

   .   .   .

" Here Milton's eyes strike piercing-dim,
 The shapes of suns and stars did swim
 Like clouds from them, and granted him
 God for sole vision.

   .   .   .   .

" And Burns, with pungent passionings
 Set in his eyes.   Deep lyric springs
 Are of the fire-mount's issuings.

   .   .   .   .   .

" And poor, proud Byron, — sad as grave
 And salt as life : forlornly brave,
 And quivering with the dart he drave.

" And visionary Coleridge, who
  Did sweep his thoughts as angels do
  Their wings, with cadence up the blue.

" These poets faced, and many more,
  The lighted altar looming o'er
  The clouds of incense dim and hoar.

" And all their faces in the lull
  Of natural things looked wonderful
  With life, and death, and deathless rule."

And such an altar we may have in our memory
and our inner being, where all these men, and
others, the priests of science and the great servants of good, shall be our companions, teachers,
and friends.   The title to it is taste for literature,
reading with our eyes open, reading with rigid
selection and exclusion, reading with a sense of
its privilege, reading for an end.

1861.

XI.

THE PRIVILEGE AND DUTIES OF PATRIOTISM.*

LET us waste no words in introduction or preface. I am to speak to you of the Privilege and Duties of American Patriotism.

First the Privilege. Patriotism is love of country. It is a privilege that we are capable of such a sentiment. Self-love is the freezing-point in the temperature of the world. As the heart is kindled and ennobled it pours out feeling and interest, first upon family and kindred, then upon country, then upon humanity. The home, the flag, the cross, — these are the representatives or symbols of the noblest and most sacred affections or treasures of feeling in human nature.

We sometimes read arguments by very strict moralists which cast a little suspicion upon the value of patriotism as a virtue, for the reason that the law of love, unrestricted love, should be our guide and inspiration. We must be cosmopolitan by our sympathy, they prefer to say. Patriotism, if it interferes with the wider spirit of humanity, is

* From an Address before the "Sumner Light Guard," November 18, 1862.

sectionalism of the heart. We must not give up to country " what is meant for mankind."

Such sentiments may be uttered in the interest of Christian philanthropy, but they are not healthy. The Divine method in evoking our noblest affections is always from particulars to generals. God " hath set the solitary in families," and bound the families into communities, and organized communities into nations ; and he has ordained special duties for each of these relationships, and inspired affections to prompt the discharge of them, and to exalt the character.

The law of love is the principle of the spiritual universe just as gravitation is the governing force of space. It binds each particle of matter to every other particle, but it attracts inversely as the square of the distance, and thus becomes practically a series of local or special forces, holding our feet perpetually to one globe, and allowing only a general unity, which the mind appropriates through science and meditation, with the kindred but far-off spheres. The man that has most of the sentiment of love will have the most intense special affections. You cannot love the whole world and nobody in particular. If you try that, it will be true of you as of the miser who said, " what I give is nothing to nobody." However deep his baptism in general good-will, a man must look with a thrill that nothing else can awaken, into the face of the mother that bore him ; he cannot cast off the ties that bind him to filial

responsibilities and a brother's devotion ; and
Providence has ordained that out of identity of
race, a common history, the same scenery, literature, laws, and aims, — though in perfect harmony
with good-will to all men, — the wider family
feeling, the distinctive virtue, patriotism, should
spring. If the ancient Roman could believe that
the yellow Tiber was the river dearest to Heaven ;
if the Englishman can see a grandeur in the
Thames which its size will not suggest ; if the Alpine storm-wind is a welcome home-song to the
Swiss mountaineer ; if the Laplander believes that
his country is the best the sun shines upon ; if the
sight of one's own national flag in other lands will
at once awaken feelings that speed the blood and
melt the eyes ; if the poorest man will sometimes
cherish a proud consciousness of property in the
great deeds that glow upon his country's annals
and the monuments of its power, — let us confess
that the heart of man, made for the Christian law,
was made also to contract a special friendship for
its native soil, its kindred stock, its ancestral
traditions, — let us not fail to see that where the
sentiment of patriotism is not deep, a sacred
affection is absent, an essential element of virtue
is wanting, and religion barren of one prominent
witness of its sway.

But why argue in favor of patriotism as a
lofty virtue ? History refuses to countenance the
analytic ethics of spiritual dreamers. It pushes
into notice Leonidas, Tell, Cincinnatus, Camillus,

Hampden, Winkelried, Scipio, Lafayette, Adams, Bolivar, and Washington, in whom the sentiment has become flesh, and gathered to itself the world's affections and honors. It asks us, " What do you say of these men? These are among the brighter jewels of my kingdom. Thousands of millions fade away into the night in my realm, but these souls shine as stars, with purer lustre as they retreat into the blue of time. Is not their line of greatness as legitimate as that of poets, philosophers, philanthropists, and priests?"

Nay, the Bible is opened for us, to stimulate and increase our love of country. Patriotism is sanctioned and commended and illustrated there by thrilling examples : — by the great patriot-prophet Moses, who, during all those wilderness-years, bore the Hebrew people in his heart; by Joshua, who sharpened his sword on the tables of stone till its edge was keen as the righteous wrath of Heaven and its flame fierce as a flash from Sinai, as it opened a path through an idolatrous land for the colonization of a worthier race and a clean idea ; (O that there were enough of that steel in America to-day to make a sword for the leader of the Union armies !) by the great statesman Samuel, to whom every Jew may point with pride as the Hebrew Washington; by David, who, for the glory of his nation, wielded the hero's sword and tuned the poet's harp; by the long line of the fire-tongued prophets, whose hearts burned for their country's redemption while they pro-

claimed the "higher law"; by the lyric singers
of the exile, like him who chanted the lament,
which seems to gush from the very heart of patriotism, "How shall we sing the Lord's song in
a strange land? If I forget thee, O Jerusalem, let
my right hand forget her cunning. . . . . Let my
tongue cleave to the roof of my mouth, if I prefer
not Jerusalem above my chief joy!"

Yes, and when we pass higher up than these
worthies of the older inspiration, to Him the
highest name, Him from whom we have received
our deepest life, Him whose love embraced the
whole race in its scope, the eternal and impartial
Love made flesh, who pronounced the parable of
the Good Samaritan, and shed the warmth of that
spirit through his life into the frosty air of human
sentiment, do we not read that he felt more keenly
the alienation of his countrymen according to the
flesh than he felt the spear-point and the nails,
and paused over the beautiful city of David to
utter a lament whose burden swept away the pros-
pect of his own lowering destiny,—"O Jerusalem,
Jerusalem, ... how often would I have gathered
your children together, even as a hen gathereth
her chickens under her wings, and ye would
not. Behold, your house is left unto you desolate."

Although the highest office of revelation is to
point to and prepare us for "a better country, even
a heavenly," no one can rightly read the pages
of the Bible without catching enthusiasm for his

earthly country, the land of his fathers, the shelter of his infancy, the hope of his children.

It is a privilege of our nature, hardly to be measured, that we are capable of the emotion of patriotism, that we can feel a nation's life in our veins, rejoice in a nation's glory, suffer for a nation's momentary shame, throb with a nation's hope. It is as if each particle of matter that belongs to a mountain, each crystal hidden in its darkness, each grass-blade on its lower slopes, each pebble amid its higher desolation, each snow-flake of its cold and tilted fields, could be conscious, all the time, of the whole bulk and symmetry and majesty and splendor of the pile, — of how it glows at evening, of how it blazes at the first touch of morning light, of its pride when it overtops the storm, of the joy it awakens in hearts that see in it the power and glory of the Creator. It is as if each could exult in feeling — I am part of this organized majesty; I am an element in one flying buttress of it, or its firm-poised peak; I contribute to this frosty radiance; I am ennobled by the joy it awakens in every beholder's breast!

Think of a man living in one of the illustrious civilized communities of the world, and insensible to its history, honor, and future, — say of England! Think of an intelligent inhabitant of England so wrapped in selfishness that he has no consciousness of the mighty roots of that kingdom, nor of the toughness of its trunk, nor

of the spread of its gnarled boughs! Runny-
mede and Agincourt are behind him, but he is
insensible to the civil triumph and the knightly
valor. All the literature that is crowned by
Bacon, Shakespeare, and Milton, the noblest this
earth ever produced from one national stock,
awakens in him no heart-beat of pride. He
reads of the sturdy blows in the great rebellion,
and of the gain to freedom by the later and more
quiet revolution, and it is no more to him than
if the record had been dropped from another
planet. The triumphs of English science over
nature, the hiss of her engines, the whirl of her
wheels, the roar of her factory drums, the crackle
of her furnaces, the beat of her hammers, the
vast and chronic toil that mines her treasures,
affect him with no wonder and arouse no exult-
ant thrill of partnership. And he sees nothing
and feels nothing that stirs his torpid blood in
the strokes and sweep of that energy, before
which the glory of Waterloo and Trafalgar is
dim, which has knit to the English will colonies
and empires within a century which number
nearly one fourth of the inhabitants of the globe.
The red flag of England hung out on all her
masts, from all her house tops, and from every
acre of her conquests and possessions, would
almost give this planet the color of Mars, if seen
through a telescope from a neighboring star.
What a privilege to be a conscious fibre of that
compacted force! If I were an Englishman, I

should be proud every hour of every day over my heritage. I believe I should now and then imitate the man who sat up all night to hate his brother-in-law, and sit up all night to exult in my privilege. And as an Englishman I should keep clear of the pollution of sympathy with the American rebellion. The man who is dead to such pride ought not to be rated as a man.

And is it any less a privilege to be an American? Suppose that the continent could turn towards you to-morrow at sunrise, and show to you the whole American area in the short hours of the sun's advance from Eastport to the Pacific! You would see New England roll into light from the green plumes of Aroostook to the silver stripe of the Hudson; westward thence over the Empire State, and over the lakes, and over the sweet valleys of Pennsylvania, and over the prairies, the morning blush would run and would waken all the line of the Mississippi; from the frosts where it rises, to the fervid waters in which it pours, for three thousand miles it would be visible, fed by rivers that flow from every mile of the Alleghany slope, and edged by the green embroideries of the temperate and tropic zones; beyond this line another basin, too, the Missouri, catching the morning, leads your eye along its western slope till the Rocky Mountains burst upon the vision, and yet do not bar it; across its passes we must follow, as the stubborn courage of American pioneers has forced its way, till

again the Sierra and their silver veins are tinted
along the mighty bulwark with the break of day ;
and then over to the gold-fields of the western
slope, and the fatness of the California soil, and
the beautiful valleys of Oregon, and the stately
forests of Washington, the eye is drawn, as the
globe turns out of the night-shadow, and when
the Pacific waves are crested with radiance, you
have the one blending picture, nay, the reality,
of the American domain ! No such soil, so varied
by climate, by products, by mineral riches, by forest and lake, by wild heights and buttresses, and
by opulent plains, — yet all bound into unity of
configuration and bordered by both warm and
icy seas, — no such domain was ever given to
one people.

And then suppose that you could see in a picture as vast and vivid the preparation for our
inheritance of this land : — Columbus haunted by
his round idea and setting sail in a sloop to see
Europe sink behind him, while he was serene in
the faith of his dream ; the later navigators of
every prominent Christian race who explored the
upper coasts ; the Mayflower with her cargo of
sifted acorns from the hardy stock of British
puritanism, and the ship, whose name we know
not, that bore to Virginia the ancestors of Washington ; the clearing of the wilderness, and the
dotting of its clearings with the proofs of manly
wisdom and Christian trust ; then the gradual interblending of effort and interest and sympathy

into one life, the congress of the whole Atlantic slope to resist oppression upon one member, the rally of every State around Washington and his holy sword, and again the nobler rally around him when he signed the Constitution, and after that the organization of the farthest West with North and South into one polity and communion; when this was finished, the tremendous energy of free life, under the stimulus and with the aid of advancing science, in increasing wealth, subduing the wilds to the bonds of use, multiplying fertile fields, and busy schools, and noble workshops, and churches hallowed by free-will offerings of prayer, and happy homes, and domes dedicated to the laws of states that rise by magic from the haunts of the buffalo and deer, all in less than a long lifetime; and if we could see also how, in achieving this, the flag which represents all this history is dyed in traditions of exploits, by land and sea, that have given heroes to American annals whose names are potent to conjure with, while the world's list of thinkers in matter is crowded with the names of American inventors, and the higher rolls of literary merit are not empty of the title of our "representative men " : — if all that the past has done for us and the present reveals could thus stand apparent in one picture, and then if the promise of the future to the children of our millions under our common law, and with continental peace, could be caught in one vast spectral exhibition, the wealth in store, the power, the privilege, the freedom, the learning, the expansive and varied and mighty unity in fellowship, almost fulfilling the poets dream of

" The Parliament of man, the federation of the world,"

you would exclaim with exultation, " I, too, am an American ! " You would feel that patriotism, next to your tie to the Divine Love, is the greatest privilege of your life ; and you would devote yourselves, out of inspiration and joy, to the obligations of patriotism, that this land so spread, so adorned, so colonized, so blessed, should be kept forever against all the assaults of traitors, one in polity, in spirit, and in aim !

Gentlemen, this is what we ought to do, what we should try to do ; we should seize by our imagination the glory of our country, that our patriotism may be a permanent and a lofty flame. Patriotism is an imaginative sentiment. Imagination is essential to its vigor ; not imagination which distorts facts, but which sweeps a vast field of them and illumines it. It comprehends hills, streams, plains, and valleys in a broad conception, and from traditions and institutions, from the life of the past and the vigor and noble tendencies of the present, it individualizes the destiny and personifies the spirit of its land, and then vows its vow to that.

It is of the very essence of true patriotism, therefore, to be earnest and truthful, to scorn the flatterer's tongue, and strive to keep its native

land in harmony with the laws of national thrift
and power. It will tell a land of its faults, as a
friend will counsel a companion. It will speak
as honestly as the physician advises a patient.
And if occasion requires, an indignation will
flame out of its love like that which burst from
the lips of Moses when he returned from the
mountain and found the people to whom he had
revealed the austere Jehovah, and for whom he
would cheerfully have sacrificed his life, worship-
ping a calf.

We condense all the intimations of these last
thoughts in saying that true patriotism is pledged
to the idea which one's native country represents.
It does not accept and glory in its country merely
for what it is at present and has been in the past,
but for what it may be. Each nation has a representative value. Each race that has appro-
priated a certain latitude which harmonizes with
its blood has the capacity to work out special
good results, and to reveal great truths in some
original forms. God designs that each country
shall bear a peculiar ideal physiognomy, and he
has set its geographical characteristics as a bony
skeleton, and breathed into it a free life spirit,
which, if loyal to the intention, will keep the
blood in health, infuse vigor into every limb, give
symmetry to the form, and carry the flush of a pure
and distinct expression to the countenance. It
is the patriot's office to study the laws of public
growth and energy, and to strive with enthusiastic

love to guard against every disease that would cripple the frame, that he may prevent the lineaments of vice and brutality from degrading the face which God would have radiant with truth, genius, and purity.

He was the best patriot of ancient Greece who had the widest and wisest conception of the capacities and genius of Greece, and labored to paint that ideal winningly before the national mind, and to direct the flame of national aspiration, fanned by heroic memories, up to the noblest possibilities of Grecian endeavor. The truest patriot of England would be the man whose mind should see in the English genius and geography what that nation could do naturally and best for humanity, and, seizing the traditional elements that are in harmony with that possibility, should use them to enliven his own sympathies, and to quicken the nation's energy. We might say the same of Russia and of Italy. The forward look is essential to patriotism.

And how much more emphatically and impressively true is this when we bring our own country into the foreground ! We have been placed on our domain for the sake of a hope. What we have done, and what has been done for us, is only preparation, the outline-sketching of a picture to be filled with color and life in the next three centuries. Shall the sketch be blurred and the canvas be torn in two ? That is what we are to decide in these bitter and bloody days.

Our struggle now is to keep the country from falling away from the idea which every great patriot has recognized as the purpose towards which our history, from the first, has been moving. God devised the scheme for us of one republic. He planted the further slope of the Alleghanies at first with Saxon men ; he has striped the Pacific coast with the energy of their descendants, protecting thus both avenues of entrance to our domain against European intrusion ; but the great wave of population he has rolled across the Alleghanies into the central basin. That is the seat of the American polity. And an imperial river runs through it to embarrass, and to shame, and to balk all plans of rupture. The Mississippi bed was laid by the Almighty as the keel of the American ship, and the channel of every stream that pours into it is one of its ribs. We have just covered the mighty frame with planking, and have divided the hull into State compartments. And the rebels say, " Break the ship in two." They scream, " We have a right to, on the ground of the sovereignty of the compartments, and the principles of the Declaration of Independence ; we have a right to, and we will ! " The loyal heart of the nation answers, " We will knock out all your Gulf compartments and shiver your sovereign bulkheads, built of ebony, to pieces, and leave you one empty territory again, before you shall break the keel." This is the right answer. We must do it, not only for our own safety, but to preserve the idea which the nation has been called to fulfil, and to which patriotism is called and bound to be loyal. Ay, even if there were one paragraph or line in the Declaration of Independence that breathed or hinted a sanction of the rebellion! Geology is older than the pen of Jefferson; the continent is broader than the Continental Congress; and they must go to the foundations to learn their statesmanship.

The Procrustes bed of American patriotism is the bed of the Mississippi, and every theory of national life and every plan for the future must be stretched on that; and woe to its wretched bones and sockets if it naturally reaches but halfway!

Providence made the country, too, when the immense basin should be filled with its fitting millions, to show the world the beauty and economy of continental peace. It is a destiny radically different from that of Europe, with its four millions of armed men, that has been indicated for us. By the interplay of widely different products into one prosperity — cotton and cattle, tobacco and corn, metals and manufactures, shipyards and banking-rooms, forests and fields, — and all under one law, and all enjoying local liberty, — sufficient centralization, but the mildest pressure on the subordinate districts and the personal will — Providence designed to bless us with immense prosperity, to develop an energy unseen before on this globe, and to teach the nations a lesson which would draw them into universal fraternity and peace.

The rebels have tried to frustrate this hope and scheme. Patriotism, which discerns the idea to which the nation is thus called, arms to prevent its defeat. They say that there shall not be such unified prosperity and all-embracing peace for the future hundreds of millions on our domain. We say that there shall. And we arm to enforce our vision.

But is not that a strange way to establish peace, by fighting on such a scale as the republic now witnesses? Is it not a novel method to labor for economy of administration and expense in government by a war which will fetter the nation with such a debt? We answer, the rebellion gave the challenge, and now victory at any cost is the only economy. Carnage, if they will it, is the only path to peace.

> "For our own good
> All causes shall give way; we are in blood
> Stept in so far, that, should we wade no more,
> Returning were as tedious as go o'er."

Yes, if we return, all our blood and treasure are wasted. The peace we gain by victory is for all the future, and for uncounted millions. The debt we incur by three years' fighting will be nothing compared with the new energy and security aroused, nothing to the next hundred years. And it will establish the idea to which the land was dedicated.

But do you say that if we conquer the rebellious area, we must hold it in subjection by a standing army which will be very costly, and is contrary to the American idea? Very well, if we do not conquer, if the rebels gain a strong and arrogant independence, we must keep up an immense standing army. It would cost more to watch them than it will to hold them. For we should be obliged in watching them to watch Europe too. We prefer to pay money to hold rather than to watch; and if we pay our money I suppose we can take our choice. Patriotism says, and says it in the interest of peace and economy and final fraternity, "Fight and conquer even at the risk of holding them for a generation under the yoke." Fight, though, on such a scale, that there will be no need of holding them; that they will gladly submit again to the rule which makes the republic one, and blesses all portions with protection and with bounty. Fight till they shall know that they kick against fate and the resistless laws of the world! Patriotism calls on the Cabinet and the head of the nation and the generals who give tone to the campaign to forget the customs and interests of peace till we shall gain it by the submission of the rebels and the shredding of their last banner into threads.

The stake is worth this style of fighting. For it is the peace of our grandchildren, the inter-blended prosperity of the continent, the economy of centuries, the abolition of standing armies for a thousand years, the indefinite postponement of war, the idea of America, that we are to bend up thus "each corporal agent" to secure. Fight with hose-pipes and lavender-water if you want perpetual hatred and indefinite slaughter ; fight with sheets of schrapnel and red-hot shot if you want to see the speedy dawn again of American peace and good-will!

And Providence, still further, dedicated this land as the better home for labor, and to a polity that honors and blesses labor. Not equal rights, so much as new honor to the workman, is the idea which our polity is divinely called to emblazon and to guard. For this and to help this our immense fields were shrouded in darkness until a race should be ready who would bring a free ballot-box with them, and an untitled church, and a free Bible, and the seed of public schools, and a spirit that should shake at last the "glittering generalities" of the Declaration of Independence into literature, like dew-drops in the morning from a tree. Into whatever movement or conceptions the doctrine of the sacredness of man and the worth of labor flows, there patriotism discerns the proper march of the tide of American thought and spirit. Whatever denies and cramps and opposes, that is hostile to the call and destiny of the younger continent. For whatever in America blasphemes the rights of labor and bars the education of the workman, smites the soil to that extent with blight, degrades literature, drains public spirit, chains the wheel of progress, insults

the New Testament, and flouts the nobler traditions of the land.

I need not tell you that the rebellion is guilty
of this too.   It sins against the Mississippi ; it
sins against the coast line ; it sins against the
ballot-box ; it sins against oaths of allegiance ; it
sins against public and beneficent peace ; and
it sins, worse than all, against the corner-stone of
American progress and history and hope, — the
worth of the laborer, the rights of man.   It
strikes for barbarism against civilization.   We
have taken the carbon of labor from Europe, and
tried to promote it into the diamond.   Under the
true American system a journeyman machinist in
his striped shirt becomes General Nathaniel P.
Banks.   The rebel idea is hostile to all this
crystallization.   Keep all labor in its grimy and
carbon state, they say ; and so they choose it
and perpetuate it of a color that will fulfil their
arrogant conception.

Patriotism calls us to brace our sinews against
this hideous apostasy, and to see that the land is
not severed by it.   Our unity gone, our economical peace broken up, standing armies imposed on
us forever, European intrigue and antagonism our
law, — and all for the doctrine that labor may
rightfully be trodden into the mire, — what a
close of the book of our national story !   What
a robbery of the crown from our once proud
forehead !

Gentlemen, it is a privilege that we can feel

a patriotism which sets our present struggle in such relations, and coolly sees that our country has been dedicated to a mission and a service so vast and eminent. The duties correspond to the privilege. One great duty is to feel the privilege more keenly, and by the inspiration of it stand strong for the country's unity.

Especially against any intimation from foreign powers of intervention to stop our war and break our integrity. If France tries it, we will arm as France armed against the intervention of Europe in her great Revolution, and hurled the circling armies back ! If England tries it, we will say to her as Macaulay said, with admirable vigor and eloquence in the House of Commons, when the secession of Ireland was threatened : " The Repeal of the Union we regard as fatal to the empire, and we never will consent to it ; never, though the country should be surrounded by dangers as great as those which threatened her when her American Colonies, and France, and Spain, and Holland were leagued against her, and when the armed neutrality of the Baltic disputed her maritime rights ; never, though another Bonaparte should pitch his camp in sight of Dover Castle ; never, till all has been staked and lost ; never, till the four quarters of the world have been convulsed by the last struggle of the great English people for their place among the nations." It was an island, utterly disjoined from England, and separated more widely by blood and belief than by the chafing sea, of whose threatened secession these words were spoken by the most widely read English orator of this generation. How much more fitly and honorably can we urge the spirit of them if England should attempt to break our hold upon integral portions of our empire, the very courses of our rivers, the very land for which we have paid our millions and our blood! Let the spirit sweep through our loyal millions which Macaulay thus uttered; let us become such a battery that fervor and determination of that temperature shall leap out whenever the thought of foreign intervention is breathed. Then Europe will be careful enough how she touches the awful galvanic pile. Patriotism of that temper will be a peace-preserver.

And another duty of patriotism now is to call for the declaration of a new policy in the war.

Many of you have heard of the eloquent sailor-preacher of Boston, Father Taylor. No man is more patriotic; no man is more powerful in prayer. A few weeks ago he prayed thus for our excellent Chief Magistrate in Boston : (those of you who have heard him will conceive with what vitality and emphasis he shot out the adjectives :) "O Lord, guide our dear President, our Abraham, the friend of God like old Abraham! Save him from those wriggling, intriguing, politic, piercing, slimy, boring keel-worms ; don't let them go through the sheathing of his integrity !" Now we ought to begin to beseech Abraham, and to

18

pray Heaven in his behalf and ours, that the "keel-worms" shall not, through his delay or scruples, bore through the sheathing of the nation's integrity.

The time has come when we must look more at the actual Constitution of the nation than at the paper constitution through which the rebel chiefs have struck their daggers. The time has come when it should be said and known and proclaimed with the trumpet of the President, that we strike to exterminate the power of the slave-aristocracy of the rebel region.

The slave-oligarchy of the rebel States, if the war is to end in our favor, must be shorn of all their power for mischief. Otherwise the war, though we conquer, does not end in our favor. By the necessity of their position they stand thus hostile. Hostility to the American spirit steams like an intellectual malaria from their plantations. They breathe it invisibly and perforce. They are enemies by fate to all that as loyal Americans we honor, and all that we are fighting to save.

In the now rebellious States there are less than three hundred thousand of them. We must crush their power. Any other issue to the war is simply chopping off the rattles from the snake instead of drawing the fangs. And to crush their power, we must strike the fetters from their bondmen. And we must say soon that our purpose is nothing less than this, that we shall hold on until we accomplish this.

Some would do this as a crusade in favor of the freedom of the black race. I would do it as a wise and statesmanlike blow for the permanent interest of all the white race in our empire, and to insure the unity and peace of the Continent for centuries. Thus we make America homogeneous. . . . . Thus we give the war a principle. Thus we strike at the root of our differences, our dangers, our sorrows, and our mighty wrong. The rebel aristocracy have staked their power upon this challenge. If they fail they have lost, and we must see that they both fail and lose. . . . .

O that the President would soon speak that electric sentence, — inspiration to the loyal North, doom to the traitorous aristocracy whose cup of guilt is full! Let him say that it is a war of mass against class, of America against feudalism, of the schoolmaster against the slave-master, of workmen against the barons, of the ballot-box against the barracoon. This is what the struggle means. . Proclaim it so, and what a light breaks through our leaden sky! The war-wave rolls then with the impetus and weight of an idea.

> " The sword! — a name of dread! — yet when
>   Upon the freeman's thigh 't is bound, —
>   While for his altar and his hearth,
>   While for the land that gave him birth,
>   The war-drums roll, the trumpets sound, —
>   How sacred is it then!
>
> " Whenever for the truth and right
>   It flashes in the van of fight, —
>   Whether in some wild mountain pass,

> As that where fell Leonidas ;
> Or on some sterile plain and stern, —
> A Marston or a Bannockburn ;
> Or mid fierce crags and bursting rills, —
> The Switzer's Alps, gray Tyrol's hills;
> Or, as when sunk the Armada's pride,
> It gleams above the stormy tide ; —
> Still, still, whene'er the battle's word
> Is Liberty, — when men do stand
> For Justice and their native land, —
> Then Heaven bless the sword ! "

Yes, gentlemen, then Heaven will bless the sword ! . . . .

1862.

XII.

INTELLECTUAL DUTIES OF STUDENTS IN THEIR ACADEMIC YEARS.*

I CONGRATULATE you all, students, officers of this college, and patrons and friends of it, upon this anniversary, upon the excellence of the exercises to which we have listened, and upon the good auspices for the future.

None of you, young men, are Alumni yet. The highest class here has one year more of academic opportunity before assuming the responsibility of active life, or turning to the narrower lines of an exclusive professional training. Many of you look forward to several years of privilege in the quiet absorption of preliminary knowledge. Years of opportunity and privilege, I say. Would that you might account them as precious as those who are engaged in the wear and waste of professional toil know and feel that they are !

The preparatory school and the college lay the basis of the power and the satisfaction with which, in after years, the work of life will be discharged. Young men do not go to college to complete their

---

* An address before the students of Oakland College, California, June 4, 1862.

education, but to draw the ground-plan of it, and
to lay the under courses of a future building deep
and firm.   To use the words of St. Paul in a secular sense, they are then "laying up for themselves
a good foundation against the time to come."
And the years are profitably used just to the
extent that habits of mental industry are formed,
loyalty to truth confirmed, and the principles
which underlie and support knowledge and culture are laid and cemented imperishably by the
masonry of application.

Nobody can become wise, in the best college
on this planet, between twelve and twenty.   But
a youth of capacious powers can do more in those
years towards enlarging the resources and ennobling the proportions of his mental character and
influence, than in any twice eight years after he
shall have taken up the tasks of life.   It is no
time to look to the lower tiers of the edifice after
the rafters are up and the roof is on.   It is no
time to be attending to a crack in the basement,
or a leaning wall, after the builder has moved
into the house with his family.   The best he can
do is to move out of it and buy another, or spend
largely to have it put in friendship with mathematics and gravitation.   But a student cannot
remove from his mental house, in his busy years,
although he may see that the ground-tier of stone
is not based right, and that the walls are not
thick enough for the weight they must bear.

And then the misery that comes !   To be

obliged to apply principles and not to be sure of them! To feel the need of fundamental instruction, which might once have been thoroughly acquired, while the mind must act, and in responsible callings too, as though it felt secure! To be under the necessity of being student and worker, journeyman and artist, in the same hour, without the satisfactions that belong to either branch of toil, and with the burden of practical, and perhaps very important duty upon the hands and conscience, — this is a species of refined and exquisite agony which many a professional man in our day experiences, and which is the penalty either of an enforced adoption of the duties of a profession without ample preparation, or of wasted academic hours.

Do not be so eager, young men, to advance in knowledge as to become masters of elementary knowledge, so that it can never slip from your grasp, but becomes incorporated with your mental substance. There is no intellectual wretchedness more keen, as I have said, than conscious inadequacy of the mental furniture to the mental duties, especially in the grasp of primal truths. And there is no intellectual pleasure more sweet than the assurance, tested in arduous labor, of being grounded in truth, of finding that you have built your house upon a rock, — than the repose that comes when you know something positively and know that you know it, and feel the mastery of a practical field because of that consciousness.

This pain or reward a student in the seclusion of college may store up for himself. If he is to be called to any prominent professional position, he is laying it up by his sloth or his diligence. Be more careful for elements and principles than for results, for the multum than the multa. Think less of harvests than of the supply and temper of reaping-instruments and the knowledge of the composition of the soil. In English composition do not try to write something as imaginative as Burke or as sinewy as Webster, — ten chances to one you will not succeed in the attempt, — but study as thoroughly as you can the structure and forces of the English tongue, the powers of words, their shades of distinction, their relative purity and excellence in the immense scale of our composite and wonderful language. This is the proper employment of the years of training. If you are ever to rival Burke or Ruskin, Macaulay or Webster, it will be by dissolving and digesting the English dictionary as they did. And if you should never rival either of them, you will fit yourself to express your thought, whatever its grade may be, in a pure and scholarly way, and you will not be obliged to begin to learn the principles of language when you need to use it.

In mathematics, do not be afraid of learning Euclid too thoroughly, or of wielding too easily the formulæ that lead towards the adytum of the Calculus. In chemistry, or botany, or geology, or physiology, keep your eye on the ground-plan

of each science, and care for the outline more than
the filling up.   You can fill up easily in odd hours
in after years, if you are not to pursue science as
a devotee ; but no odd hours will clear up for
you the basis and scope of each science as you
can master it in college.   And if you are never
to study geology minutely, let me beseech you to
learn enough of it to prevent you from saying
" a strata," which is so common a mistake, even
among intelligent people in our State.   We cannot make the article " a " plural even by the utmost exaggeration which is sometimes attributed
to all Californians in their dealing with truth ; we
cannot make strata singular unless we fuse the
crust of the earth into " conglomerate " in a most
ungeological way.   And therefore we had better
refrain from the combination, unless we are willing to speak of " an oxen " or " a teeth."

In the study of history, too, the most practical
use of the academic years is to become acquainted
with the skeleton facts and the great articulations
of national experience, and to master them thoroughly, rather than to seek wide information by
reading on a narrower scale.   The first is basis-
knowledge, which must be gained by drilling the
memory when the mind is undistracted by practical cares; and when it is gained, all after reading
readily takes its place as part of a rich organism
of truths.

Let me apply the same principle to the classic
languages.   In American colleges, as in the Euro-

18 *

pean system, the study of classic literature takes
the most honored rank in the scheme of scholarly
training.   Yet how many graduated students, in
proportion to the whole number, could read, ten
years after leaving college, a page of Æschylus
easily, an ode of Catullus, or a satire of Horace?
It may be of very little consequence to a man
in the press of American life that he can meet
such a test, but his failure throws an unpleasant
light back upon the economy of his time in the
years of training.   If it is worth while to spend
so much time on Latin and Greek between ten
and twenty, it is worth while to spend it in such
a way that the results cannot be wiped out by the
ten years of active life next succeeding the college
commencement.   The true scholarly object is not
to read a few pages more of this classic author or
that, in the junior and senior years, but to conquer the Latin and Greek tongues by exploring
the nooks in which difficulties hide, by mastery
of exceptions, by exercise in synonymes, by faithful study of measure, by appreciation of niceties
of construction and phrase.   It lies with students
to do this, by their persistent devotion to the
groundwork of these noble languages in their
groundwork years.   They can lay in the substructure of memory the grammar of the classic
tongues and enough of their vocabulary by the
time of leaving college, if they study wisely and
with systemized will, so that they shall never lose
the power of receiving delight from the elegant

majesty of Virgil, or of being lifted up with conscious joy on the ground-swell of Cicero's philosophic eloquence, or of feeling upon any page of his printed triumphs the momentum and force of the furious logic of Demosthenes. I should not care to live over again the last twenty years of my life ; but I should consider it an unspeakable boon to be able, with my present conviction of their importance, to re-live the season of training between ten and seventeen. I am sure that by using to the full the opportunities of that period I could easily have doubled the productiveness, worth, and intellectual satisfaction of the twenty years of active life that have been allotted to me.

Do not fail, then, young men, to use carefully the months, the days, the hours, in which as yet you are secluded from all cares but those of tillage. Do not be in a hurry to reach responsibility. Strive to be furnished for it. And in every line of inquiry that you open, be eager for the facts that belong to the substructure, rather than for those that belong to the finish of culture. The deeper you go now into principles, the higher you will rise in results in the years to come, when the bulk of your powers must be pledged to work, and only the uncertain leisure can be devoted to further acquisition.

Another point of which I would speak, and in the light of which the college years are critical, is the choice of occupation. For ordinary labor there is a law of demand and supply which the political economists interpret to us. The coarser necessities of a community determine how, during a period of five years, the laboring force of a state shall be distributed into bridge-builders, miners, carpenters, blacksmiths, masons ; and without much trouble the general force can be turned over from one department to another. But in the higher or finer domains of industry the tendency of the individual is to be consulted. The destiny is seated within, not without. In the selection of your life-work follow your bent.

How wonderful and how beautiful is the secret working of Providence by which intelligent power is diversified into ten thousand varieties and specialties, — men of equal intellectual energy and altitude being so marked for different lines and services that they are infants if taken out of their track and fastened to another style of task ! The laws of society are wiser than the wisest laws that can issue from human reflection. The struggle of the race is to throw off the hampers of human ignorance and quackery, that the inwrought forces of society may have free play. Then we get order, symmetry, freedom. In the development of civilization there would be an immense stride towards happiness, and the establishment of public sanity, if everybody could follow the bent of his nature, except the bent for wickedness, which, in an Orthodox Church and in this presence, I am not going to say is weak. If from birth the leanings of the nature could be known, and education could be applied to it, so that at manhood and womanhood each soul could find itself in its own place, the Fourier dream of attractive industry would not be so wild, the millennium would receive a push hitherward, and Dr. Cumming might fix his dates with less fear of the elasticity of prophetic arithmetic.

Students ought to revere this stirring of Providence within, and recognize the peculiar talent as the call. Inclinations are to be searched and scrutinized and weighed, perhaps utterly disregarded. Aptitudes are to be respected and obeyed. If you are by direction a mathematician, find a calling where your prime mental faculty will be called prominently into play. If you are an artist, not by desire simply to handle a brush, but by competence and by the chronic passion to express thought in form and color, do not be forced into law or medicine. Break your way by obstinate denials and sacrifices through the thorniest social chapparal, although it take you years to do it, that you may get into the path where your instincts will be like the wings of Mercury to your feet.

What losses of force, what raggedness of service, what wretchedness of heart, have resulted from maladjustment of powers to stations, — blacksmiths in pulpits, preachers in counting-rooms, artists in the rough holding trowels, artisans disguised as architects, admirable subjects for the Inebriate Home wearing shoulder-straps and stars, thieves spelling their titles in three syllables, " Contractors," and traders appearing as politicians, till statesmanship means, " How will you swop ? "

Think what a change in the fortunes of the race if Columbus had not been able to get aboard his sloop ; if Bacon had been kept in politics so exclusively that he had not written the " Novum Organum " ; if Newton had not happened to hear of a new measurement of the earth's radius, and of a degree of latitude, which was the occasion of the final demonstration of the force and law of gravity ; if Milton had not found his fit setting in English history ; if Watt had been placed in circumstances that would have quenched his intellectual enthusiasm.   Artemus Ward tells us that Shakespeare would have been entirely unfit to be a reporter of a New York newspaper, because he had not imagination and fancy enough. How fortunate, therefore, that he was drawn to and held in a sphere where his more limited supply attracted the attention of the world !

Every student is bound to honor the law that the talent is the divine commission, and then to fit his own talent to the field he enters, so that he shall extend the bounds of light in his department.   Subdivision is the condition of intellectual eminence and solid reputation, and of the advance of science.   If you go into law, or medicine, or theology, or any avenue of physical research, or become a student in literature, select, besides the general practical duties of your calling, one narrow district or vein of the great treasury of truth in your department, and work in that till you master all that has been done in it, and then try to push the line of darkness a little further out.

Every intellect is forced now to be a parasite of some branch, leaf, organ of the mighty structure of universal truth. Concentrate power upon one line of your profession, one narrow line, and you shall win mental satisfaction to fill a portion of every day with sweetness, and shall find your study advancing you to a clear and powerful knowledge of the whole domain into whose larger paths your chosen and tiny district opens by modest and delightful aisles.

Another duty of students in their preparatory years is to form the habit of intellectual respect and hospitality.

The world of truth is immense, the mind of man is fragmentary, and the heart of man is narrow. When we get harnessed into the toils and conflicting interests of practical life, truth does not have a fair chance at our hands. We have taken sides. We are soon organized by friendships and by customs into the partial antagonism of movements, schools, and creeds. We cannot devote ourselves to the culture of broad sympathies, but must act where the very channels of action, the only channels through which we can do efficient service, are barriers of division, and tend to alienate sympathies, and to narrow the mental vision.

A man who has been devoted for years to one theory in a science, and whose fame and interests are involved in its security, is not in the free condition to give the kind of welcome to a rival hypothesis which it has a right to claim. All it asks is severe, unprejudiced logic. But the logic which will be applied by the famous representative of a theory that will be displaced by it, can hardly be unprejudiced, however sure it may be to prove sufficiently severe. The homœopath and allopath will hardly do justice to each other's philosophy of medicine when each is winning patients from the other in the fluctuations of a city experience. It is only clergymen who are always clear of partisanship, and able to look at competing doctrines through an achromatic lens!

Providence made us to be workers ; made us to choose sides, and forbids us to be perpetual inquirers, always pampering an intellectual charity which restrains us from saying things positive, and from striking, now and then, hard blows. Still, mental tolerance is one of the chief graces and glories of character, and the time to lay the substructure of it is in the studious years, before we become pledged to the duties and interests that exercise the will, and indispose the mind to turning new pages in the book of truth. Youth is the time for wide views, and to fix the habit of intellectual respect founded on the knowledge of the breadth of the field of truth and speculation.

In our unfettered studious years we see that, in spite of all that Plato taught and wrote, Aristotle had an immense deal to say for himself, that stoicism kept rising from repeated rebuffs, that materialism and idealism renew in every age their desperate contests through consummate athletes, and that the shores of history are littered with the wrecks of systems which once pretended to account for nature, and claimed to be able to rule human thought forever. The student should not learn from this that he must not be a party man. He must be. He will never be able to settle and harmonize what millions of minds and a score of centuries have not reduced to consistent symmetry. But he must learn not to be a partisan, and to keep clean of the infection of intellectual contempt towards thinkers and systems that have a long lineage.

God has diversified the world of souls into various classes of temperament; he has made no mind competent to manage and harmonize the profoundest mysteries of moral and spiritual life ; and he has disposed certain classes of souls by their temperament to turn in certain directions of the spiritual universe for their nutriment, that many groups may illustrate by their character the riches of the mighty realm.

Conservatives have a right to exist, as the bark and trunk of an oak have no apology to offer for themselves. The tree needs muscle and weight. Advance thinkers have a call to exist, for the tree needs leaves and expansion. Gravitation and opposition to gravitation are equal requisites of tree-truth. Let the fibres settle the philosophy of the business and its contradiction among themselves, if they can. They are called to choose sides, but they will be wise if they recognize the mystery in their organism, and work with a feeling of common wonder and mutual toleration.

Take a High Churchman, an earnest Methodist, a devoted Quaker, and excite the religious sentiment in them to fervor. The Churchman drops on his knees before the printed prayer of St. Chrysostom; the Methodist will ache if he cannot cry out, not from Chrysostom, but from the sacred tumult in his private breast; the Quaker is quiet as the mountain lake at midnight reflecting the calm of the quivering stars. Are their intellects made to agree, when their souls are thus formed to take different hues, and live in different airs of sentiment? No religious philosophy is ample that does not justify the ritualism, the hallelujah, and the silence. Nobody was made to live on error, but living on a part of the truth is not living on error, any more than the persistent redness of the rose and the chronic whiteness of the lily prove that one or the other of them rejects the sun. Apostolical succession! Yes, but there were twelve Apostles with different types of grace expressed in their spiritual organization; and then Paul comes in to make a generous dozen ; and each church can have an apostolical succession of its own.

We hear of the five points of Calvinism. Do not fear that I am going to attack them, under the delusion that it is Sunday and that I am in my own church. If I were there I should not. Brethren, you claim too little. I believe that Calvinism has more than five points. It has as many as one hundred and eighty ; that is the number of degrees in half a circle, is n't it? And I believe that its philosophic roots run down to the foundations of intellectual and spiritual truth. But truth, like the earth, is a globe ; and the foundation is the centre ; and Arminius has another one hundred and eighty degrees and he comes down to the centre too ; and Swedenborg gets there also ; and I have a suspicion that Channing once sank his shaft as far. A score of sects on some lines get down to the centre, and there is room enough there for all the shafts, and power enough there to hold all the systems firm.

Dr. Bushnell, a name to be mentioned nowhere but with the heartiest respect, and with peculiar reverence and affection before this college, once said that he could sign as many creeds as might be offered to him, since words are so elastic and truth so comprehensive. Let us thank Heaven for the Doctor and the vigor of his mental digestion, and be stimulated by his words to a nobler temper than contemptuous dogmatism. And as students, in the years of inquiry, before the feet are fettered and the hands tethered to practical responsibilities and vows, let us bow before the vastness and mystery of the world and "the Word," and prepare to enter diverging paths of confession and service, with joy in the breadth of the wisdom which can use such variety of temperament, and view, and organization in the illustration of its composite and blinding light. Students are called to the duty of so surveying the expanse of the domain of truth, that all diversity, where the foundations of morals are not touched, shall be genial in temper, and all discussion between permanent classes of belief dignified, candid, catholic, and calm.

And now I cannot refrain, young men, from referring to another duty of American scholars, in their studious years, namely, to fill their hearts with patriotism by feeding their minds from the wonderful annals of their country's history.

Whatever path a young man chooses in the intellectual world, whatever severity of study he may impose upon himself in the ambition to master it, two volumes must always be pouring their influence into his nature, the New Testament and the volume of records of his native land. Religion and patriotism must stream into every fibre of his brain, into every duct of his blood.

There is no danger now that the sentiment of patriotism will fail in the masses of the American people. How suddenly in the hour of need it

arose! How it swelled from unsuspected fountains! The wisest statesman, the most sagacious
politician, did not predict or suspect the possibility
of such a surge. It came with a Bay of Fundy
sweep and speed! Nay, more marvellous than that.
It was akin rather to an earthquake wave we read
of sometimes in a tropic country. Just at the
outbreak of treason there was, you know, a strange
stillness in the air, heavy and oppressive. The
sea was listless. The beaches were bare. It
seemed as though mammon-worship had paralyzed
manhood. And then the volcanic moment came,
the rumble, the roar, the upheaval of the very
bed of the sea under the flame of the country's
maddened heart. And the billow rose — the
moral billow — along the line of a continent ; and
it rolled from that calm ocean dark, massive, sublime, till its edge whitened with sacred wrath,
and the track of its tremendous dash is marked
by the broken forts, the flying hosts, the sub-
merged banners, of the rebellion. Disloyalty to
the imperial republic will never care to tempt
again the anger of that sleeping deep.

You know the prophecies of a little more than
a year ago, the prophecies of foreign critics, and
of their emissaries here, that the national life was
dying. Our imperial bird was spiritless, they said,
and mortally sick. They did not see how Milton's wonderful passage had been waiting till now
for fulfilment: "Methinks I see in my mind a
noble and puissant nation rousing herself, like

a strong man after sleep, and shaking her invincible locks; methinks I see her as an eagle mewing her mighty youth, and kindling her undazzled eyes at the full midday beam ; purging and unsealing her long-abused sight at the fount itself of heavenly radiance ; whilst the whole noise of timorous and flocking birds, with those also that love the twilight, flutter about amazed at what she means, and in their envious gabble would prognosticate a year of sects and schisms." It has been no year of schism, but such an affirmation of national unity as will banish all future dreams of conspiracy.

The heart of the nation is sound in patriotism. But the time will soon pass when it will be stimulated by public peril, and will be expressed through powder, steel, and a gorgeous wilderness of banners. The scholars of the country must sustain and chasten and direct it. We must not fall back from our attainment. The academies, the colleges, the churches, must secrete the passion for our country's honor and mission, and be ready to pour inspiration at needed moments into the popular soul.

Let the students turn now with new zeal and reverence to the pages of our national past, and fit themselves to be intelligent centres of patriotic fervor, guides and purifiers of the national passion. Let them learn more of the training of this people in the last two centuries, the preparations for the present instinct of unity and the spontaneously compacted patriotism to preserve it. Let them arm themselves with the story of American growth and the mysterious aids to it, and be equipped with knowledge to guide and interpret, as with sentiment to echo, the devotion of our loyal millions to their intrusted land.

If there had been a deeper study of the history of America in the last twenty years in the rebellious districts, and a baptism in the spirit which that study liberates, this war could not have been. But rebel memories do not run back farther than the vice-presidency of Calhoun. Before him, to their vision, America was a blank, — or if anything existed worth recalling, it was the Resolutions of 1798.

See what a difference in the motives and appeals that incite and animate the hostile sections ! On one side, self-will. No appeal to a principle, no cry that a great truth is in danger, no rally around a noble charter, no invocation of the memories and service and advice of canonized fathers, no geographical unity to guard, no invasion to avert, no guaranteed rights trampled or wrested away, but a schism entailing infinite mischief determined, completed, and justified by pure hatred and self-will. On the other side, history appealed to, memories of a noble past recalled, a majestic charter, never broken, put forward, the labors, hopes, and prayers of great men from all sections adjured, common battles and triumphs rekindled, a majestic and symmetrical geography to guard, a great commission acknowledged and accepted, the sentiment of freedom chanted in stirring rhythms, and a cause whose success gives the same blessing to vanquished as to victors!

Drink of the fountains, young men, that are pouring such power and nobility into the nation's heart to-day. Make the history of your land part of your mental substance. Resolve that every year shall introduce you to some new department or treasure of it. Fill up by some regular reading, if it is only a chapter a week, the outline story of the early colonization, the dotting of the surface with various nuclei of Saxon energy, the early passion for self-government, the sweeping away of the French competition, the Revolution, the controversies about the Mississippi, the wretchedness and dissolution of the early confederation, the rise of the Constitution, the gathering of the breadth of the continent under its ægis and banner, and the march of the nation, by strides unmatched in the experience of ages, towards the first rank in the synod of states. Make some noble biography every year more familiar to your heart. In this way the scholars of the country can contribute more than tons of powder, more than sheaves of steel, more than parks of Dahlgreens, more than bombproof forts, a fleet of monitors, to the defences of the republic. They contribute power, the very core of power, — inspiration to the character of the land, — energy that will use the material forces to some noble purpose. Fit yourselves to bear part in this mission of baptizing the nation in its traditions through which God will sustain its renewed vitality.

Lay the foundations of knowledge firm in the years of your academic privilege; follow your bent if possible in seeking your profession; learn from your outlook over the field of knowledge the lesson of mental tolerance and respect; live for your country by the patriotism of your studies as of your feeling : thus much I have hinted to you in fragmentary and incompetent pages, of the duties of students in their academic years. And here we must close. Yet to close here with no further word would be to leave our walls, humble as they are, unroofed. The elements and the heights of knowledge are revelations to man of the Infinite intellect, sparks and streams from the insufferable brightness. The aptitudes of the mind and soul are from him whose inspiration giveth us understanding, and who supplies diversities of gifts with his one Spirit. We are called to toleration because all schools in science, philosophy, and faith are classes which he is leading by various · explorations towards the home of light. And it is he whose dial marks the age of states, and whose finger determines the times before appointed and the bounds of their habitations. Knowledge has its source and crown and nobleness, its motive and vigor, in him and his service and his blessing.

Him we discern in every star and in the mystic

fellowship of stars ; him and a word from him in
the laws and bounty of the world ; him in the
breadth of truth which no finite capacities can
drain ; him in man ; him in the head of humanity
and nations, " the Word made flesh." Knowledge
is dark and goodness discrowned that do not bow
before his light and consecrate themselves to his
will.   I have spoken of patriotism, and the foster-
ing of it by scholars in their vocation.   Hear
these words of an American patriot and scholar,
himself for years the head of the oldest university
of New England, a patriarch now, a connecting
link, almost the last, between this age and the
Revolution, born before the first continental Congress, a youth of seventeen at the inauguration
of President Washington, now in the full pos-
session of his faculties at fourscore and ten, and
believing in the eloquent words which I am to
quote more devoutly as he steps nearer and
nearer the light which looks like shadow to our
fleshly eyes : " Human happiness hath no perfect
security but freedom ; freedom none but virtue ;
virtue none but knowledge ; and neither freedom
nor virtue nor knowledge has any vigor or immortal hope except in the principles of the Christian
faith and the sanctions of the Christian religion."

1862.

Cambridge : Electrotyped and Printed by Welch, Bigelow, & Co.

www.ingramcontent.com/pod-product-compliance
Lightning Source LLC
Chambersburg PA
CBHW071401090426
42737CB00011B/1309